Capital Market Equilibria

Edited by

Günter Bamberg and Klaus Spremann

With Contributions by

G. Bamberg M. Brennan V. Firchau R. Geske B. Rudolph
E.S. Schwartz K. Spremann S. Trautmann

With 4 Figures and 12 Tables

Springer-Verlag
Berlin Heidelberg New York Tokyo

Prof. Dr. Günter Bamberg
Institut für Statistik und Mathematische Wirtschaftstheorie
Universität Augsburg
Memminger Straße 14, D-8900 Augsburg, FRG

Prof. Dr. Klaus Spremann
Abteilung Wirtschaftswissenschaften
Universität Ulm
Oberer Eselsberg, D-7900 Ulm, FRG

ISBN-13: 978-3-642-70997-5 e-ISBN-13: 978-3-642-70995-1
DOI: 10.1007/978-3-642-70995-1

Library of Congress Cataloging-in-Publication Data. Capital market equilibria. Includes bibliographies and indexes. 1. Capital market–Mathematical models. 2. Equilibrium (Economics)–Mathematical models. 3. Efficient market theory–Mathematical models. I. Bamberg, Günter, 1940-. II. Spremann, Klaus.
HG4523.C33 1986 332.6'0724 86-10104
ISBN 0-387-16248-8 (U.S.)

Softcover reprint of the hardcover 1st edition 1986

Offsetprinting: Beltz Offsetdruck, Hemsbach/Bergstrasse
Binding: J. Schäffer OHG, Grünstadt

2142/3140-543210

Preface

Both introductory surveys and results of individual research on a selection of six issues of modern finance form the content of this volume:

- The Hybrid Model and Related Approaches to Capital Market Equilibria
- Portfolio Decisions and Capital Market Equilibria under Incomplete Information (by Volker Firchau)
- Option Valuation: Theory and Empirical Evidence (by Robert Geske and Siegfried Trautmann)
- The Value of Security Agreements (by Bernd Rudolph)
- Asset Pricing in a Small Economy: A Test of the Omitted Assets Model (by Eduardo S. Schwartz and Michael J. Brennan)
- The Simple Analytics of Arbitrage.

The main idea was to help students in their work and to provide material for seminars.

The book originated from a cooperation between the authors coming from the USA, Canada, and West Germany. Support was granted by the Allianz Lebensversicherung Stuttgart, the Badenia Bausparkasse Karlsruhe, the Landeszentralbank in Baden-Württemberg, and the Stifterverband für die Deutsche Wirtschaft.

Finally, we want to express our thanks to Birgit Emmrich for her help during the different stages of manuscript preparation, and, last but not least, to Werner A. Müller from the Springer-Verlag for the readiness to publish our volume.

Günter Bamberg
University of Augsburg

Klaus Spremann
Ulm University

Table of Contents

Prologue

Günter Bamberg and Klaus Spremann

1. Equilibrium versus Market Imperfections

People working in the field of finance are sometimes divided into two groups. There are those who "believe" in capital market equilibria on the one hand, on the other hand, those who think that the most interesting phenomena find their rationale in market imperfections and transactions costs. In fact, what in the field of finance could be called to be "institutional" or "managerial", i.e., what essentially emerged from the traditions of financial practice, banking, and financial intermediation (rather than from microeconomic theory) seems to be contradictory to the concept of capital market equilibria: Market imperfections due to transactions costs, informational asymmetry, incentive incompatibility, and moral hazard, dominate real life situations. Perhaps the best example is the discussion of the capital structure of a firm in view of the irrelevance theorems by Franco Modigliani and Merton H. Miller (1958): Although the equity-debt ratio serves as an indicator of trustworthyness in real business life, the capital structure is irrelevant to the value of the firm if a capital market equilibrium prevails (or to be more precise: under free entry, equal access to information, and absence of transactions costs and taxes).

Nevertheless, in many fields of scientific knowledge better ways of understanding existing real phenomena originate from a thorough study of abstract theory. The metaphorical expressions in each theory are the concepts of structural interrelations, that is, idealizations. The most prominent idealization which, of course, is not only fruitful in finance is the concept of equilibrium. Thus, in our point of view, capital market equilibria is not only the issue in the theory of finance which should be one of the first topics to study, but in addition, it provides a basic platform where subsequent analysis of imperfections could start.

Thus, we suggest to study concepts of equilibrium first not because we claim that real phenomena can best be described as equilibrium. Rather than that, the philosophy is that the study of capital market

Capital Market Equilibria. Ed. by G. Bamberg and K. Spremann

equilibria provides a conceptual basis of reference and is a prerequisite for addressing real phenomena in the world of finance. Philosophy, that directly brought us to the idea ef editing a portfolio of surveys as well as state-of-the-art research contributions on fundamental issues concerning capital market equilibria. This well diversified portfolio was consequently termed "CAPITAL MARKET EQUILIBRIA". The volume is neither a textbook in the usual sense nor an arbitrary collection of papers as they are published in each of the professional journals. What is the rationale? Referring the interested student to one of the standard textbooks which treat finance from the equilibrium point of view - an excellent example is "The Theory of Finance" by Eugene F. Fama and Merton H. Miller (1972) - requires today additional backup in several directions. To these directions of current research belong issues such as arbitrage theory and option pricing, testing for efficiency, presentation and analysis of actual data, heterogeneous and incomplete information, security agreements and the role of collateralization which can rarely be found in textbooks. Professional journals, on the other hand, do not select submitted papers according the criterion to come up with a sound and diversified presentation of current lines of knowledge.

The volume CAPITAL MARKET EQUILIBRIA aims at filling this gap between textbooks and professional journals. Students in the field of finance are invited to enter into a discussion of the subjects selected and grouped in this volume.

2. Questions and Answers

In order to have the portfolio of papers in CAPITAL MARKET EQUILIBRIA sufficiently diversified we asked six questions:

1. Which is the "best" decision-theoretic approach to portfolio selection?
2. How are portfolios selected if investors have incomplete information only?
3. What is the actual evidence in the field of option pricing?
4. Since more financial instruments become irrelevant under equilibrium conditions - can a similar hypothesis of collateral irrelevance hypothesis be stated?
5. What can and what cannot be tested in Capital Asset Pricing Models?

6. What is the basic idea of arbitrage theory?

More questions, of course, could have been asked. So to speak: although the portfolio of contributions to CAPITAL MARKET EQUILIBRIA is diversified, some systematic risk remains. Not everything can be done by two editors in one book. Nevertheless, eight scientists agreed to enter into the project which was to provide answers in the twin style of presenting both introductory surveys and results of individual research. In alphabetical ordering of authors' names the answers provided can shortly be stated as follows.

1. In "The Hybrid Model and Related Approaches to Capital Market Equilibria", Günter Bamberg focusses on the variety of decision theoretic approaches to portfolio selection. Portfolio selection, of course, is an essential element in the evaluation of equilibrium prices in capital markets. While many of the approaches compared result in implicit characterizations of equilibrium prices, it is shown that exactly under two specific assumptions explicit valuation formulas can be obtained. These assumptions form the so-called hybrid model, i.e., exponential utility of investors and normal distributions of returns. The proof is based on the argumentation by Thomas W. Epps (1981). Applications of the hybrid model are presented; so, for example, the implication of alternative tax schedules and short sales restrictions on equilibrium prices.

2. Problems of "Portfolio Decisions and Capital Market Equilibria under Incomplete Information" are analyzed by Volker Firchau. After surveying different types of preknowledge and concepts such as the Bayes approach and generalized minmax he concludes that knowing the true distribution of returns is not necessary for making what could be termed "the best portfolio decision". Rather than that, partial knowledge provides a sufficient basis of information for investors. This is a considerable generalization of the approach suggested by Winston T. Lin (1981) which is appropriate only in the case of completely known prior distributions.

3. Modern option pricing theory orginated from the seminal paper by Fisher Black and Myron Scholes (1973). They used a partial equilibrium model and assumed that the stock price changes are continuous with a constant variance of relative changes. The famous Black/Scholes formula provides an explicit representation of the call price. Meanwhile it is known that the formula exhibits some biases. For instance, it

undervalues options on low variance stock and overvalues options on high variance stocks. These biases and the restrictive assumptions underlying the Black/Scholes approach stimulated some new approaches. The paper by Robert Geske and Siegfried Trautmann reviews approaches competing with the Black/Scholes formula and gives a comprehensive survey on empirical tests performed both on American and European option markets.

4. An important issue in the analysis of contractual arrangements is to establish values of security agreements, here discussed by Bernd Rudolph. The survey on collateral policy and debt claims presents not only the argumentation of J. Scott (1977) that a firm can maximize its value through using all its assets as collateral for the creditors: Costs such as sales taxes, administrative costs of bankruptcy, and legal damage claims indicate the relevance of collateral policy. If, however, such cost vanish in a perfect capital market an irrelevance hypothesis can be established.

5. One of the basic distinctions to be made in economics is "average" versus "marginal" or "big" versus "small" respectively. A similar distinction has to be made with testing the asset pricing model. Since Richard Roll (1977) pointed out the difficulties with testing the asset pricing model for a whole economy, it seems to be preferred to aim at statistical results on the mean-variance efficiency of portfolios with respect to a small set of assets. In "Asset Pricing in a Small Economy: A Test of the Omitted Assets Model", Eduardo S. Schwartz and Michael J. Brennan are concerned with testing the asset pricing model in a small economy where the issue of integration or segmentation of different national markets cannot be decided beforehand. Their study focusses on the Canadian experience and is similar in spirit so that by Richard Stehle (1977). Extensions are made with respect to the methods of statistical inference. In particular, Dimson's aggregated beta eximation has been combined with Gibbons' maximum likelihood approach.

6. Arbitrage is a traditional analytical tool to derive the conditions that must prevail in equilibrium. Arguments of arbitrage are largely independent of individual characteristics such as endowments and preferences, i.e. initial wealth and particular attitudes toward risk. In "The Simple Analytics of Arbitrage" Klaus Spremann presents the basic idea of arbitrage from the most elementary point of view. So it becomes evident that the arbitrage of an investor with respect to uncertainty and futures contracts exhibits the same structural

pattern as the arbitrage of a producing firm. The paper presents also some of the most fruitful applications of arbitrage theory to modern finance, namely the pricing of derivative futures contracts such as options.

The Hybrid Model and Related Approaches to Capital Market Equilibria

Günter Bamberg

Summary: Single period capital-asset-pricing models provide a number of implications on capital market equilibria. Familiar notions as, for instance, the market price of risk or the market portfolio can be derived from the equilibrium conditions without having explicit representations of the equilibrium prices. However, such explicit solutions are required to conduct other investigations successfully. The availability of explicit solutions facilitates the analysis of changes in the value of firms under a variety of circumstances. The paper concentrates on the chances to obtain explicit solutions. It makes precise in which sense the hybrid model, characterized by multivariate normally distributed returns and constant risk aversion of the investors, is the most convenient model of capital market equilibrium. Some applications are surveyed concerning taxes, heterogeneous expectations, short sales restrictions, and imperfect capital markets.

Table of Contents:

Capital Market Equilibria. Ed. by G. Bamberg and K. Spremann

1. Introduction

The familiar single-period two-parameter model for portfolio decisions and capital market equilibrium presupposes risk averse individuals maximizing an objective function $\Phi(E,V)$ of mean E and variance V of end-of-period-wealth. A bulk of papers and books discusses the pros and cons of the approach.[1] The mean-variance approach seems to be indispensable, at least at the present time, for illustrative and especially teaching purposes, for empirical studies etc. Therefore, we will take the mean-variance framework as the basis of the main sections (3 and 4). Prominent results of the mean-variance approach are

- the equation determining the expected rate of return R_i on asset i in equilibrium

$$E(R_i) = r_f + \frac{E(R_m) - r_f}{Var(R_m)} Cov(R_m, R_i) \tag{1}$$

- the equation determining the equilibrium value V_i of asset i

$$V_i = \frac{E(X_i) - \lambda \, Cov(R_m, X_i)}{1 + r_f} . \tag{2}$$

Hereby the symbols have the following meaning:

r_f = risk free rate of interest

R_i = rate of return on asset i (in equilibrium)

R_m = rate of return on the (E-V) market portfolio

X_i = stochastic end-of-period value of asset i .

λ = market price of risk,

$$\lambda = \frac{E(R_m) - r_f}{Var(R_m)} . \tag{3}$$

---

1) For instance, Tobin (1958,1969), Markowitz (1959), Schneeweiß (1967), Borch (1969,1974), Feldstein (1969), Hakansson (1972), Tsiang (1972,1974), Chipman (1973), Bierwag (1974), Levy (1974), Williams (1977b), Gonzales/Litzenberger/Rolfo (1977), Baron (1977), Rudolph (1979), Drukarczyk (1980), Copeland/Weston (1983).

An equation of type (1) which relates the "required rate of return" to appropriate risk and market characteristics is termed as CAPM (= capital asset pricing model)-equation. If X_i in equation (2) is interpreted as stochastic end-of-period value of a single share, V_i is identical with the equilibrium price of one share.

Note that the market price of risk (λ) contains each individual firm value V_i by virtue of

$$R_m = \frac{\sum_{j=1}^{n} V_j R_j}{\sum_{j=1}^{n} V_j} \qquad (n = \text{number of assets}) \tag{4}$$

in a rather involved manner. Therefore, equation (2) merely is an *implicit representation* of the equilibrium value. Lintner (1965) argued that (2) can be regarded as explicit representation if the "small firm assumption" is valid. This assumption means that any individual firm is so small in relation to the entire market that the market price of risk (3) is independent of the value V_i of firm i. As this "small firm assumption" is justified in the majority of capital market investigations the implicit character of (2) often escapes from awareness. One of the main objectives of the paper is to stress this implicity and to look for *explicit representations* of the firm values. The availability of explicit solutions facilitates comparative static analyses concerning the firm values under variations of regulations or parameters of the end-of-period values. Explicit solutions are indispensable for investigations concerning big firms occurring, for instance, in monopolistic or oligopolistic capital market studies.

A second objective is to check the "rationality" of the different approaches, i.e. to investigate whether the different approaches are consistent with the expected utility hypothesis.

Some attempts to develop models based on other parameters (than E-V) are surveyed in section 2. Section 3 analyzes simultaneous restrictions on tastes and beliefs, delineates how to get rid of the unfashionable quadratic utility function, focusses on explicit solutions and provides the rationale of the hybrid model. Section 4 is devoted to several applications of the hybrid model. Portions of the proofs of a supportive and more technical nature are contained in the appendix.

2. Portfolio Models Based on Different Sets of Parameters

2.1 One-Parameter Models

In the one-parameter case the random payments X (or rates of return stemming from different portfolios) are ranked according to a preference functional Φ depending only on a single distributional parameter, for instance

$\Phi(X) = E(X)$: expected value of X

or

$\Phi(X) = MED(X)$: median of X .

Portfolio selection procedures of this type are quite unrealistic since they don't take into account a risk characteristic. Of course, the sole consideration of a risk measure, for instance

$$\Phi(X) = -Var(X) \; ,$$

is just as unreasonable.

Throughout we will only discuss *rational portfolio models*, i.e. models which are consistent with the expected utility hypothesis. Judged from this point of view the rule $\Phi(X) = E(X)$ implies a linear (increasing) utility function, and $\Phi(X) = MED(X)$ violates the expected utility hypothesis provided that all probability distributions are feasible. The latter statement follows from the well known result[1] that a rule $\Phi(X)$ depending only on the median and defined on all probability distributions is consistent with the expected utility hypothesis if and only if the utility function and hence Φ are constant. Put another way: the rationality axioms underlying the expected utility hypothesis are consistent with median-oriented portfolio selection procedures only in the trivial case of complete indifference.

---

[1] going back to Massé (1953); it was generalized to other ordinal parameters and restricted classes of probability distributions by Schneeweiß (1967).

Since there don't exist reasonable one-parameter portfolio models we will turn to the two-parameter models. The most prominent two-parameter approach is the mean-variance (E-V) approach. As this concept is dealt with in some detail in the course of the next sections we will focus on two-parameter approaches different from the E-V aproach.

2.2 Two-Parameter Models: Mean-Semivariance Approach

Whereas the use of the expected value $E(X)$ as a measure of return seems to be uncontroversial, several scale or dispersion parameters have been proposed as measures of risk. A large number of authors[1] prefers the semivariance (lower partial moment) as a measure of risk. Semivariance S^2 of a random rate of return X with respect to a target value t is defined by

$$S^2 = \int_{-\infty}^{t} (x-t)^2 \, dF(x) = E[\min(0, X-t)]^2 ,$$

where F is the probability distribution function of X. Natural target values t are the expected value $E(X)$ or the risk free rate of return r_f. Semivariance S^2 and semistandard-deviation S have the advantage to concentrate on the failure to earn a realistic target rate. Advocates of the semivariance concept argue that S is more consistent with investor's intuitive perception of risk than variance. One of the first advocates was Markowitz (1959) but familiarity and simplicity of computation induced him to prefer the variance after all. We will discuss some advantages and disadvantages of the E-S approach.

To start with, a major *advantage* is the before-mentioned consistency of S with the intuitive feeling of risk. A secondadvantage is the fact that many of the results and methods of the E-V approach can be carried over to the E-S model. For instance, the efficient set in the S-E-plane is a concave curve provided that a risk free asset is excluded. If a risk free asset is available, combinations of the

---

[1] Mao (1970), Hogan/Warren (1974), Porter/Bey/Lewis (1975), Jahankhani (1976), Bawa/Lindenberg (1977), Nantell/Price (1979), Price/Price/Nantell (1982), Nantell/Price/Price (1982).

risk free asset with another fixed portfolio plot along a straight line of the plane. Consequently, notions like the capital market line and the market portfolio (as tangency portfolio) can be equally applied to the E-S model. Additionally, an E-S CAPM can be derived. Following the procedure used by Sharpe (1964), Hogan and Warren (1974) obtained the result:

$$E(R_i) = r_f + \frac{E(R_m) - r_f}{S^2(R_m)} CS(R_m, R_i) \tag{5}$$

where the (new) symbols have the meaning:

R_m = rate of return on the E-S market portfolio (in equilibrium)

$S^2(R_m)$ = semivariance of the return on the market portfolio with respect to r_f as target rate

$CS(R_m, R_i)$ = co-semivariance between R_m and R_i defined by

$$E\{[\min(0, R_m - r_f)](R_i - r_f)\} . \tag{6}$$

Note that the co-semivariance (unlike the covariance) is not symmetric, i.e. $SC(X,Y) \neq SC(Y,X)$. Moreover, the fixed target rate entails, for instance, that the well-known equation $Var(aX) = a^2 Var(X)$ is violated with respect to semivariances; i.e. in general we have $S^2(aX) \neq a^2 S^2(X)$. These somewhat less familiar properties are illustrated by the following simple example.

Example 1:

Let R_m and R_i be dependent discrete random variables characterized by the joint probability distribution

R_m \ R_i	0.05	0.10
0.06	0.2	0.1
0.09	0.1	0.6

The target rate $t = r_f = 0.07$ gives rise to the co-semivariance

$$\begin{aligned} CS(R_m, R_i) &= 0.2(-0.01)(-0.02) + 0.1(-0.01)\cdot 0.04 + 0.1\cdot 0 + 0.6\cdot 0 \\ &= 0.00001 \end{aligned}$$

and the semivariance

$$S^2(R_m) = (0.01)^2 \cdot 0.3 = 0.00003 \; .$$

By interchanging the role of R_m and R_i we obtain the co-semivariance

$$CS(R_i, R_m) = 0.2(-0.01)(-0.02) + 0.1(-0.01)\cdot 0.03 + 0.1\cdot 0 + 0.6\cdot 0$$
$$= 0 \neq CS(R_m, R_i) \; .$$

Multiplication of R_m by the factor 2 leads to $S^2(2R_m) = 0$, whereas

$$4 \cdot S^2(R_m) = 0.00012 \neq 0 \; .$$

To conclude the example, we will turn to the question whether our numerical values (with respect to r_f and the probabilities) are consistent with the equilibrium condition (5) on the capital market.

From

$$E(R_m) = 0.06 \cdot 0.3 + 0.09 \cdot 0.7 = 0.074$$

$$E(R_i) = 0.05 \cdot 0.3 + 0.10 \cdot 0.7 = 0.085$$

one can see that the left hand side of (5) is greater than the right hand side. Equilibrium would require a slightly modified value of r_f which is, however, irrelevant for our illustrative purposes. ∎

From our point of view which is characterized by two main objectives

- compatibility with expected utility
- development of explicit formulas for the equilibrium values of the firms (given the stochastic end-of-period values)

the mean-semivariance approach shows the following *disadvantages*:

a) A ranking of arbitrary random rates of return X according to a preference functional depending only on expected value $E(X)$ and semivariance with *target value* $t = E(X)$ is consistent with the expected utility hypothesis if and only if the ordering depends on $E(X)$ only (and not on $S^2(X)$). In other words: If all probability distributions are taken into account and if the semivariance is defined by the mean value as target rate, an E-S approach is consistent with the expected utility hypothesis if and only if risk neutrality prevails. This result was shown by Schneeweiß (1967, p. 112). On the other hand, target value $t = E(X)$ combined with the restriction on a class of symmetric distribution (such that consistency with expected utility holds) provides no new results since semivariance is half of variance and co-semivariance is half of covariance.

b) If the *target rate t is exogeneously fixed* (this was the case in the E-S CAPM of Hogan and Warren), objection a) is not applicable. The well known corresponding utility function is composed of a quadratic and a linear part. But the derivation of explicit valuation formulas seems to be extremely difficult. Porter/Bey/Lewis (1975) tried to develop valuation formulas from the E-S CAPM relation (5). They delineate problems arising in the conversion from rates of return to dollar returns. According to Lintner's (1965) E-V approach they circumvent the problem by making the "small firm assumption", which means that the E-S market price of risk

$$\frac{E(R_m - r_f)}{S^2(R_m)}$$

may be considered as independent from the value V_i of firm i. The valuation formula obtained by Porter, Bey and Lewis is much less tractable than the corresponding E-V valuation formula (2). As both valuation equations are contingent on this "small firm assumption" they are not suitable to cope with monopolistic, dyopolistic or oligopolistic capital markets.

2.3 Other Two-Parameter Approaches

If consistency with the expected utility hypothesis is called for and arbitrary probability distributions are taken into account no reasonable two-parameter approach different from the E-V or the E-S approach seems to exist. Results obtained by Schneeweiß (1967) show that ranking procedures for portfolios X according to the following rules are incompatible with the expected utility hypothesis unless they degenerate to the E-rule (μ-criterion):

- any rule depending on the expected value E and an *ordinal* [1] parameter as, for instance, the median, the mode, a fractile, the maximum or the minimum of the support of X
- any rule depending on E and a second parameter which is a function of ordinal parameters as, for instance, the range, differences between pairs of fractiles like the semi-interquartile range
- any rule depending on E and the mean absolute deviation [2] $E[|X-E(X)|]$
- any rule depending on E and the lower semi-expectation $E\{\min[0,X-E(X)]\}$
- and finally, the already discussed E-S rule with target value $t=E(X)$.

If we take into account only a rather restricted class of probability distributions the scope for preference functionals consistent with the expected utility hypothesis increases considerably. The most popular proposal is the restriction on normal distributions. Since this proposal is discussed in section 3 other proposals made in the literature should be reported at this place.

Fama (1965), Roll (1970), Fama/Miller (1972) and others advocate the restriction on *stable distributions*. Roughly speaking, the distribution of independent random variables is stable if it is closed under the formation of linear combinations (of random variables). The stable class is a four-parameter class. Evidence from empirical date seems to justify the restriction on *symmetric stable distributions*, which constitute a three-parameter class. One parameter, the "characteristic exponent" α must be in the range $0<\alpha\leq 2$. The expected value exists iff $1<\alpha\leq 2$, and the variance exists iff $\alpha=2$. The restriction on $\alpha=2$ uniquely determines the class of normal distri-

---

1) A distributional parameter γ is denoted as ordinal if $\gamma(X)=\gamma(Y)$ entails $\gamma[g(X)]=\gamma[g(Y)]$ for arbitrary strictly increasing transformations $g:\mathbb{R}\rightarrow\mathbb{R}$.

2) The use of average deviations (not necessarily around the mean value) has been recently advocated by Denneberg (1984). He argues that the stronger empirical evidence offsets the disadvantage of violating the expected utility property.

butions.Fama/Miller (1972) introduce the restriction on symmetric stable distributions with given characteristic exponent α between 1 and 2 . The resulting class is characterized by two parameters, the usual mean value (which exists for $\alpha > 1$) and a second parameter which plays the role of a dispersion parameter (and is identical to the variance iff $\alpha = 2$) . Fama/Miller (1972) show that such classes have the property that for a risk averter expected utility is an increasing function of expected portfolio return and a decreasing function of the return dispersion. Based on this fact the efficient set analysis continues as in the E-V framework. However, the development of a generalized two-parameter CAPM meets with some additional difficulties concerning the generalization of the covariance notion and the independency assumption underlying stable distributions. Stable distributions are indeed taylormade for weighted addition of *independent* random variables, whereas a salient feature of asset returns is their interdependence. Agnew (1971) demonstrated by counterexamples that stability against weighted addition does not characterize the stable distributions if the basic random variables (from which the nontrivial linear combinations are formed) are dependent. Fama/Miller (1972) tried to maintain their symmetrical stable class and by-passed the problems by taking recourse to the "one factor market model" whose market factor and disturbance term are assumed to be independent and symmetric stable (with the same α) .

With respect to the desired closedness against linear combinations of dependent random variables the most appropriate distributions seem to be the *elliptical distributions*. Agnew's counterexample belongs to this class too. Reference is made to Owen/Rabinovich (1983) who delineate the relevance of this class to portfolio and capital market theory. Based on this class they derive a general two-parameter CAPM and a corresponding (implicit) valuation equation. There seem to be some open questions concerning the consistency with the expected utility hypothesis and the overlap and nonoverlap which exists between stable and elliptical distributions.

2.4 Extensions to Three or More Parameters

Jean (1971 and 1973) extended the two-parameter analysis to three parameters. In addition to the mean value and the variance he considered the third moment around the mean. Under suitable assumptions about the (two-dimensional) efficient set and the structure of the indifference surfaces he derived a three-parameter CAPM. In a similar manner he derived an n-parameter CAPM. Of course, there are still many open questions. If, for instance, all probability distributions are taken into account and the investors are risk averse this three-parameter approach cannot be consistent with the expected utility hypothesis.

Additional contributions to the three-parameter approach were made by Arditti/Levy (1975), Kraus/Litzenberger (1976) and Simkowitz/Beedles (1978). Simkowitz and Beedles demonstrate that diversification is not necessarily desirable for investors who base their decisions on the first three moments of return distributions.

Taken by and large, three - or more - parameter approaches or even parameter-free approaches did not get very much response in the literature.

3. Rationale of the Hybrid Model

3.1 Consistency of the Mean-Variance Approach with Expected Utility and Stochastic Dominance

It is well known that the mean-variance approach is consistent with the expected utility hypothesis only if certain assumptions hold. Weak (strong) restrictions on the utility functions imply strong (weak) restrictions on the probability distributions and vice versa.

If, for instance, any increasing utility function is taken into account the random vector of asset returns R must be spherically distributed[1] (up to a linear transformation). To be more precise, the latter result which is contained in Chamberlain's (1983) paper presupposes the existence of a risk free asset, and exploits the structure of the end-of-period wealth. In the case under consideration the end-of-period wealth X can be written as

---

[1] An n dimensioned random vector R with mean vector $E(R) = 0$ is said to be spherically distributed about the origin, if AR has the same distribution as R for every orthogonal $(n \times n)$ matrix A .

$$X = \beta' R + \beta_0 \ , \tag{7}$$

where β is a weighting vector and β_0 is a scalar. Free short sales are permitted, so that there are no non-negativity or other restrictions on β or β_0 .

Theorem 1 (Chamberlain): Suppose that a riskless asset exists and that the vector R *of random asset returns has a nonsingular covariance matrix. The expected utility* $E\,u(X)$ *resulting from an arbitrary increasing utility function* u *and the end-of-period wealth (7) is a function of* $E(X)$ *and* $Var(X)$ *if and only if there is a nonsingular matrix* T *such that*

$$T[R - E(R)]$$

is spherically distributed about the origin.

If, on the other hand, any probability distribution of the returns is taken into account, an E-V-preference functional Φ is consistent with the expected utility hypothesis if and only if Φ is derived from a quadratic utility function (which may be written as)

$$u(x) = 2a\,x - x^2 \tag{8}$$

and is therefore given (up to a strictly increasing transformation) by

$$\Phi(E,V) = 2a\,E - E^2 - V \ . \tag{9}$$

The partial derivative of (9),

$$\Phi_E = 2a - 2E \ ,$$

exhibits "wealth preference" iff $E \leq a$. But this condition is not sufficient to avoid violations of the (first degree) stochastic dominance principle, as Borch (1969) pointed out. Borch considered an arbitrary system of upward sloping indifference curves in the standard deviation - mean plane and any two points on a given indifference curve for which he constructed suitable Bernoulli distributions with the prescribed moments such that one Bernoulli distribution stochastically dominates the other (in the strong sense). As the two points were arbitrary, his example works for points with $E \leq a$ too. In order to protect against such infringements of the stochastic dominance principle one has to impose the stronger condition that no realization (of the end-of-period wealth) can exceed the parameter a defined in (8).

The most serious disadvantage of the quadratic utility function is its ever increasing absolute risk aversion; i.e. it implies reduced risk taking as wealth increases. Sarnat (1974) summarizes the criticism in the following way "The shortcomings of a quadratic utility function are so serious and so widely known that by now one might assume that it would simply have been dropped from consideration". This view seems to be too extreme. The quadratic utility function is still useful, at least for computation purposes as Kallberg and Ziemba (1984) show. Nevertheless we will try to avoid the quadratic utility function.

Fortunately the mean-variance approach in capital market theory - though often mixed up with the quadratic utility function - does not hinge on this function. The crucial point to get rid of it is the restriction on certain classes of relevant probability distributions. The necessity to introduce suitable restrictions has been emphazised by Tobin (1969): "To get propositions with significantly more content than the prescription that the investor should maximize expected utility, it is necessary to place restrictions on this utility function or his subjective probability estimates or both."

In taking heed of Tobin's advise we will first consider restrictions on the probability distributions. If such restrictions will be introduced the scope for feasible preference functionals Φ will increase considerably. A drastic and frequently proposed limitation is the restriction on normally distributed returns. This (of course not uncontroversial) proposal is based on arguments such as:

- The family of normal distributions is closed under (non-degenerated) linear blends.
- Even if the returns on the single assets differ from a normal distribution the return on the portfolio (which is relevant for the end-of-period wealth) tends to be approximately normally distributed.

But the main reasons for the restriction on normally distributed returns are the enhanced choice of rational E-V-preference functionals Φ, the avoidance of the quadratic utility function, and the mathematical convenience stemming from the explicity of the resulting solutions.

Allais (1953), Schneeweiß (1967) and Chipman (1973) analyzed necessary and sufficient conditions which ensure the rationality of preference functionals Φ . Their main result is:

Theorem 2: With respect to the class of normal distributions an E-V-preference functional $\Phi(E,V)$ is rational only if it satisfies the partial differential-functional equation (where g is an arbitrary function):

$$\Phi_{EE} - 2\Phi_V = (\Phi_E)^2 \, g(\Phi) \ . \tag{10}$$

Under slight regularity conditions (10) is even sufficent to ensure the rationality of Φ .

Example 2:

With respect to the family of normal distributions preference functionals like

$$\Phi(E,V) = E - \frac{\alpha}{2} V \qquad (\alpha > 0) \tag{11}$$

or

$$\Phi(E,V) = \frac{E+a}{\sqrt{V+b}} \qquad (b > 0) \tag{12}$$

are consistent with the expected utility hypothesis and the stochastic dominance principle. The validity of (10) can easily be checked. We have to verify that the ratio

$$\frac{\Phi_{EE} - 2\Phi_V}{(\Phi_E)^2}$$

depends on E and V only through the value Φ . The functional (11) entails

$$\frac{\Phi_{EE} - \Phi_V}{(\Phi_E)^2} = \frac{0 + \alpha}{1} = \alpha$$

which is even a constant function. (12) entails

$$\frac{\Phi_{EE} - 2\Phi_V}{(\Phi_E)^2} = \frac{E+a}{\sqrt{V+b}} = \Phi = g(\Phi) \ .$$

The utility function corresponding to (11) is

$$u(x) = -e^{-\alpha x} \tag{13}$$

and that corresponding to (12) is [comp. Schneeweiß (1967, p. 153)]

$$u(x) = F\left(\frac{x+a}{\sqrt{b}}\right) \ , \tag{14}$$

where F is the cumulative distribution function of a standardized normally distributed random variable. ■

As we will consider only risk averse investors utility functions such as (14) and corresponding preference functionals are ruled out. In taking heed of Tobin's third alternative we will restrict the probability estimates *and* the utility functions suitably. To be more specific, we will focus on the so called hybrid approach.

The *hybrid approach* is characterized by the twin assumptions:

(a) The returns on the different assets are normally distributed.

(b) The investors have constant absolute risk aversion, i.e. a utility function on the type described in (13).

Of course, the degree α of risk aversion can vary among investors. The combination of (a) and (b) leads to the preference functional (11). Lintner (1969,1970) was the first who combined these two assumptions about beliefs (normal distribution) and tastes (exponential utility) into a model of capital market equilibrium. The analytical advantages of this approach were striking. But it was not yet clear whether another combined restriction on beliefs and tastes would yield comparable or even better advantages. A theorem obtained by Epps (1981) and the arguments presented in section 3.3 show that these advantages can not be achieved by any other (single-period) model. In this sense the combination of the assumptions (a) and (b) is a necessary requisite of a convenient portfolio and capital market model.

3.2 Explicit Solutions of the Portfolio Problem

As the twin assumptions (a) and (b) of the hybrid model should be motivated step by step we will not start from these conditions but from the usual assumptions of the two-parameter single-period portfolio model, i.e.:

1) Investors maximize a mean-variance functional $\Phi(E,V)$; Φ operating on the end-of-period wealth satisfies $\Phi_E > 0$

(wealth preference) and $\Phi_V < 0$ (risk aversion).

2) There exists a risk-free asset such that investors may borrow or lend unlimited amounts at the risk-free rate r_f .

3) There are no market imperfections such as taxes, regulations, or restrictions on short selling; the assets are perfectly divisible, and the investors are price takers.

Some additional assumptions will be introduced later. It goes without saying that many of these assumptions are unrealistic. The relaxation of assumptions will be discussed in chapter 4.

The (stochastic) end-of-period wealth

$$W = \left(w - \sum_{i=1}^{n} x_i v_i\right)\left(1 + r_f\right) + \sum_{i=1}^{n} x_i Y_i = wr + x^T\left(Y - vr\right) \tag{15}$$

depends on

r = 1 plus risk-free rate of interest $(r = 1 + r_f)$,

w = initial wealth of the investor (at free disposal for investment)

$Y = (Y_1,\ldots,Y_n)^T$ = vector of the stochastic end-of-period values (price plus dividend per share) of the n different types of risky assets,

$x = (x_1,\ldots,x_n)^T$ = vector of the number of shares included in the portfolio (the x_i's need not be integer),

$v = (v_1,\ldots,v_n)^T$ = vector of the share-prices at the beginning of the period.

Denoting the mean vector and the covariance matrix of Y by μ and Ω , respectively, the mean and the variance of end-of-period wealth are

$$\left.\begin{aligned} E(x) &= E(W) = wr + x^T(\mu - vr) \\ V(x) &= \mathrm{Var}(W) = x^T \Omega x \ . \end{aligned}\right\} \tag{16}$$

An optimal portfolio is a minimizer x of

$$\Phi[E(x),V(x)] \ . \tag{17}$$

We will assume that (17) is a convex function of x . Portfolio optimum then calls for

$$(\mu - vr)\Phi_E + 2\Omega x \Phi_V = 0 \ . \tag{18}$$

Under the additional asssumption that the covariance matrix Ω of the basic assets is nonsingular, (18) is equivalent to

$$x = -\frac{1}{2}\,\frac{\Phi_E}{\Phi_V}\,\Omega^{-1}(\mu - vr) \ . \tag{19}$$

Whether (19) represents an *explicit* solution of the portfolio selection problem or merely an *implicit* optimum condition is crucially dependent on the behavior of the ratio Φ_E/Φ_V of partial derivatives. (19) represents a true solution for x if

$$\frac{\Phi_E}{\Phi_V} \text{ is constant (i.e. independent of } E,V) \ . \tag{20}$$

Obviously, the simplest case is characterized by this independency condition (20). Explicit solutions may also be attainable if Φ_E/Φ_V contains E and V (and hence x) in a rather innocent manner; this topic will be analyzed in section 3.3. For the moment we will start out from the independency condition (20). As we know from the theory of partial differential equations [e.g. John (1982, p. 4)] the general solution of the partial differential equation corresponding to (20),

$$\Phi_E = c\,\Phi_V \ , \tag{21}$$

is given by

$$\Phi = h(E + \frac{1}{c}V) \ , \tag{22}$$

where h is an arbitrary differentiable function. Together with our normative assumptions $\Phi_E > 0$, $\Phi_V < 0$ we have $h' > 0$ and $c < 0$. As a preference functional is only determined up to an arbitrary increasing transformation, the independency condition (20) is satisfied if and only if Φ is of type (11) used in the hybrid model. Indeed, Epps (1981) showed that (20) entails not only constant absolute risk aversion but also multivariate normality of the end-of-period values Y .

Theorem 3 (Epps): The preference functional $\Phi(E,V)$ satisfies (20) and is consistent with the expected utility hypothesis if and only if the twin assumptions of the hybrid model are valid.

Some clarification about the independency condition (20) seems to be in order. Epps assumed that the constant c [defined in (21)] is independent from variations of w,x,v,r,μ and Ω . Actually, the consideration of some of these variations is dispensable; variations in the initial wealth w , the portfolio vector x and the price vector v are sufficient to ensure Epps' result. The following proof makes this point more transparent. In contrast to Epps' proof which works in a pure multivariate context we will mainly stay in a one dimensional setting. Nevertheless essential ideas of Epps' proof will be maintained. The sufficiency part of theorem 3 is well known and needs no further discussion; c is equal to $-\frac{2}{\alpha}$, where α is the absolute risk aversion of the investor [compare (11) and (13)]. The core of the necessity part is theorem 4 which focusses on a class of one-dimensional random variables generated by one fixed random variable. This class emerges in a natural way from the representation (15) of the end-of-period wealth. Given fixed proportions between the components of the portfolio vector x, (15) may be written in the form

$$W = wr + a(\hat{x}^T Y - \hat{x}^T vr) , \tag{23}$$

where the portfolio vector $x \neq 0$ is factorized into a (positive or negative) stretching factor a and a normalized vector $\hat{x}$ (normalized e.g. by $\Sigma \hat{x}_i^2 = 1$). If r, Y and $\hat{x} \neq 0$ remain fixed whereas a, v and w remain variable, (23) describes a three-parameter class of one-dimensional random variables

$$Z = a(X - b) + d , \tag{24}$$

where a, b, d are arbitrary real numbers and X is a *fixed* random variable with $0 < \mathrm{Var}(X) < \infty$.

Theorem 4: *Assume that a mean-variance rule* $\Phi(E,V)$ *satisfies*

$$\Phi_E > 0 , \ \Phi_V < 0 \ \text{ and } \ \Phi_E = c\,\Phi_V \quad (c \neq 0) \tag{25}$$

and is consistent with the expected utility hypothesis (u *having the properties* $u' > 0$ *and* $u'' < 0$) *on the class* (24) *of random variables. Then the utility function* u *must exhibit constant (positive) risk aversion and* X *must be normally distributed.*

A proof of theorem 4 is given in the appendix. The existence of a risk-free asset is essential with regard to the structure of the three-parameter class (24) and the course of the proof. Insofar the question whether Epps' theorem could be extended to the case without a risk-free asset should deserve further attention but will not pursued here.

From theorem 4 the following conclusions can be drawn:

- If the independency condition means that c is constant with respect to variations of the stretching factor a, the vector v of the share prices and the initial wealth w, then $\hat{x}^T Y$ and the end-of-period wealth W must be normally distributed.

- If moreover c is constant with respect to variations of the portfolio vector x then all components $Y_1,\ldots,Y_n$ of Y and all linear combinations must be normally distributed; hence Y must be multivariate normally distributed.

Within the hybrid model the explicit solutions of the portfolio problem directly can be taken from the optimality condition (19):

$$x^* = -\frac{1}{2} c\,\Omega^{-1}(\mu - vr)$$

Denoting the absolute risk aversion by α $(= -\frac{2}{c})$ we get the optimal portfolio of the investor in the form

$$x^* = \frac{1}{\alpha}\,\Omega^{-1}(\mu - vr) \quad . \tag{26}$$

Note that the optimal portfolio is independent of the initial wealth w and that the composition of the optimal portfolio is independent of the degree α of risk aversion (separation property).

Example 3:

We will restrict ourselves on $n = 2$ risky assets, whose price vector v, vector μ of expected end-of-period values and covariance matrix Ω are given by

$$v = \begin{pmatrix}140\\80\end{pmatrix}, \quad \mu = \begin{pmatrix}200\\100\end{pmatrix}, \quad \Omega = \begin{pmatrix}100 & 20\\ 20 & 60\end{pmatrix}.$$

We will assume that the risk-free (borrowing and lending) rate is $r_f = 0.1$ and the risk aversion coefficient is $\alpha = 10^{-5}$.

The optimal portfolio x^*, defined by (26), is

$$x^* = \frac{1}{\alpha}\,\Omega^{-1}(\mu - vr) = 10^5\,\frac{1}{5600}\begin{pmatrix}60 & -20\\ -20 & 100\end{pmatrix}\begin{pmatrix}200 - 140\cdot 1.1\\ 100 - 80\cdot 1.1\end{pmatrix} = \begin{pmatrix}45000\\ 5000\end{pmatrix}.$$

The resulting numbers of shares are positive and integer. In other numerical examples both properties could be violated since formula (26) was derived without taking into account integer restrictions and without ruling out short sales. Doubling the risk aversion coefficient α would divide the numbers of shares in half. As stated above, the composition (here 90% shares of asset 1 und 10% shares of asset 2) remains the same for all (positive) numerical values of the risk aversion coefficient α.

An increase of v_2 (share-price of asset 2) from 80 to 90 would alter the optimal portfolio into

$$x^* = \begin{pmatrix} 45000 \\ -14642.86 \end{pmatrix} .$$

Asset 2 is now overpriced; it is favorable to sell it short and to invest the money obtained from short-selling into the remaining assets (asset 1 and the risk free asset). ■

The portfolio problem as defined till now started out from exogenously given stochastic end-of-period values Y and share-prices v. Sometimes a vector R of stochastic rates of return is exogenously given instead of Y and v. The optimal vector x_R^* of amounts which should be invested in the different opportunities can be derived as easily (provided that the hybrid model is valid). The result is

$$x_R^* = \frac{1}{\alpha}\,\Omega^{-1}[E(R) - r_f e] \tag{26a}$$

where Ω_R is the covariance matrix of the rates of return and e is a vector of ones.

Example 4:

We will start with two risky opportunities characterized by the mean vector $E(R)$ and the covariance matrix Ω_R as follows:

$$E(R) = \begin{pmatrix} 0.08 \\ 0.11 \end{pmatrix} , \quad \Omega_R = \begin{pmatrix} 0.01 & -0.005 \\ -0.005 & 0.04 \end{pmatrix}$$

The risk-free rate of return and the risk aversion coefficient are assumed to be

$$r_f = 0.05 \quad , \quad \alpha = 10^{-6} .$$

Formula (26a) yields:

$$x_R^* = 10^6 \frac{1}{0.00375} \begin{pmatrix} 0.04 & 0.005 \\ 0.005 & 0.01 \end{pmatrix} \begin{pmatrix} 0.08 - 0.05 \\ 0.11 - 0.05 \end{pmatrix} = \begin{pmatrix} 40 \\ 2 \end{pmatrix} 10^6 ;$$

i.e. the decision maker should invest 40 or 2 million $ in opportunity 1 or 2, respectively. Of course, the derivation of (26a) rests upon the assumption that the rates of return are not influenced by the level of investment; Arrow (1970) terms this assumption as "constant stochastic returns to scale".

For the sake of comparison we will calculate the amounts to be invested in the different opportunities if only one of them is available. In this case R is a scalar (random variable) and (26a) gives

$$x^* = \frac{E(R) - r_f}{\alpha \, \mathrm{Var}(R)} = \begin{cases} 10^6 \dfrac{0.03}{0.01} = 3 \cdot 10^6 & \text{for opportunity 1} \\ 10^6 \dfrac{0.06}{0.04} = \dfrac{2}{3}\, 10^6 & \text{for opportunity 2} \end{cases} .$$

Both amounts are lower than before. This is quite natural since the correlation coefficient between the two rates of return is negative. Due to the diversification effect, the existence of the other risky opportunity is of mutual benefit. In monopolistic capital markets both opportunities could not rise as much funds than in the dyopolistic case. ■

3.3 Explicit Solutions of the Equilibrium Conditions

We extend the market assumptions stated at the beginning of section 3.2 by the additional assumption of *homogeneous expectations*; i.e. investors' perceptions of the distribution of the end-of-period values should be identical. Hence μ and Ω are the same for all investors. Provided that the hybrid model is valid the derivation of the equilibrium share-prices proceeds as follows:

According to (26) the optimal portfolio x^k of investor k is

$$x^k = \frac{1}{\alpha^k} \Omega^{-1} (\mu - vr) , \tag{27}$$

where α^k denotes the risk aversion of investor k . The aggregation of the optimal portfolio yields the (vector-valued) demand functions

$$\sum_k x^k = \sum_k \frac{1}{\alpha^k} \Omega^{-1} (\mu - vr) = \frac{1}{\alpha} \Omega^{-1} (\mu - vr) , \tag{28}$$

where α , the risk aversion of the entire market, is determined by Lintner's inverse additivity rule

$$\frac{1}{\alpha} = \sum_k \frac{1}{\alpha^k} .$$

Furthermore, denote by N_i the number of outstanding shares of security i and by $N = (N_1, \ldots, N_n)'$ the corresponding vector, then the equilibrium share-prices are determined by equating (28) to N :

$$N = \frac{1}{\alpha} \Omega^{-1} (\mu - vr) \tag{28a}$$

These market clearing conditions yield the explicit representation of the *equilibrium share-prices*

$$v = \frac{\mu - \alpha\Omega N}{r} \quad . \tag{29}$$

According to (27) and (29) the optimal portfolio x^k of investor k in equilibrium is

$$x^k = \frac{\alpha}{\alpha^k} N \, . \tag{30}$$

Observe that in equilibrium short sales are ruled out.

<u>Example 5:</u>

Suppose 10^5 investors are involved in a capital market with $r_f = 0.1$ on which (only) two risky assets are traded. The stochastic end-of-period values of the shares are characterized - as in example 3 - by

$$\mu = \begin{pmatrix} 200 \\ 100 \end{pmatrix} \quad , \quad \Omega = \begin{pmatrix} 100 & 20 \\ 20 & 60 \end{pmatrix} \quad .$$

The set of investors falls into two strata of equal size. The members of the first stratum have a risk aversion coefficient $\alpha = 10^{-5}$; the members of the second stratum are more risk averse and have $\alpha = 10^{-4}$. The numbers of the outstanding shares are

$$N_1 = 3 \cdot 10^6 \quad , \quad N_2 = 10^6 \quad .$$

The first step to calculate the equilibrium share-prices is the determination of the aggregated risk aversion. By Lintner's inverse additivity rule we get

$$\alpha = \alpha_{\text{Market}} = \left(\sum_k \frac{1}{\alpha^k}\right)^{-1} = \left(\frac{1}{2}\, 10^5 \cdot 10^5 + \frac{1}{2}\, 10^5 \cdot 10^4\right)^{-1} = 1.82 \cdot 10^{-10} \quad .$$

According to (29) we obtain the equilibrium share-prices

$$v = \frac{1}{r}\left[\mu - \alpha\Omega N\right] = \frac{1}{1.1}\left[\begin{pmatrix} 200 \\ 100 \end{pmatrix} - 1{,}82 \cdot 10^{-10} \begin{pmatrix} 100 & 20 \\ 20 & 60 \end{pmatrix} \begin{pmatrix} 3 \cdot 10^6 \\ 10^6 \end{pmatrix}\right] = \begin{pmatrix} 181.77 \\ 90.98 \end{pmatrix} \quad .$$

Since the entire market behaves as a single investor with a very low risk aversion the equilibrium share-prices are not far away from the discounted expected end-of-period values. The optimal portfolio of an investor from the first stratum is

$$x^k = \frac{\alpha}{\alpha^k} N = 1.82 \cdot 10^{-10} \cdot 10^5 \cdot 10^6 \begin{pmatrix} 3 \\ 1 \end{pmatrix} = 18.2 \begin{pmatrix} 3 \\ 1 \end{pmatrix} \quad ,$$

whereas the optimal portfolio of an investor belonging to the second stratum is

$$x^k = \frac{\alpha}{\alpha^k} N = 1.82 \cdot 10^{-10} \cdot 10^4 \cdot 10^6 \begin{pmatrix} 3 \\ 1 \end{pmatrix} = 1.82 \begin{pmatrix} 3 \\ 1 \end{pmatrix} .$$ ∎

If the i-th component of (29) ,

$$v_i = \frac{\mu_i - \alpha \sum_j \sigma_{ij} N_j}{r} , \quad \Omega = (\sigma_{ij})$$

will be multiplied by the number N_i of corresponding shares, an equation for the value of firm i in equilibrium will be obtained:

$$v_i N_i = \frac{\mu_i N_i - \alpha \sum_j N_i \sigma_{ij} N_j}{r} ,$$

which can be transformed into the explicit valuation formula

$$V_i = \frac{E(X_i) - \alpha \sum_j Cov(X_i, X_j)}{r} , \qquad (29a)$$

where

V_i is the equilibrium value of firm i

$X_i = N_i Y_i$ is the stochastic end-of-period value of firm i .

Note that the outer shape of (29a) is similar to the implicit formula (2). However, the terms on the right side of (29a) do not contain the equilibrium values $V_1, \ldots, V_n$.

The well known implicit valuation formulas can be generated by bringing up the rate of return R_m on the market portfolio (4) and observing

$$R_j = \frac{X_j}{V_j} - 1 \quad \text{or} \quad X_j = V_j R_j + V_j ,$$

$$\sum_j Cov(X_i, X_j) = Cov(X_i, \sum_j X_j) = Cov(X_i, \sum_j V_j R_j + V_j) =$$
$$= Cov(X_i, \sum_j V_j R_j) = (\sum_j V_j) Cov(X_i, R_m) .$$

Insert this expression into (29a) to get

$$V_i = \frac{E(X_i) - (\alpha \sum_j V_j) Cov(X_i, R_m)}{r} , \qquad (29b)$$

from which an alternative equation for the market price of risk (λ)

results:

$$\lambda = \alpha \sum_j V_j \quad ,$$

i.e. the market price of risk (3) is the product of the aggregated risk aversion and the sum of the equilibrium firm values.

Of course, (29b) coincides with the implicit valuation formula (2) mentioned in the introduction. By the way, valuation formula (29b) is often designated as *certainty-equivalent valuation formula* since the numerator may be interpreted as a kind of certainty-equivalent which is discounted at the rate r in the denominator. In contrast to this, a valuation formula in which the numerator is identical to the expected end-of-period value $E(X_i)$ and the denominator is identical to r up to a positive or negative correction (for risk) is termed a *risk-adjusted rate of return formula*. The latter can be derived very easily taking into account that

$$\mathrm{Cov}(X_i, R_m) = V_i \ \mathrm{Cov}(R_i, R_m) \ .$$

Inserting into (29b) yields

$$V_i = \frac{E(X_i) - \lambda V_i \ \mathrm{Cov}(R_i, R_m)}{r} \ ,$$

which, solved for V_i is identical to the result looked for:

$$V_i = \frac{E(X_i)}{r + \lambda \ \mathrm{Cov}(R_i, R_m)} \qquad (29c)$$

Finally, both valuation formulas (29b) and (29c) could be expressed in terms of the *volatility* (or β-factor) of asset i ,

$$\beta_i = \frac{\mathrm{Cov}(R_i, R_m)}{\mathrm{Var}(R_m)} \ .$$

For instance, (29c) then reads as follows:

$$V_i = \frac{E(X_i)}{r + \lambda \beta_i \ \mathrm{Var}(R_m)} \ . \qquad (29d)$$

3.4 Which Mean-Variance Approaches Provide Explicit Solutions?

In this section we will fathom the chances to obtain closed form solutions for the optimal portfolio x and the equilibrium prices v . The optimality condition (19) can be solved for x analytically only if the ratio Φ_E/Φ_V does not contain the vector x in a rather involved manner. Disregarding the case of a constant ratio which leads to the hybrid model the next best case is given if the ratio is a linear function of x . From (16) we see that this is true if and only if the ratio is a linear function of E ,

$$\frac{\Phi_E}{\Phi_V} = \beta + \gamma E \; . \tag{31}$$

To simplify the analysis we will restrict on separable preference functionals

$$\Phi(E,V) = f(E) + g(V) \; . \tag{32}$$

Since preference functionals are determined only up to an arbitrary increasing transformation, the investigation of additive separable functionals includes the investigation of multiplicative separable functionals too. Combining (31) and (32) we obtain the condition

$$\frac{f'(E)}{\beta + \gamma E} = g'(V) \; , \tag{33}$$

which implies the constancy of both sides. Hence Φ must be of the following type

$$\Phi(E,V) = c_1 E + c_2 E^2 + c_3 V \; , \tag{34}$$

where c_1, c_2, c_3 are constants of a suitably chosen sign.

Theorem 5: Let the preference functional $\Phi(E,V)$ be additively or multiplicatively separable. Then the determination of the optimal portfolio merely requires the solution of a linear equation system if and only if Φ is (up to an arbitrary increasing transformation) identical with (34).

If the separability assumption will be dropped the complete solution of the partial differential equation (31) can only be given implicitly. This is done in section 5.2 of the appendix. But as it seems, the complete solution does not include further special cases which are relevant for portfolio theory.

The functions (9) and (11) are of the type described by (34). The preference functional (9), based on the quadratic utility function, plays a dominant role in Mossin's (1973) textbook. With respect to the task to determine the optimal portfolio x the difference between the model based on (9) and the hybrid model is not very significant. But things change and the advantages of the hybrid model become more apparent if we switch over to the determination of the equilibrium share-prices. According to the hybrid model the aggregation and the market clearing conditions lead to formula (28a). According to the alternative model an analogue to (28a) results in which the (constant) factor $1/\alpha$ from (28a) is replaced by a (variable) factor which is a linear function of the vector v . Therefore, the analogue to (28a) is an interdependent quadratic system which hardly can be evaluated analytically unless Mossin's trick is adopted. He eludes the analytical problems by introducing an additional market clearing condition, namely that lending and borrowing among investors must cancel; what is borrowed by one must be lent by another. The closedness condition on the money market reduces the quadratic system to a linear one from which Mossin's explicit share-prices formulas result. Concerning this closedness condition another point of view may be adopted: As there are many participants on the money market which are no typical investors in risky securities (e.g. pure savers, the government, persons who lend money exclusively for consumption purposes etc.) borrowing and lending among investors must not all cancel. Note that the equilibrium share-prices derived in the framework of the hybrid model do not presuppose the closedness assumption on the money market.

So far we have discussed the cases of a constant ratio Φ_E/Φ_V and a ratio which is linear in E . In terms of separable functionals (32) the cases in which the ratio is a function of E or V alone can be analyzed very easily.

<u>*Theorem 6:*</u> *Let the preference functional* Φ *satisfy the separability condition and the condition*

$$\frac{\Phi_E}{\Phi_V} = h(V) \tag{35}$$

or the condition

$$\frac{\Phi_E}{\Phi_V} = h(E) \ , \tag{36}$$

where h *is an arbitrary function. Then* Φ *must be of the type*

$$\Phi(E,V) = c_0 + c_1E + c_1 \int \frac{dV}{h(V)} \quad \textit{if (35) holds,} \tag{37}$$

$$\Phi(E,V) = c_0 + c_1 \int h(E)\,dE + c_1V \quad \textit{if (36) holds.} \tag{38}$$

It should be noted that (37) and (38) were derived only from the separability condition and the behavior (35) or (36) of the ratio.

If we call for the compatibility with the expected utility property or for a convenient analytical treatment in portfolio theory, most of the general functions (37) and (38) are ruled out. If we are willing to tolerate quadratic systems (for the determination of the optimal portfolio x) we are compelled to restrict ourselves on ratios of the type

$$\beta + \gamma E + \delta E^2 \qquad (39)$$

or

$$\beta + \gamma V \qquad (40)$$

or the sum of (39) and (40). Especially with respect to (40) theorem 6 yields (if $\gamma \neq 0$)

$$\Phi(E,V) = c_0 + c_1 E + \frac{c_1}{\gamma} \ln|\beta + \gamma V| \ . \qquad (41)$$

Of course, the solution of the corresponding quadratic system is less delightful and the solution of the resulting market clearing conditions is even more cumbersome. Moreover, there is an incompatibility to the expected utility property. Clearly (41) violates the expected utility property if all probability distributions are taken into account. Even if we restrict ourselves on normal distributions serious problems continue to exist. The normative assumption $\Phi_E/\Phi_V < 0$ rules out γ-values different form zero; of course, the same holds true for γ in (31). However, $\gamma = 0$ leads us again back to the hybrid model.

Obviously, the results of this section substantiate the conjecture that there is no virtual alternative to the hybrid model provided that the objective to obtain closed form equilibrium solutions is given high priority. In this sense the hybrid model is the most convenient model in capital market theory.

4. Applications of the Hybrid Model

The discussion in chapter 3 made it clear that the hybrid model plays a special role among the single-period models. The closed form solution (29) can be used for the purpose of comparative static investigations. Some examples of such investigations which hardly could be conducted in terms of the implicit valuation formulas of the usual CAPM framework are presented in sections 4.1 to 4.4

Since we do not get something for nothing the critisism of our basic assumption (constant risk aversion and normality) is the price for the considerable simplifications resulting from the hybrid model. Some criticism can be invalidated by suitable counter arguments or by an appropriate modification of the way of looking at a problem. For instance, an important objection is the incompatibility of the normality assumption with the limited or nonexistent liability of common stock holders. This drawback can be overcome by considering the "true price" of the limited liability-share as the price of a call option with an exercise price of zero. Brennan (1979) developed suitable call price formulas in a one-period model and pointed out that the twin assumptions of the hybrid model are sufficient to ensure the derivation of so called "risk neutral valuation relationships" for contingent claims.

4.1 Consideration of Income Taxation

The impact of corporate taxes on capital market equilibria is well known. The capital-structure decision is affected by corporate taxes provided that interest payments of the firm's debt are tax-deductible. In what follows we will disregard corporate taxes; we will focus on income taxes. Tax law is supposed not to discriminate between dividends and capital gains income. Therefore we need not split up rates of return or end-of-period values into corresponding terms.

According to (15), the period income resulting from portfolio decision x is

$$wr + x^T(Y - vr) - w \ .$$

Taking into account an additional (nonstochastic) basic income b and a *proportional tax schedule* with tax rate t , the net income is

$$(1-t)[b + wr_f + x^T(Y - vr)] \ . \qquad (42)$$

In order to justify the representation (42) of net income we have to introduce two assumptions:

$$\left.\begin{array}{l}\text{There are full loss-offset provisions.}\\ \text{The proportional tax schedule is valid}\\ \text{for negative incomes too.}\end{array}\right\} \qquad (43)$$

In real life the period income resulting from a positive basic income, from interest income and from the proceeds of a well diversified portfolio is expected to be positive. However, the normality assumption of the hybrid model does not exclude negative period incomes (though realistic vavlues of μ and Ω will yield a negligible probability for that case). The second assumption of (43) prevents from cumbersome case distinctions; it means that an individual with a negative period income has a negative tax liability, i.e. he or she gets money from the tax authorities.

The derivation of the optimal portfolio is now straightforward. According to (11), the objective function (the certainty-equivalent of the end-of-period wealth) is

$$\Phi(W) = w + (1-t)[b + wr_f + x^T(\mu - vr)] - \frac{\alpha}{2}(1-t)^2 x^T \Omega x \ .$$

The gradient of this concave function is

$$\text{grad}_x \ \Phi(W) = (1-t)(\mu - vr) - \alpha(1-t)^2 \Omega x$$

and the maximizer x^* is (provided that Ω is regular and $t < 1$):

$$x^* = \frac{1}{\alpha(1-t)} \Omega^{-1}(\mu - vr) \ . \qquad (44)$$

<u>Theorem 7:</u> *Under the assumptions of the hybrid model and a proportional income tax schedule satisfying (43) the optimal portfolio is given by (44).*

Recall that the mean vector μ and the covariance matrix Ω refer to the end-of-period values before taxes. A comparison of (44) and (26) shows that the introduction of proportional income taxes (with full loss-offset) leads to an increase in the number of risky shares in the portfolio; i.e. risk-taking is increased. This result is in accordance with the findings of Mossin (1968), Stiglitz (1969), Allingham (1972) and others.

We will turn to the investigation of equilibrium share-prices. Denote by α^k the (constant absolute) risk aversion of investor k, and by t^k his marginal tax rate (which is assumed to be independent of the actual portfolio decision). By the same assumption and the procedure which led to (44) we obtain the optimal portfolio of investor k:

$$x^k = \frac{1}{\alpha^k(1-t^k)} \Omega^{-1}(\mu - vr) \ . \qquad (45)$$

The case of a uniformly valid proportional tax rate corresponds to

$$t^k = t \quad \text{for all} \quad k \ .$$

The variability of the tax rate implicitly takes into account a progressive taxation scheme, different basic incomes (b^k), and tax-exempt amounts. In Germany there is a tax allowance of DM 800 per family and year for dividends and interest income. Hence $t^k = 0$ is appropriate for "small" investors. According to German tax laws $t^k = 0.56$ is the appropriate marginal tax rate of "big" investors and corporations. Constant but individually varying marginal tax rates provide a standard framework which has been used, for instance, by Brennan (1970) and Saelzle (1976).

Aggregating the portfolios (45) and equating the sum to the vector N (numbers of outstanding shares) results in the equilibrium share-prices

$$v = \frac{\mu - \alpha_t \Omega N}{r} \tag{46}$$

where

$$\alpha_t = \left[\sum_k \frac{1}{\alpha^k (1 - t^k)} \right]^{-1} . \tag{47}$$

The only difference between (29a) and (46) is the substitution of α through the aggregated risk aversion after taxes (α_t).

The dependence of α_t on the marginal tax rates t^k is as follows:

- α_t is a decreasing function of (each individual) t^k.
- If t_{max} and t_{min} are the maximal and minimal tax rates, and α is the aggregated risk aversion before taxes, we have

$$\alpha(1 - t_{max}) \le \alpha_t \le \alpha(1 - t_{min}) \le \alpha \tag{48}$$

Example 6:

Assume that $n = 10^6$ investors are involved in the capital market, each of which has a (constant) risk aversion $\alpha^k = 10^{-6}$. Then α is given by

$$\alpha = \left(\sum_k \frac{1}{\alpha^k} \right)^{-1} = \left(\sum_k 10^6 \right)^{-1} = 10^{-12} .$$

If the investors are faced with the marginal tax rates

$$t^1 = \dots = t^K = 0 \quad , \quad K = 5 \cdot 10^5$$

$$t^{K+1} = \dots = t^{10^6} = 0.56 \quad ,$$

(47) yields

$$\alpha_t = \left[\sum_{k=1}^{K} 10^6 + \frac{1}{0.44} \sum_{k=K+1}^{10^6} 10^6 \right]^{-1} = 0.61 \cdot 10^{-12} = 0.61\alpha \ .$$

If all investors have the same marginal tax rate $t^k = 0.56$, the corresponding value is $\alpha_t = 0.44 \cdot 10^{-12} = 0.44\alpha$. ■

We are now in a position to answer the question: How does the inclusion of income taxes affect the share prices, the firm values, and the portfolio in equilibrium?

Insert (46) into (45) to get

$$x^k = \frac{1}{\alpha^k(1-t^k)} \Omega^{-1}[\mu - (\mu - \alpha_t \Omega N)] = \frac{\alpha_t}{\alpha^k(1-t^k)} N \ . \qquad (49)$$

(48) allows to rewrite α_t as

$$\alpha_t = \alpha(1-\bar{t}) \ , \qquad (50)$$

where $\bar{t}$ is an appropriate "average" tax rate. Hence we have

$$x^k = \frac{\alpha}{\alpha^k} \cdot \frac{1-\bar{t}}{1-t^k} \cdot N \ . \qquad (51)$$

We summarize the result in the following

Theorem 8: *Under our assumption on the tax system (fixed tax rate t^k for investor k) the optimal portfolio in equilibrium is given by (51), where the average tax rate $\bar{t}$ is defined by (47) and (50). If $t^k = t$ for all k , the portfolio before taxes is the same as the portfolio after taxes; the numerical value of the uniformly valid tax rate t is irrelevant. If $t^k < \bar{t}$ (i.e. k is a "small" investor), the taxation scheme reduces the absolute number of risky shares held by investor k . If $t^k > \bar{t}$ (i.e. k is a "big" investor), the taxation scheme increases the absolute number of risky shares held by investor k .*

Example 7:

We will resume the situation of example 6. The (already determined) relation $\alpha_t = 0.61\alpha$ means

$$\bar{t} = 1 - 0.61 = 0.39 \ .$$

Taxation leads to the optimal portfolio in equilibrium given by

$$x^k = \frac{1-0.39}{1-0} \frac{\alpha}{\alpha^k} N = 0.61 \frac{\alpha}{\alpha^k} N \quad \text{if } k \text{ is a "small" investor} \ ,$$

$$x^k = \frac{1-0.39}{1-0.56}\,\frac{\alpha}{\alpha^k}\,N = 1.39\,\frac{\alpha}{\alpha^k}\,N \quad \text{if } k \text{ is a "big" investor .}$$

A taxation scheme of the kind under consideration induces "small" investors to hold only 61% and "big" investors to hold 139% of the numbers of shares held in a world without taxes. ■

To analyze the effect on the equilibrium share-prices or the firm values we transform the i-th component of (46) into the analogue of (29b),

$$V_i = \frac{E(X_i) - \alpha_t \sum_j Cov(X_i, X_j)}{r}$$

or to

$$V_i = \frac{E(X_i) - \alpha_t \; Cov(X_i, \sum_j X_j)}{r} \quad . \tag{52}$$

From (52) we can see that the effect of the taxation scheme is crucially dependent on the covariance between X_i (the stochastic-end-of period value of firm i) and $\sum_j X_j$ (the sum of the end-of-period values of all firms).

<u>*Theorem 9:*</u> *Under our assumptions on the tax system the equilibrium value* V_i *of firm* i *is given by* (52).
If $Cov(X_i, \sum_j X_j) = 0$, *there is no taxation effect on* V_i .

If $Cov(X_i, \sum_j X_j) > 0$ *(resp.* < 0*) the taxation scheme increases (resp. reduces) the equilibrium firm value* V_i .

<u>Example 8:</u>

Suppose $n = 1000$ firmsare offering shares on a capital market whose aggregated risk aversion is 10^{-8} .

Let $r = 1.1$ and

$Var(X_i) = 10^{10}$ for $i = 1, \ldots, 1000$

$Cov(X_i, X_j) = 0.5 \cdot 10^{10}$ for $i \neq j$

$E(X_1) = 700\ 000$.

The equilibrium value V_1 of firm 1 (without taxes) is

$$V_1 = \frac{700\ 000 - 10^{-8} \cdot 10^{10}(1 + 999 \cdot 0.5)}{1.1} = 590\ 864\ \$$$

If all investors are faced with a tax rate of 56% V_1 increases to

$$V_1 = \frac{700\ 000 - 0.44 \cdot 10^{2}(1 + 999 \cdot 0.5)}{1.1} = 616\ 344\ \$\ .$$ ■

The qualitative results of theorem 9 can be obtained even in a more general mean-variance setting, compare for instance Saelzle (1976, p. 230) who gives an illustrative explanation of the results.

Since (52) is equivalent to

$$v_i = \frac{E(Y_i) - \alpha_t \operatorname{Cov}(Y_i, \sum_j X_j)}{r} \tag{53}$$

similar conclusions are valid with respect to the equilibrium share-prices v_i .

4.2 Heterogeneous Expectations

The assumption of homogeneous expectations will be dropped, the other assumptions (no market imperfections, risk free rate r_f , hybrid model) will be maintained. The distinct beliefs are characterized by

μ^k , the mean (vector) of the end-of-period values and
Ω_k , the covariance matrix as perceived by investor k . [1)]

Equation (27) yields the optimal portfolio of investor k ,

$$x^k = \frac{1}{\alpha^k} \Omega_k^{-1} (\mu^k - vr) \; . \tag{54}$$

Aggregation over all investors gives the total demand for risky assets

$$\sum_k x^k = \sum_k \frac{1}{\alpha^k} \Omega_k^{-1} (\mu^k - vr)$$

which may be written as

$$\sum_k x^k = \frac{1}{\alpha} \Omega^{-1} (\mu - vr) \; , \tag{55}$$

where

$$\alpha = \left[\sum_k \frac{1}{\alpha^k} \right]^{-1} \tag{56}$$

$$\Omega = \left[\sum_k \frac{\alpha}{\alpha^k} \Omega_k^{-1} \right]^{-1} \tag{57}$$

---

1) As before, the k superscript denotes the k-th investor. The subscript at Ω_k is an exception in order to write the inverse Ω_k^{-1} without ambiguity. Of course, the existence of Ω_k^{-1} is an assumption which we have to introduce.

$$\mu = \Omega \Sigma \frac{\alpha}{\alpha^k} \Omega_k^{-1} \mu^k \quad . \qquad (58)$$

A comparison of (55) with (54) shows that the entire market behaves like a "big" investor having constant risk aversion of size α and expectations given by (57) and (58).

Equating the aggregated demand (55) to the vector N of outstanding shares determines the market clearing share-prices

$$v = \frac{\mu - \alpha \Omega N}{r} \quad . \qquad (59)$$

(59) differs from the corresponding formula (29) only in the definition of the aggregated parameters (57),(58).

In equilibrium the optimal portfolio of investor k turns into

$$x^k = \frac{1}{\alpha^k} \Omega_k^{-1} (\mu^k - \mu + \alpha \Omega N) \quad . \qquad (60)$$

Some remarks are in order:

- Formulas (55) to (60) were established by Lintner (1969); additional reference is made to Williams (1977a), Jarrow (1980), Peterson/Peterson (1982), and Firchau (1984).
- In contrast to the case of homogeneous expectations, (60) does not exclude short sales.
- (59) does not exclude the occurrence of negative share-prices in equilibrium. While short sales can be excluded by a slight modification of the model (compare section 4.3), negative equilibrium prices can only be avoided by assuming that the given data satisfy

  $$\mu \geq \alpha \Omega N \ .$$

  Negative share-prices affect the end-of-period wealth (15) in the following way: A positive number x_i of negatively priced shares i means additional cash $x_i |Y_i|$ at the beginning of the period. This cash can be invested elsewhere and may be interpreted as a kind of premium to offset the risk $(x_i Y_i)$ to be borne at the end of the period.

Both negative share-prices and short sales occur in the subsequent example.

Example 9:

We will restrict on two investors and $n = 2$ risky assets.

Risk aversions: $\alpha^1 = 10^{-5}$, $\alpha^2 = \frac{1}{2} \cdot 10^{-5}$

Mean vectors: $\mu^1 = \begin{pmatrix} 6 \\ 13 \end{pmatrix}$, $\mu^2 = \begin{pmatrix} 12 \\ 10 \end{pmatrix}$

Covariances: $\Omega_1 = \Omega_2 = \begin{pmatrix} 10 & 5 \\ 5 & 20 \end{pmatrix}$

Numbers of outstanding shares: $N_1 = 10^5$, $N_2 = 3 \cdot 10^5$.

Hence the aggregated parameters are

$$\alpha = (3 \cdot 10^5)^{-1} \; , \; \Omega = \begin{pmatrix} 10 & 5 \\ 5 & 20 \end{pmatrix} \; , \; \mu = \frac{1}{3} \begin{pmatrix} 6 \\ 13 \end{pmatrix} + \frac{2}{3} \begin{pmatrix} 12 \\ 10 \end{pmatrix} = \begin{pmatrix} 10 \\ 11 \end{pmatrix}$$

The calculation of the equilibrium prices and the portfolios in equilibrium proceeds according to (59),(60) and results in:

$$v = \frac{1}{r} \left[\begin{pmatrix} 10 \\ 11 \end{pmatrix} - \frac{10^{-5}}{3} \begin{pmatrix} 10 & 5 \\ 5 & 20 \end{pmatrix} \begin{pmatrix} 1 \\ 3 \end{pmatrix} 10^5 \right] = \frac{1}{r} \begin{pmatrix} 1.67 \\ -10.67 \end{pmatrix}$$

$$x^1 = 10^5 \frac{1}{175} \begin{pmatrix} 20 & -5 \\ -5 & 10 \end{pmatrix} \begin{pmatrix} -4 \\ 2 \end{pmatrix} + 10^5 \cdot \frac{10^{-5}}{3} \cdot 10^5 \begin{pmatrix} 1 \\ 3 \end{pmatrix} = \begin{pmatrix} -18{,}095 \\ 122{,}857 \end{pmatrix}$$

$$x^2 = 2 \cdot 10^5 \frac{1}{175} \begin{pmatrix} 20 & -5 \\ -5 & 10 \end{pmatrix} \begin{pmatrix} 2 \\ -1 \end{pmatrix} + 2 \cdot 10^5 \cdot \frac{10^{-5}}{3} \cdot 10^5 \begin{pmatrix} 1 \\ 3 \end{pmatrix} = \begin{pmatrix} 118{,}095 \\ 177{,}143 \end{pmatrix}$$

Investor 1 sells short 18,095 shares of asset 1. The negatively priced asset 2 is contained in both portfolios. Note that the two portfolios are not proportional, i.e. the separation theorem (valid for homogeneous expectations) fails to be true for heterogeneous expectations. ■

4.3 Restrictions on Short Sales

Till now we allowed unrestricted short sales with full use of the proceeds. In real world investors do not receive funds equal to the value of assets which they sell short.[1] The assumption of unrestricted short sales facilitated the analysis insofar as the optimal portfolio could be obtained without consideration of nonnegativity restrictions. As already mentioned, in equilibrium short sales can occur if heterogeneous expectations are present; short sales are ruled out if homogeneous expectations prevail. Accordingly, it turns

1) Compare for instance Jarrow (1980) or Sharpe (1981, p. 36) about the current US-regulations concerning short sales.

out that short sales are only relevant in the case of heterogeneous expectations. Miller (1977) argued that the direction of the effect is always unambiguous: Short selling restrictions increase the prices of risky assets above those which would occur in a world with no restrictions. A rigorous reconsideration of Miller's conjecture by Jarrow (1980) revealed that the direction of the effect is ambiguous unless special conditions are met. Since Jarrow used the hybrid model framework his analysis will be surveyed in the sequel.

Recall that the optimal portfolio (54) of investor k has been obtaned by equating the gradient (of the objective function $\Phi(E(x), V(x))$ to zero, i.e.

$$\mu^k - vr - \alpha^k \Omega_k x^k = 0 . \tag{61}$$

In the presence of nonnegativity restrictions $x^k \geq 0$ the relevant optimality condition is

$$\mu^k - vr - \alpha^k \Omega_k x^k + \lambda^k = 0 , \tag{62}$$

where λ^k is an $(n \times 1)$-vector of Lagrangean multipliers (n = number of different basic assets). To be more exactly: A portfolio-vector $x^k \geq 0$ is optimal if and only if $\lambda^k \geq 0$ exists such that (62) is satisfied together with the well-known slackness-conditions

$$\lambda_i^k x_i^k = 0 \quad (i = 1, \ldots, n) . \tag{63}$$

Rearranging (62) gives the optimal portfolio

$$x^k = \frac{1}{\alpha^k} \Omega_k^{-1} (\mu^k - vr) + \frac{1}{\alpha^k} \Omega_k^{-1} \lambda^k . \tag{64}$$

A comparison with (54) shows that the additional term

$$\frac{1}{\alpha^k} \Omega_k^{-1} \lambda^k \tag{65}$$

reflects the effect of short sales restrictions. Though λ^k is nonnegative the sign of (65) is ambiguous as shown by Jarrow. Clearly the effect of short sales restrictions vanishes if all nonnegativity restrictions are nonbinding (i.e. $\lambda^k = 0$) .

We will now switch from exogenously given prices v to equilibrium prices. The first step consists in the aggregation of the individual portfolios (64).

$$\sum_k x^k = \sum_k \frac{1}{\alpha^k} \Omega^{-1}(\mu^k - vr) + \sum_k \frac{1}{\alpha^k} \Omega_k^{-1}\lambda^k$$

$$= \frac{1}{\alpha} \Omega^{-1}(\mu - vr) + \frac{1}{\alpha} \lambda \ , \qquad (66)$$

where α, μ and Ω are defined by (56),(57),(58), and λ is defined through

$$\lambda = \sum_k \frac{\alpha}{\alpha^k} \Omega_k^{-1}\lambda^k \ . \qquad (67)$$

Note that the components of λ (unlike the components of λ^k) may have different signs.

The market clearing conditions

$$N = \frac{1}{\alpha} \Omega^{-1}(\mu - vr) + \frac{1}{\alpha}\lambda$$

result in the equilibrium prices

$$v = \frac{\mu - \alpha \Omega N}{r} + \frac{\Omega\lambda}{r} \ . \qquad (68)$$

The first term of (68) is identical to the equilibrium prices (59) in the absence of short sales restrictions. The second term,

$$\frac{1}{r} \Omega\lambda \qquad (69)$$

is caused by the introduction of short sales restrictions. In general, both Ω and λ contain positive and negative elements. Jarrow (1980) demonstrates the ambiguity of the sign of (69) by the following example.

Example 10:

Suppose a capital market consists of two individuals and two risky assets. The data are

$$\alpha^1 = \alpha^2 = 1 \ , \ N_1 = N_2 = 1$$

$$\mu^1 = \begin{pmatrix} 2 \\ 1 \end{pmatrix} , \ \mu^2 = \begin{pmatrix} 1 \\ 3 \end{pmatrix} , \ \Omega_1 = \begin{pmatrix} 1 & 1 \\ 1 & 3 \end{pmatrix} , \ \Omega_2 = \begin{pmatrix} 3 & 1 \\ 1 & 1 \end{pmatrix} .$$

According to (56),(57),(58), the aggregated parameters are

$$\alpha = \frac{1}{2} \ , \ \mu = \frac{1}{6} \begin{pmatrix} 13 \\ 17 \end{pmatrix} , \ \Omega = \frac{2}{3} \begin{pmatrix} 2 & 1 \\ 1 & 2 \end{pmatrix} .$$

Without short sales restrictions (i.e. $\lambda^1 = \lambda^2 = 0$), equations (59) and (60) yield

$$v = \frac{1}{r}\begin{pmatrix} 7/6 \\ 11/6 \end{pmatrix}, \quad x^1 = \frac{1}{6}\begin{pmatrix} 10 \\ -5 \end{pmatrix}, \quad x^2 = \frac{1}{6}\begin{pmatrix} -4 \\ 11 \end{pmatrix}$$

as equilibrium prices and portfolios. The corresponding vectors in the presence of short sales restrictions are

$$v = \frac{1}{r}\begin{pmatrix} 1 \\ 2 \end{pmatrix}, \quad x^{(1)} = \begin{pmatrix} 1 \\ 0 \end{pmatrix}, \quad x^{(2)} = \begin{pmatrix} 0 \\ 1 \end{pmatrix}.$$

Hence the equilibrium price of asset 1 falls while the equilibrium price of asset 2 rises as a result of the short sales restrictions. ■

Obviously, the impacts of short sales restrictions on the equilibrium prices are ambiguous unless additional knowledge about the individual data α^k, μ^k and Ω_k is available. The impacts are unambiguous if the beliefs about the covariances are not too different in the following sense:

- Investor agree that the returns are uncorrelated; i.e. the covariance matrix Ω_k is diagonal (the diagonal elements may differ from investor to investor)
- The covariance matrices are identical up to a positive factor, i.e. $\Omega_k = a^k \Omega_0$.

A glance on the definitions (57) and (67) of Ω and λ shows that these conditions are sufficient to guarantee the nonnegativity of the term (69). We summarize the result in

Theorem 10 (Jarrow): *Equilibrium asset prices rise (or stay constant) due to short sales restrictions either if the different covariance matrices Ω_k are diagonal or if they are proportional.*

4.4 Some Other Market Imperfections

Of the many market imperfections which deserve further attention we will single out some problems resulting from deficiencies of the competition among the participants on the capital market. Deficiencies of this kind are present if the number of investors or the number of companies (n = number of basic assets) are too small. Instead of going into detail we will prefer to give some references.

The aggregation procedure leading to equilibrium prices works for arbitrary numbers of investors and companies. However, if there are only a few investors, the calculated equilibrium prices seem to be doubtful since the assumption of price-taking investors may be frowned upon. Capital markets of this type have been analyzed by Rudolph (1982).

If, on the other hand, the number n of companies (or basic assets) is very small, the "small company assumption" cannot be adopted. The implicit valuation formula (2) is unsuitable to investigate the impacts of different policies on the market value of the own company and the other companies. Clearly, the explicit valuation formula (29a) of the hybrid model is much more appropriate to conduct such investigations. Based on the valuation equation (29a), Bamberg/ Spremann (1981b) and Spremann/Bamberg (1981) consider a company, say company number i, who achieves to reduce the variance $Var(X_i)$ of its end-of-period value X_i (as perceived by the investors). In real life this could be done, for instance, by converting fixed charges into variable charges (proportional to gross sales) or by persistently pursued income smoothing. Under the simplifying assumption that the variance reduction does not change the mean values and the correlation structure the results of the comparative static analysis are:

Variance reducing efforts of company i

- increase its own value V_i if the covariance of X_i with the rest of market, i.e.

  $$Cov(X_i, \sum_{j \neq i} X_j)$$

  is positive; otherwise both an increase and a reduction of V_i is possible (depending on the remaining variance)
- increase (reduce) the value V_j of those companies j whose end-of-period values X_j are positively (negatively) correlated with X_i.

The effect on the values of the other firm is expected to provoke reactions on the part of these firms: a game theoretical situation arises. Bilateral variance reducing efforts lead to a dyopolistic capital market which has been analyzed by Bamberg (1984).

The final example refers to a company whose risk characteristic (in terms of real rate of return) differs from those of the other companies; the extreme case of a single company (i.e. $n = 1$) offering risky shares to the public is included. This kind of imperfection of the capital market could suggest issuing strategies. The company under consideration (or the initial shareholders) could try to ration the public by a suitable issuing policy. Bamberg/Spremann (1983a,1984) and Spremann (1984) discuss these topics on the basis of the hybrid model. The optimal amount of capital is determined which should be financed by issuing new shares, the relation between inital and final shareholders is analyzed in some detail and, finally, some results on incentive compatibility are derived.

5. Appendix

5.1 Proof of Theorem 4

The proof is facilitated if the differentiation and the expectation operator are interchangeable. To avoid technical tangentialities we will assume that the corresponding regularity conditions are satisfied. (Of course, these regularity conditions are satisfied in the case of the hybrid model.)

First we will compare the a-values which maximize $E[u(Z)]$ on the one hand and $\Phi(E,V) = h(E + \frac{1}{c}V)$ on the other hand.

$$\frac{d}{da} E[u(Z)] = E[u'(aX - ab + d)(X - b)] \tag{70}$$

$E[u(Z)]$ is a concave function of a since

$$\frac{d^2}{da^2} E[u(Z)] = E[u''(aX - ab + d)(X - b)^2] < 0 .$$

Hence a^* , the optimal a-value, will be obtained by equating (70) to zero. The optimal a^* is a function of the two other parameters b and d . Differentiating the optimality condition with respect to b yields:

$$E[u''(a^*X - a^*b + d)(\frac{da^*}{db} X - b \frac{da^*}{db} - a^*)(X - b)] =$$

$$= E[u'(a^*X - a^*b + d)] ,$$

or

$$\frac{da^*}{db} = \frac{E[u'(a^*X-a^*b+d)] + a^*E[u''(a^*X-a^*b+d)(X-b)]}{E[u''(a^*X-a^*b+d)(X-b)^2]} . \tag{71}$$

Application of the same procedure on the mean-variance rule yields:

$$\frac{d}{da} h[a\ E(X) - ab + d + \frac{1}{c}\ a^2\ Var(X)] =$$

$$= h'[a\ E(X)-ab+d + \frac{1}{c} a^2\ Var(X)][E(X)-b + \frac{2a}{c}\ Var(X)] \overset{!}{=} 0 \qquad (72)$$

By virtue of $h' > 0$, (72) leads to

$$a^* = \frac{c}{2} \cdot \frac{b-E(X)}{Var(X)} \quad \text{and} \quad \frac{da^*}{db} = \frac{c}{2\ Var(X)}\ . \qquad (73)$$

From (73) we have

$a^* = 0$ if $b = E(X)$.

Hence the comparison of the two dervatives $\frac{da^*}{db}$ at the point $b = E(X)$ results in

$$\frac{E[u'(d)]}{E[u''(d)(X - E(X))^2]} = \frac{u'(d)}{u''(d)Var(X)} = \frac{c}{2\ Var(X)}\ .$$

Consistency between the mean-variance rule and the expected utility hypothesis consequently implies:

$$-\frac{u''(d)}{u'(d)} = -\frac{2}{c} \quad \text{for all} \quad d \in \mathbb{R}\ . \qquad (74)$$

(74) is equivalent to the constancy of the absolute risk aversion. Pratt (1964) allows to infer

$$u(d) = -e^{\frac{2}{c}d} \quad \text{for all} \quad d \in \mathbb{R} \qquad (75)$$

(up to an arbitrary increasing linear function).

With respect to the utility function (75) rationality of the mean-variance rule means the equality:

$$E[u(Z)] = -E\left[e^{\frac{2}{c}Z}\right] = h[E(Z) + \frac{1}{c}\ Var(Z)] \qquad (76)$$

for a suitable chosen function h and all Z generated by (24). Denote the probability function of X by $F(\zeta)$ and insert (24) into (76) to get

$$-\int_{-\infty}^{\infty} \exp[\frac{2}{c}(a\zeta-ab+d)]dF(\zeta) = h[aE(X)-ab+d + \frac{1}{c} a^2\ Var(X)]\ , \qquad (77)$$

which (evaluated at $a = 0$) gives

$$-\exp[\frac{2}{c}d]\int_{-\infty}^{\infty} dF(\zeta) = h(d) \quad \text{or}$$

$$h(d) = -\exp[\frac{2}{d}d] \quad \text{for all} \quad d \in \mathbb{R} \ . \tag{78}$$

(77) and (78) can be transformed into

$$\int_{-\infty}^{\infty} \exp[\frac{2}{c}a\zeta]\, dF(\zeta) = \exp[\frac{2}{c}a\, E(X) + \frac{2}{c^2}a^2 Var(X)]$$

or

$$M(t) = \exp[t\, E(X) + \frac{t^2}{2} Var(X)] \quad \text{for all} \quad t \in \mathbb{R} \ , \tag{79}$$

where M is the moment generating function of X .

$M(t)$ thus coincides with the well known moment generating function of a normally distributes random variable. The uniqueness of the moment generating function ensures that X is normally distributed.

■

5.2 Solution of Partial Differential Equation (31)

Equation (31) is a simple quasi-linear partial differential equation. According to the pertinent literatur, e.g. John (1982), its general solution can be characterized by the following steps:

1. Let s and t be two auxiliary variables and $\varphi\ (t), \varphi_2(t), \varphi_3(t)$ arbitrary functions (but subject to some regularity conditions).

2. The equations $E = s + \varphi_1(t)$, $V = [\beta+\gamma\ \varphi_1(t)]s + \gamma \frac{s^2}{2}\varphi_2(t)$ have to be solved for s and t ; actually we need only $t = t(E,V)$.

3. The general solution $\Phi(E,V) = \varphi_3[t(E,V)]$ is obtained by varying $\varphi_1(t), \varphi_2(t)$ and $\varphi_3(t)$.

References*)

Agnew, R.A. (1972): Conter-Examples to an Assertion Concerning the Normal Distribution and a New Stochastic Price Fluctuation Model, RES 38, 381-383

Allais, M. (1953): L'extension des théories de l'équilibre économique général et du rendement social au cas du risque, Econometrica 19, 269-290

Allingham, M.G. (1972): Risk-Taking and Taxation, Zeitschrift für Nationalökonomie 32, 203-224

Arditti, F.D.; Levy, H. (1975): Portfolio Efficiency Analysis in Three Moments: The Multiperiod Case, JoF, 797-809

Arrow, K.J. (1970): Essays in the Theory of Risk-Bearing, Amsterdam-London

Bamberg, G.; Firchau, V. (1981): Some Remarks on the Aggregation Theorem for Divergent Borrowing and Lending Rates, Methods of Operations Research 44, 465-476

Bamberg, G.; Spremann, K. (1981a): Implications of Constant Risk Aversion, Zeitschrift für Operations Research 25, 205-224

Bamberg, G.; Spremann, K. (1981b): Financial Smoothing and Firm Values, Methods of Operations Research 44, 477-488

Bamberg, G.; Spremann, K. (1983): The Impacts of Several Emission Policies in an Imperfect Capital Market, in: Göppl, H.; Henn, R. (Eds.): Proceedings of the 2. Symposium on Money, Banking, and Insurance, Karsruhe, 531-536

Bamberg, G. (1984): The Impacts of Variance Reducing Strategies in Dyopolistic Capital Market, in: Bamberg, G.; Spremann, K. (Eds.): Risk and Capital, Berlin-Heidelberg-New York-Tokyo, 52-63

Bamberg, G.; Spremann, K. (Eds.) (1984): Risk and Capital, Berlin-Heidelberg-New York-Tokyo

Baron, D.P. (1977): On the Utility Theoretic Foundations of Mean-Variance Analysis, JoF 32, 1683-1697

---

*) Abbreviations

AER	American Economic Review
JFE	Journal of Financial Economics
JFQA	Journal of Financial and Quantitative Analysis
JoF	Journal of Finance
RES	Review of Economic Studies
ZfB	Zeitschrift für Betriebswirtschaft
ZfbF	Zeitschrift für betriebswirtschaftliche Forschung

Bawa, V.S.; Lindenberg, E.B. (1977): Capital Market Equilibrium in a Mean-Lower Partial Moment Framework, JFE 5, 189-200

Bierwag, G.O. (1974): The Rationale of the Mean-Standard Deviation Analysis: Comment, AER 64, 431-433

Borch, K. (1969): A Note on Uncertainty and Indifference Curves, RES 36, 1-4

Borch, K. (1974): The Rationale of the Mean-Standard Deviation Analysis: Comment, AER 64, 428-430

Brennan, M.J. (1970): Taxes, Market Valuation and Corporate Financial Policy, National Tax Journal 23, 417-427

Brennan, M.J. (1979): The Pricing of Contingent Claims Discrete Time Models, JoF 24, 53-68

Brenner, M. (1983) (Ed.): Option Pricing. Theory and Applications, Lexington

Chamberlain, G. (1983): A Characterization of the Distributions that Imply Mean-Variance Utility Functions, Journal of Economic Theory 29, 185-201

Chipman, J.S. (1973): The Ordering of Portfolios in Terms of Mean and Variance, RES 40, 167-190

Copeland, T.E.; Weston, J.F. (1983): Financial Theory and Corporate Policy (second ed.), Reading (Mass.)

Denneberg, D. (1984): Elements of Finance under Risk.An Average Deviation Approach to Risk, Economi Appliquée 37, 165-199

Drukarczyk. J. (1980): Finanzierungstheorie, München

Dyer, J.S.; Sarin, R.K. (1982): Relative Risk Aversion, Management Science 20, 875-886

Epps, T.W. (1981): Necessary and Sufficient Conditions for the Mean-Variance Portfolio Model with Constant Risk Aversion, JFQA 16, 169-176

Fama, E.F.; Miller, M.H. (1972): The Theory of Finance, Hindsdale (Ill.)

Fama, E.F. (1965): The Behavior of Stock Market Prices, Journal of Business 38, 34-105

Feldstein, M.S. (1969): Mean-Variance Analysis in the Theory of Liquidity Preference and Portfolio Selection, RES 36, 5-12

Firchau, V. (1983): Informationsbewertung und Portfolioplanung, in: Göppl, H.; Henn, R. (Eds.): Proceedings of the 2. Symposium on Money, Banking, and Insurance, Karlsruhe, 551-555

Firchau, V. (1984): Variable Information and Capital Market Equilibria, in: Bamberg, G.; Spremann, K. (Eds): Risk and Capital, Berlin-Heidelberg-New York-Tokyo, 52-63

Geske, R. (1978): The Pricing of Options with Stochastic Dividend Yield, JoF 33, 617-625

Gonzales, N.; Litzenberger, R.; Rolfo, J. (1977): On Mean-Variance Models of Capital Structure and the Absurdity of their Predictions, JFQA 12, 165-179

Hakansson, N.H. (1972): Mean-Variance Analysis in a Finite World, JFQA 7, 1873-1880

Hogan, W.W.; Warren, J.M. (1974): Toward the Development of an Equilibrium Capital Market Model Based on Semivariance, JFQA 9, 1-11

Jahankhani, A. (1976): E-V and E-S Capital Asset Pricing Models: Some Empirical Tests, JFQA 11, 513-528

Jarrow, R. (1980): Heterogeneous Expectations, Restrictions on Short Sales, and Equilibrium Asset Prices, JoF 35, 1105-1113

Jean, W. (1971): The Extension of Portfolio Analysis to Three or More Parameters, JFQA 6, 505-515

Jean, W. (1973): More on Multidimensional Portfolio Analysis, JFQA 8, 475-490

John, F. (1982): Partial Differential Equations (4ed.), New York-Heidelberg-Berlin

Kallberg, J.G.; Ziemba, W.T. (1981): Remarks on Optimal Portfolio Selection, Methods of Operations Research 44, 19-40

Kallberg, J.G.; Ziemba, W.T. (1984): Mis-Specifications in Portfolio Selection Problems, in: Bamberg, G.; Spremann, K. (Eds.): Risk and Capital, Berlin-Heidelberg-New York-Tokyo, 74-87

Kraus, A.; Litzenberger, R. (1976): Skewness Preference and the Valuation of Risky Assets, JoF 31, 1085-1100

Levy, H. (1974): The Rationale of the Mean-Standard Deviation Analysis: Comment, AER 64, 434-441

Lintner, J. (1964): The Valuation of Risk Assets and the Selection of Risky Investments in Stock Portfolios and Capital Budgets, RES 47, 13-37

Lintner, J. (1969): The Aggregation of Investor's Diverse Judgements and Preferences in Purely Competitive Securities Markets, JFQA 4, 347-400

Lintner, J. (1970): The Market Price of Risk, Size of Market and Investor's Risk Aversion, RES 52, 87-99

Mao, J.C.T. (1970): Models of Capital Budgeting, E-V versus E-S, JFQA 5, 657-675

Markowitz, H.M. (1959): Portfolio Selection, New York

Massé, P. (1953): Reflexions sur les Comportements Rationnels en Economie Aléatoire, Cahiers Seminaire d'Econométrie 2, 11-58

Miller, E. (1977): Risk Uncertainty, and Divergence of Opinion, JoF 32, 1151-1168

Mosler, K.C. (1982): Entscheidungsregeln bei Risiko. Multivariate Stochastische Dominanz, Berlin-Heidelberg-New York

Mossin, J. (1968): Taxation and Risk-Taking: An Expected Utility Approach, Economica 35, 74-82

Mossin, J. (1973): Theory of Financial Markets, Englewood Cliffs

Müller, S. (1985): Arbitrage Pricing of Contingent Claims, Berlin-Heidelberg-New York-Tokyo

Nantell, T.J.; Price, B. (1979): An Analytical Comparision of Variance and Semivariance Capital Market Theories, JFQA 14, 221-242

Nantell, T.J.; Price, K.; Price, B. (1982): Mean-Lower Partial Moment Asset Pricing Model: Some Empirical Evidence, JFQA 17, 763-783

Owen, J.; Rabinovich, R. (1983): On the Class of Elliptical Distributions and their Applications to the Theory of Portfolio Choice, JoF 38, 745-752

Peterson, D.; Peterson, P. (1982): The Effect of Changing Expectations upon Stock Return, JFQA 17, 799-813

Porter, R.B.; Bey, R.P.; Lewis, D.C. (1975): The Development of a Mean-Semivariance Approach to Capital Budgeting, JFQA 10, 639-649

Pratt, J.W. (1964): Risk Aversion in the Small and in the Large, Econometrica 32, 122-136

Price, K.; Price, B.; Nantell, T.J. (1982): Variance and Lower Partial Moment Measures of Systemtic Risk: Some Analytical and Empirical Results, JoF 37, 843-885

Roll, R. (1970): The Behavior of Interest Rates: The Application of the Efficient Market Model to US Treasury Bills, New York

Ross, S.A. (1978): Mutual Fund Separation in Financial Theory - The Separating Distributions, Journal of Economic Theory 17, 254-286

Rudolph, B. (1979): Kapitalkosten bei unsicheren Erwartungen, Berlin-Heidelberg-New York

Rudolph, B. (1982): Portfeuille- und Aktienkursbildung bei monopolistischem Anlegerwettbewerb, ZfB 52, 471-490

Saelzle, R. (1976): Investitionsentscheidungen und Kapitalmarkttheorie, Wiesbaden

Samuelson, P.A. (1970): The Fundamental Approximation Theorem of Portfolio Analysis in Terms of Means, Variances and Higher Moments, RES 37, 537-542

Sarnat, M. (1974): A Note on the Implications of Quadratic Utility for Portfolio Theory, JFQA 9, 687-689

Schneeweiß, H. (1967): Entscheidungskriterien bei Risko, Berlin-Heidelberg-New York

Schneider, D. (1980): Investition und Finanzierung (5ed.), Wiesbaden

Sengupta, J.K. (1985): Optimal Decisions Under Uncertainty, Berlin-Heidelberg-New York-Tokyo

Sharpe, W.F. (1964): Capital Asset Prices: A Theory of Market Equilibrium Under Conditions of Risk, JoF 19, 425-442

Sharpe, W.F. (1981): Investments (2ed.), Englewood Cliffs

Simkowitz, M.A.; Beedles, W.L. (1978): Diversification in a Three-Moment World, JFQA 13, 927-941

Spremann, K. (1984): A Firm in Statu Nascendi-Initial and Final Shareholders, in: Bamberg, G.; Spremann, K. (Eds.): Risk and Capital, Berlin-Heidelberg-New York-Tokyo, 103-121

Spremann, K.; Bamberg, G. (1982): Bilanzpolitik, Mehrperioden-Diversifikation und kapitaltheoretische Unternehmenswerte, ZfB 51, 1204-1222

Spremann, K.; Bamberg, G. (1983a): Emissionslimitierung und Kursbildung in einem unvollkommenen Kapitalmarkt, ZfbF 35, 302-314

Spremann, K.; Bamberg, G. (1983b): Local Consistency of Risk Preferences, Statistische Hefte 24, 73-83

Stiglitz, J.E. (1969): The Effect of Income, Wealth, and Capital Gains Taxation on Risk Taking, Quarterly Journal of Economics 83, 263-283

Swoboda, P. (1981): Betriebliche Finanzierung, Würzburg-Wien

Tobin, J. (1958): Liquidity Preference as Behavior Towards Risk, RES 25, 65-86

Tobin, J. (1969): Comment on Borch and Feldstein, RES 36, 13-14

Tsiang, S.C. (1972): The Rationale of the Mean-Standard Deviation Analysis, Skewness Preference, and the Demand for Money, AER 62, 354-371

Tsiang, S.C. (1974): The Rationale on the Mean-Standard Deviation Analysis: Replay and Errata for Original Article, AER 64, 442-450

Vickson, R.G. (1977): Stochastic Orderings from Partially Known Utility Functions, Math. Operations Research 2, 244-252

Wilhelm, J.E.W. (1983): Finanztitelmarkt und Unternehmensfinanzierung, Berlin-Heidelberg-New York

Wilhelm, J.E.W. (1985): Arbitrage Theory, Berlin-Heidelberg-New York

Williams, J.T. (1977a): Capital Asset Prices with Heterogeneous Beliefs, JFE 5, 219-239

Williams, J.T. (1977b): A Note on Indifference Curves in the Mean-Variance Model, JFQA 12, 121-126

Zachow, E.W.; Schmitz, N. (1977): Eine Axiomatisierung des erwarteten Nutzens, in: Henn, R.; Möschlin, O. (Eds.): Mathematical Economics and Game Theory (Essays in Honor of Oskar Morgenstern), Berlin-Heidelberg-New York, 250-264.

Portfolio Decisions and Capital Market Equilibria Under Incomplete Information

Volker Firchau

Summary: In the scope of the hybrid model which is characterized by the assumptions of an exponential utility function and of normally distributed end-of-period values of the risky assets, the optimum portfolio decisions are determined in the case of incompletely known prior parameters. Risk and uncertainty approaches are examined. The problems of the determination of equilibrium prices are dealt with.

Table of Contents:

1. Introduction

In the following the hybrid model so designated under the influence of Bamberg, Spremann [1981] is considered. It is characterized by two relatively restrictive assumptions: The considered decision maker starts prior from multidimensional normally distributed end-of-period values and has an exponential utility function, i.e. a constant absolute risk aversion.

Hence, it is started with an investor, whose utility function which is defined on a real result g of a decision is given by

$$u(g) = -e^{-\alpha g} \qquad \forall\, g \in \mathbb{R} \,. \tag{1}$$

The real number $\alpha > 0$ is the constant absolute risk aversion independent of the special result,

$$\alpha = -\frac{u''(g)}{u'(g)} \qquad \forall\, g \in \mathbb{R} \,.$$

The investor endowed with the initial wealth $w \in \mathbb{R}$ is offered within the scope of a one periodic portfolio planning problem a total of n risky investment opportunities. The total value of an asset is equal to the actual price of one share, multiplied by the number of shares in the market. The total value of asset i at the beginning is denoted by v_i and the stochastic end-of-period value by X_i :

Capital Market Equilibria. Ed. by G. Bamberg and K. Spremann

$$v = (v_1,\dots,v_n)^T$$
$$X = (X_1,\dots,X_n)^T \quad .$$

While $v \in \mathbb{R}^n$ is supposed to be known to the decision maker, the end-of-period values X are unknown at the beginning of the period. X is correspondingly interpreted as n-dimensional random variable. The realization of X, i.e. the actual, only ex post known price vector at the end of the period is designated by x. The investor defines his preknowledge by a prior distribution of X, described by a density φ. It is presupposed that the prices X are evaluated by the investor as prior normally distributed with expectation vector $\mu \in \mathbb{R}^n$, and positive definite covariance matrix $\Omega \in \mathbb{R}^{(n,n)}$:

$$X \sim N(\mu,\Omega) \quad . \tag{2}$$

φ is, therefore, the density of an $N(\mu,\Omega)$-distribution.

Let the portfolio vector chosen by the investor be

$$y = (y_1,\dots,y_n)^T \in \mathbb{R}^n \quad ,$$

where y_i denotes the fraction of the asset i which the investor holds. Usually, $0 \le y_i \le 1$; negative components of y correspond to short sales and components greater than one to a 'corner'. The end-of-period wealth then yields as result of the decision and depends on the end-of-period values. Under the assumptions of a perfect capital market the end-of-period wealth is

$$g(x,y) = (w - \sum_{j=1}^{n} y_j v_j)(1+r) + \sum_{j=1}^{n} y_j x_j \tag{3}$$
$$= w(1+r) + y^T(x - (1+r)v) \quad \forall x,y \in \mathbb{R}^n \quad ;$$

r stands for the risk-free interest rate at which any amount can be borrowed or saved.

In the scope of a decision theoretic approach as the hybrid model represents it, the evaluation of a decision is made corresponding to the Bayes principle by the expected utility or by the certainty equivalent of the result. The certainty equivalent of the decision y depending on φ is defined by

$$\upsilon_\varphi(g(X,y)) = u^{-1}(E_\varphi\, u(g(X,y))) \quad . \tag{4}$$

As φ is the density of a normal distribution and as g according to (3) is a linear function in x, $g(X,y)$ is also normally distributed.[1)]

1) if $y \neq 0$. Yet, all following statements are also valid analogously for $y = 0$.

In this case the determination of υ_φ is particularly simple:[1]

$$\upsilon_\varphi(g(X,y)) = E_\varphi\, g(X,y) - \frac{\alpha}{2}\,\mathrm{Var}_\varphi g(X,y) \qquad (5)$$

$$= w(1+r) + y^T(E_\varphi\, X - (1+r)v) - \frac{\alpha}{2}\, y^T(\mathrm{Cov}_\varphi\, X)y$$

$$= w(1+r) + y^T(\mu - (1+r)v) - \frac{\alpha}{2}\, y^T \Omega y\ .$$

Using (5), the optimum portfolio decision, i.e. the decision y^*, which maximizes (4), can easily be determined:

$$y^* = \frac{1}{\alpha}\,(\mathrm{Cov}_\varphi\, X)^{-1}(E_\varphi\, X - (1+r)v) \qquad (6)$$

$$= \frac{1}{\alpha}\,\Omega^{-1}(\mu - (1+r)v)\ .$$

<u>Example 1:</u>

For simplification small numerical values are supposed in the following. The example may look more realistic if it is assumed that the underlyed measuring unit is one million dollars. Let $n = 2$, $\alpha = \frac{100}{7}$ [2] and

$$\mu = \begin{pmatrix} 4 \\ 5 \end{pmatrix} \qquad \Omega = \begin{pmatrix} 1.5 & 0.5 \\ 0.5 & 2.5 \end{pmatrix} \qquad v = \begin{pmatrix} 3.5 \\ 4.5 \end{pmatrix}\ .$$

The determinant of Ω is $|\Omega| = 3.5$, and obviously Ω is positive definite.With regard to

$$\Omega^{-1} = \frac{1}{7}\begin{pmatrix} 5 & -1 \\ -1 & 3 \end{pmatrix}$$

(6) gives the result

$$100\, y^* = \begin{pmatrix} 2 \\ 1 \end{pmatrix} - r\begin{pmatrix} 13 \\ 10 \end{pmatrix}$$

$$= \begin{cases} \begin{pmatrix} 0.05 \\ -0.5 \end{pmatrix} & \text{for} \quad r = 0.15 \\ \begin{pmatrix} 0.635 \\ -0.05 \end{pmatrix} & \text{for} \quad r = 0.105 \\ \begin{pmatrix} 0.7 \\ 0 \end{pmatrix} & \text{for} \quad r = 0.1 \\ \begin{pmatrix} 2 \\ 1 \end{pmatrix} & \text{for} \quad r = 0 \end{cases}$$

For example, if the interest rate r is equal to 10% then the investor will only buy 0.7% of asset one.

---

[1] See Pratt, Raiffa, Schlaifer [1965], Bamberg, Spremann [1981].

[2] more precisely: $\alpha = \frac{100}{7}\,[10^6\,\$]^{-1}$, e.g. α is rather 'small'.

If the risk-free interest rate is greater than 10% the investor will hold a short position in the second security. Supposing another investor who is a 'big' one and whose risk aversion is only a hundredth of α , then $r=0$ leads to a corner, for this big investor would hold 200% of asset one.

The amounts riskily invested by the originally considered investor are

$$\begin{pmatrix} v_1 y_1^* \\ v_2 y_2^* \end{pmatrix} = \begin{cases} \begin{pmatrix} 0.00175 \\ -0.0225 \end{pmatrix} & \text{for} \quad r = 0.15 \\ \begin{pmatrix} 0.022225 \\ -0.00225 \end{pmatrix} & \text{for} \quad r = 0.105 \\ \begin{pmatrix} 0.0245 \\ 0 \end{pmatrix} & \text{for} \quad r = 0.1 \\ \begin{pmatrix} 0.07 \\ 0.045 \end{pmatrix} & \text{for} \quad r = 0 \end{cases}$$

The total riskily invested amount is given by

$$v^T y^* = v_1 y_1^* + v_2 y_2^* = 0.115 - 0.905 \cdot r \ .$$

For $r=0.15$, this value is negative: the value of the short sale of asset two exceeds the amount invested in asset one. ■

As suggested by the example, the total riskily invested amount generally is a decreasing function of r because:

$$v^T y^* = \frac{1}{\alpha} v^T \Omega^{-1} (\mu - v) - \frac{r}{\alpha} v^T \Omega^{-1} v$$

and $v^T \Omega^{-1} v > 0$ for $v \neq 0$ since Ω^{-1} is positive definite.

Assuming the hybrid model for the portfolio planning problem - besides α , v and r - the prior data μ and Ω have, therefore, to be known to determine the optimal portfolio. Starting from an objective concept of probability, i.e. assuming that φ describes the 'true' distribution of X , then μ and Ω can be estimated by using past data. Such an estimation, however, is connected with considerable problems.[1)]

But also in the scope of the subjective approach represented here the investor can be demanded too much specifying μ and Ω . If the investor does not have any information about μ and Ω , i.e. the pre-

---

1) Regarding the estimation problems in particular under stationarity aspects see Jobson, Korkie [1980], Levy, Kroll [1980], Hsu [1982], Maier, Peterson, Van der Weide [1982], Cohen, Hawawini, Maier, Schwartz, Whitcomb [1983].

information only consists in the information that the end-of-period values are normally distributed, then the decision problem is only meaningfully solvable applying the Minimax-rule resulting in $y^* = 0$. The investor then invests his whole initial wealth without any risk and receives a secure end-of-period wealth $w(1+r)$.

The assumption of certain pre-information about μ and Ω leads to more interesting results. In the following two alternative scenarios are considered. First, two solution possibilities are discussed for a risk situation with regard to the prior parameters.[1] Then (in Sec. 4), the case of partial uncertainty about μ and Ω is treated.

Finally, problems of the determination of equilibrium prices are shortly described for this uncertainty case. It should be mentioned that in the following only the distribution assumption (2) is modified. All other model assumptions - in particular the one of an exponential utility function (1) - are always kept.

2. Risk Situation with Regard to the Prior Parameters: A Two-Level Bayes Approach

The description of the portfolio planning problem presented in Sec. 1 is not the only possibility to formulate the problem as decision problem under risk. Besides the state-preference approach[2] especially those approaches are to be mentioned which do not consider the prior parameters μ and Ω as known variables, but as the true unknown environment parameters.[3] Usually it is assumed the the investor determines a prior distribution of the parameters (μ,Ω) . As also with sure knowledge of μ and Ω the end-of-period values and therefore the end-of-period wealth are still not known by sure, it concers a two-level, hierarchical problem with (μ,Ω) as hyperparameter.[4] Such an approach is of course in principle not limited to two levels. Concerning the problems of information-processing and - evaluation for general hierarchical decision models and different uncertainty functions see Goel, DeGroot [1981], Goel [1983].

---

[1] Only risk situations with regard to μ are investigated.

[2] See for example Morris [1974], Wilhelm [1981].

[3] See for example Mao, Särndal [1966], Kalymon [1971], Barry [1974], Winkler, Barry [1975], Jennings, Barry [1983] and especially the book from Bawa, Brown, Klein [1979] which summarizes the early papers of the authors.

[4] I.e. a parameter which determines the 'true' prior distribution.

In this section, it is assumed that the two-level problem is reduced to a usual one-level problem through the formula for the total probability. Presuming only uncertainty about μ, defined in detail by a prior normal distribution, this problem can be reduced to the problem in the scope of the hybrid model:[1]

Given are $m \in \mathbb{R}^n$ and positve definite matrices $\Pi, \Omega \in \mathbb{R}^{(n,n)}$. Let M be an $N(m,\Pi)$-distributed random variable:

$$M \sim N(m,\Pi) . \tag{7}$$

Under the condition $'M = \mu'$ let X be $N(\mu,\Omega)$-distributed:

$$X\big|_{M=\mu} \sim N(\mu,\Omega) \quad \forall\, \mu \in \mathbb{R}^n , \tag{8}$$

then the marginal (unconditional) distribution of X is an $N(m,\Omega+\Pi)$-distribution:

$$X \sim N(m,\Omega+\Pi) . \tag{9}$$

(7) and (8) describe the underlying two-level decision problem. The investor has an $N(\mu,\Omega)$-distribution as a prior distribution (see (2)) where he only knows Ω precisely, and about μ a prior distribution on a higher level according to (7) is known. This two-level problem can be reduced to a one-level one according to (9). For the investor, X is therefore 'actually' prior $N(m,\Omega+\Pi)$-distributed. He knows the parameters of this distribution. Hence, the problem is reduced to a problem which can be treated in the scope of the hybrid model approach. Similarly to (6) as optimum portfolio decision $\tilde{y}^*$ now yields

$$\tilde{y}^* = \frac{1}{\alpha} (\Omega+\Pi)^{-1} (m - (1+r)v) . \tag{10}$$

Example 2:

Let the underlying data-situation be nearly the same as in example 1 except for one point. Now the expectation vector μ is not known by **sure** but is $N(m,\Pi)$-distributed with

$$m = \begin{pmatrix} 4 \\ 5 \end{pmatrix} \qquad \Pi = \begin{pmatrix} 3.5 & 0.5 \\ 0.5 & 0.5 \end{pmatrix} .$$

It should be remarked that m is equal to the expectation vector μ of example 1. Therefore, this example is a natural extension of the first one.

[1] A proof of the following standard statement about normal distributions is for example found in LaValle [1970].

With

$$(\Omega + \Pi)^{-1} = \frac{1}{14}\begin{pmatrix} 3 & -1 \\ -1 & 5 \end{pmatrix} ,$$

(10) results in

$$100\,\tilde{y}^* = \begin{pmatrix} 0.5 \\ 1 \end{pmatrix} - r\begin{pmatrix} 3 \\ 9.5 \end{pmatrix}$$

$$= \begin{cases} \begin{pmatrix} 0.05 \\ -0.425 \end{pmatrix} & \text{for} \quad r = 0.15 \\ \begin{pmatrix} 0.185 \\ 0.0025 \end{pmatrix} & \text{for} \quad r = 0.105 \\ \begin{pmatrix} 0.2 \\ 0.05 \end{pmatrix} & \text{for} \quad r = 0.1 \\ \begin{pmatrix} 0.5 \\ 1 \end{pmatrix} & \text{for} \quad r = 0 \end{cases}$$

If the risk-free interest rate is 10.5%, in contrast to example 1 now there is no short selling.

The total riskily invested amount is now given by:

$$v^T \tilde{y}^* = 0.0625 - 0.5325\, r \quad .$$

A comparison with the corresponding result of example 1 shows that - depending on r - additional uncertainty about μ can but need not decrease the total riskily invested amount. ∎

Also if - as in the specified literature - the two-level problem is interpreted in a combined objective-subjective way,[1] (9) does represent only a distribution which can be interpreted subjectively. This becomes especially clear by considering the covariances. If X is actually $N(\mu,\Omega)$-distributed, and if Ω is known, then an approximation of this objective distribution should anyway estimate the covariance by Ω . Accordingly the covariance matrix of X is $\Omega + \Pi$, i.e. the prior distribution (9) of X still considers besides Ω the subjective estimation risk of the estimation of μ .[2]

---

[1] hence, the distributions in (7) are considered as subjective and in (8) as objective.

[2] Regarding the significance of the estimation risk at the estimation of the decision parameters see Bawa, Brown, Klein [1979].

In the scope of this two-level model approach it would be in itself desirable to also treat risk situations with regard to Ω . Here, however, it is renounced on this, because the marginal distribution of X then usually[1] is not a normal distribution, i.e. the corresponding one-level problem can no longer be treated in the scope of the hybrid model.

Example 3:

Let $n = 1$, $\mu \in \mathbb{R}$ be known, and only two values $\sigma_1^2, \sigma_2^2 \ (\sigma_1^2 \neq \sigma_2^2)$ be possible for the variance σ^2 of X

$$X|_{\sigma^2=\sigma_i^2} \sim N(\mu, \sigma_i^2) \qquad i = 1,2 \ .$$

If $p = 1/2$ is the prior probability for σ_1^2 :

$$P(\sigma^2 = \sigma_1^2) = \frac{1}{2} \ ,$$

then the marginal density of X is given by

$$f(x) = \frac{\frac{1}{2}}{\sqrt{2\pi}\ \sigma_1} e^{-\frac{(x-\mu)^2}{2\sigma_1^2}} + \frac{\frac{1}{2}}{\sqrt{2\pi}\ \sigma_2} e^{-\frac{(x-\mu)^2}{2\sigma_2^2}} \ .$$

Obviously

$$E_f(X) = \mu$$

$$Var_f(X) = \frac{1}{2}(\sigma_1^2 + \sigma_2^2) \ ,$$

but f is not a density of an $N(\mu, \frac{1}{2}(\sigma_1^2 + \sigma_2^2))$ - distribution for

$$f(\mu) = \frac{\frac{1}{2}(\sigma_1 + \sigma_2)}{\sqrt{2\pi}\ \sigma_1\ \sigma_2} \neq \frac{1}{\sqrt{2\pi}\ \sqrt{\frac{1}{2}(\sigma_1^2 + \sigma_2^2)}} \ .$$ ■

3. Risk Situation with Regard to the Prior Parameters: Lin's Approach

Lin [1981] proposes an alternative possibility of solving the two-level decision problems under risk presented in Sec. 2.[2] In Sec. 2, the distributions were aggregated by the formula of the total proba-

---

[1] The marginal distribution of X of course depends on the presupposed prior distribution for Ω . Similarly simple results as above are not to be expected, because the prior distribution is to be defined on the very complex set of all positive definite matrices, provided with a suitable σ-algebra.

[2] See also Lin/Boot [1982].

bility to an adequate subjective prior distribution. Accordingly, in the scope of Lin's approach it is tried to subjectively estimate the objectively right but not completely known distribution of the end-of-period values. The result is accordingly indeed subjectively influenced, but has the character of an objective distribution.

Assume that the distributon of X is an $N(\mu,\Omega)$ - distribution and that the parameters are objectively right, but unknown. Let the investor estimate (μ,Ω) by $(\hat{\mu},\hat{\Omega})$. [1] For the evaluation of the quality of the estimation it is obvious to base on the following loss function:

$$L((\mu,\Omega),(\hat{\mu},\hat{\Omega}))=\nu_{\varphi}(g(X,y^*))-\nu_{\varphi}(g(X,\hat{y}^*)) \quad . \tag{11}$$

Thereby $\hat{y}^*$ is the optimal portfolio decision based on an $N(\hat{\mu},\hat{\Omega})$ - distribution for X :

$$\hat{y}^*=\frac{1}{\alpha}\,\hat{\Omega}^{-1}(\hat{\mu}-(1+r)v) \quad . \tag{12}$$

L specifies the opportunity costs - described by the certainty equivalents - at the end of the period, which result from the (wrong) estimation of (μ,Ω) by $(\hat{\mu},\hat{\Omega})$ and the thereby caused (wrong) decision.

Obviously it holds:

$$L((\mu,\Omega),(\hat{\mu},\hat{\Omega}))\geq 0$$
$$L((\mu,\Omega),(\mu,\Omega))=0 \quad ,$$

i.e. knowing the objectively right distribution this one is meaningfully based at decision making.

According to (5),(6),(11) and (12), the following is true:

$$\begin{aligned} L((\mu,\Omega),(\hat{\mu},\hat{\Omega})) &= \frac{1}{2\alpha}(\mu-(1+r)v)^T\Omega^{-1}(\mu-(1+r)v) \\ &- \frac{1}{\alpha}(\hat{\mu}-(1+r)v)^T\hat{\Omega}^{-1}(\mu-(1+r)v) \\ &+ \frac{1}{2\alpha}(\hat{\mu}-(1+r)v)^T\hat{\Omega}^{-1}\,\Omega\hat{\Omega}^{-1}(\hat{\mu}-(1+r)v) \quad . \end{aligned} \tag{13}$$

If a prior distribution for (μ,Ω) is given, then the estimation of (μ,Ω) has to be done in a way that the expected loss related to this prior distribution is minimal:

$$EL((\mu,\Omega),(\hat{\mu}^*,\hat{\Omega}^*)) = \min_{(\hat{\mu},\hat{\Omega})} EL((\mu,\Omega),(\hat{\mu},\hat{\Omega})) \quad .$$

---

1) whereby $\hat{\Omega}$ be positive definite.

For the situation described in Sec. 2, i.e. for the case that Ω is known and μ is prior $N(m,\Pi)$ - distributed, it holds according to (13):

$$EL((\mu,\Omega),(\hat{\mu},\hat{\Omega})) = \frac{1}{2\alpha}\,[(m-(1+r)v)^T\Omega^{-1}(m-(1+r)v) \tag{14}$$

$$+ \operatorname{tr}(\Omega^{-1}\Pi)] - \frac{1}{\alpha}(\hat{\mu}-(1+r)v)^T\hat{\Omega}^{-1}(m-(1+r)v)$$

$$+ \frac{1}{2\alpha}(\hat{\mu}-(1+r)v)^T\hat{\Omega}^{-1}\,\Omega\hat{\Omega}^{-1}(\hat{\mu}-(1+r)v)$$

$$=: Z(\hat{\mu},\hat{\Omega}) \ .$$

Since $\hat{\Omega}^{-1}\,\Omega\,\hat{\Omega}^{-1}$ is positive definite, $Z(\hat{\mu},\hat{\Omega})$ is a convex function of $\hat{\mu}$.

Partial differentiation of Z to $\hat{\mu}$ yields:

$$\frac{\partial Z}{\partial\hat{\mu}} = -\frac{1}{\alpha}\hat{\Omega}^{-1}(m-(1+r)v) + \frac{1}{\alpha}\,\hat{\Omega}^{-1}\,\Omega\,\hat{\Omega}^{-1}(\hat{\mu}-(1+r)v) \ .$$

Hence, it follows as a necessary optimality condition

$$\Omega^{-1}(m-(1+r)v) = \hat{\Omega}^{*-1}(\hat{\mu}^*-(1+r)v) \ . \tag{15}$$

(15) replaced in (14) yields:

$$Z(\hat{\mu}^*,\hat{\Omega}^*) = \frac{1}{2\alpha}\,[(m-(1+r)v)^T\Omega^{-1}(m-(1+r)v)$$

$$+ \operatorname{tr}(\Omega^{-1}\Pi)] - \frac{1}{\alpha}(m-(1+r)v)^T\Omega^{-1}(m-(1+r)v)$$

$$+ \frac{1}{2\alpha}(m-(1+r)v)^T\Omega^{-1}(m-(1+r)v)$$

$$= \frac{1}{2\alpha}\operatorname{tr}(\Omega^{-1}\Pi) \ .$$

This is no longer dependent on $(\hat{\mu}^*,\hat{\Omega}^*)$, i.e. each admissible[1] solution of (15) minimizes[2] (14). The admissible solutions of (15) obviously are:

$$\hat{\Omega}^* = A \quad \text{arbitrary (positive definite)}$$

$$\hat{\mu}^* = A\,\Omega^{-1}(m-(1+r)v) + (1+r)v \ .$$

All these solutions lead to the same optimal portfolio decision (see (6)):

$$\hat{y}^{**} = \frac{1}{\alpha}\,\Omega^{-1}(m-(1+r)v) \ .$$

---

1) $\hat{\Omega}^*$ has to be positive definite.

2) Z is continuous, non-negative and obviously has a minimum. The solutions of (15) can therefore only be minima.

Seen from a pragmatic standpoint, a more precise determination of $(\hat{\mu}^*, \hat{\Omega}^*)$ is unnecessary. As Ω was presupposed to be objectively right and known, it is obvious to choose the special solution

$$(\hat{\mu}^*, \hat{\Omega}^*) = (m, \Omega) . \tag{16}$$

A comparison with (10) shows that with the approach chosen here the covariance matrix Π need not be considered.

Example 4:

The situation of example 1 and 2 is again considered. Since m in example 2 is equal to μ in example 1, it follows from (6) and (16) that $y^* = \hat{y}^{**}$, e.g. the optimal portfolio vectors are now the same as in example 1. This result is only true if $\mu = m$ because Ω is positive definite.

But although the distributions are the same, it should be remarked again that they have to be interpreted in a different way. The distribution of X in example 1 can be a subjectively fixed distribution, while the same distribution now is the result of a Bayes-estimation of the objectively right distribution. ■

Lin's approach is preferable to the two-level Bayes approach, but it is only applicable if information about the true distribution of X is available.

Summarizing:

- If the true distribution of X , described by φ , is known, then (6) gives the best portfolio decision.
- If the true distribution of X is not exactly known but the uncertainty about this true distribution can be described by a risk situation, then Lin's approach is appropriate.
- If the true distribution of X is unknown but the preknowledge about X can be described subjectively by one prior distribution then again (6) is applicable. But φ is now the density of this prior distribution of X .
- If not even one prior distribution can be fixed subjectively but a subjective distribution for the possible prior distribution then the two-level Bayes approach of Sec. 2 can be used for determining an optimal portfolio decision.

4. Partial Uncertainty with Regard to the Prior Parameters

Both presented risk approaches for the solution of the portfolio planning problem under uncertainty about the prior parameters have, as each risk approach, the disadvantage to need the specification of a prior distribution for the parameters. As is shown in Sec.2, the decision-maker is only apparently less demanded: The specification of a prior distribution of the second level practically means the determination of a prior distribution for the actual, underlying problem. Therefore, it is obvious to start from an uncertainty approach which demands from the decision-maker the definition of few data. In the scope of a (μ,σ) - approach this was first proposed by Bühler [1977] for the portfolio problem. Within a special index model he led the decision problem back to a vector optimization problem, see also Bühler [1984].

The approach presented here corresponds to the concept of partial information based on the papers of Bierlein [1963] and Richter [1963] as it was founded as linear partial information by Kofler, Menges [1976] and extended by Kofler, Menges, Fahrion, Huschens, Kuss [1980] to the concept of the stochastic partial information. However, the following model can only be filed under this concept in a limited way, because the sets of distributions considered here are (corresponding to the hybrid model) sets of normal distributions and therefore usually extremely non-convex.

Example 5:

The convex combination of two normal distributions with the same expected values and different variances is in general not normal as example 3 shows. The same result can be derived for the case of identical variances and different expectation values, which is mainly assumed in Sec. 2 and 3. Let $n = 1$, $\sigma^2 > 0$ be known, and only two values μ_1, μ_2 $(\mu_1 \neq \mu_2)$ be possible for the expected value μ of X

$$X|_{\mu=\mu_i} \sim N(\mu_i, \sigma^2) \qquad i = 1,2 .$$

If $p = \frac{1}{2}$ is the prior probability for μ_1 :

$$P(\mu = \mu_1) = \frac{1}{2} ,$$

then the marginal density of X is given by

$$f(x) = \frac{1}{2\sqrt{2\pi}\,\sigma}\, e^{-\frac{(x-\mu_1)^2}{2\sigma^2}} + \frac{1}{2\sqrt{2\pi}\,\sigma}\, e^{-\frac{(x-\mu_2)^2}{2\sigma^2}} .$$

Obviously

$$E_f(X) = \frac{1}{2}\,(\mu_1 + \mu_2)$$

$$\mathrm{Var}(X) = \sigma^2 + \frac{1}{4}\,(\mu_1 - \mu_2)^2 ,$$

but f is not a density of an $N(\frac{1}{2}(\mu_1+\mu_2)\,,\,\sigma^2+\frac{1}{4}(\mu_1-\mu_2)^2)$ - distribution since we have

$$f(\tfrac{1}{2}(\mu_1+\mu_2)) = \frac{1}{\sqrt{2\pi}\,\sigma}\, e^{-\frac{(\mu_1-\mu_2)^2}{8\sigma^2}} \neq \frac{1}{\sqrt{2\pi}\,\sqrt{\sigma^2+\frac{1}{4}(\mu_1-\mu_2)^2}} .$$ ■

In the framework the two risk approaches presented above it was assumed that the investor considers each normal distribution[1] as a prior distribution to be possible but differently probable. Now it is presupposed that the investor only determines one class Φ of densities containing the density of the prior distribution without a more precise specification in the form of a higher level prior distribution.

In agreement to the hybrid model approach it is postulated:

Φ is non-empty and contains only densities of normal distributions.

Except in trivial special cases Φ is not convex and not a polyhedron,[2] i.e. Φ is no linear partial information in the sense of Kofler, Menges [1976].

The MaxE$_{min}$-principle (so termed by Kofler, Menges [1976]) which comprises the Bayes- and Minimax-principle as extremes is chosen as optimality criterion:[3]

$$\min_{\varphi\in\Phi} E_\varphi\, u(g(X,\tilde{\tilde{y}}^*)) = \max_{y\in\mathbb{R}^n}\min_{\varphi\in\Phi} E_\varphi\, u(g(X,y)) \tag{17}$$

or (u^{-1} is monotonously increasing):

$$\min_{\varphi\in\Phi} \nu_\varphi(g(X,\tilde{\tilde{y}}^*)) = \max_{y\in\mathbb{R}^n}\min_{\varphi\in\Phi} \nu_\varphi(g(X,y)) \quad . \tag{18}$$

---

1) with fixed covariance matrix Ω in the considered special cases.

2) A finite union of convex polyhedrons is called polyhedron. If Φ is finite, then Φ is also a polyhedron.

3) Let Φ be such that the occurring maxima and minima exist. It will turn out that this is true for the special cases considered in the following.

Then $\tilde{\tilde{y}}^*$ is the optimal decision with respect to the criterion, and (18) specifies the corresponding certainty equivalent.

As Φ only contains normal distributions, it is obvious to describe Φ by the possible (μ,Ω) - combinations:[1]

$$\Theta := \{(\mu,\Omega) \mid \exists \varphi \in \Phi : \varphi \text{ is the density of an } N(\mu,\Omega)\text{ - distribution}\} . \qquad (19)$$

Example 6:

The following modification of example 5 is considered. Let $n=1$, $\sigma^2>0$ be known, and all values between μ_1 and μ_2 $(\mu_1<\mu_2)$ be possible for the expected value μ of X,

$$X \sim N(\mu,\sigma^2) \qquad \mu \in [\mu_1,\mu_2] .$$

Obviously,

$$\Theta = \{\mu,\sigma^2) \mid \mu \in [\mu_1,\mu_2]\} \subset \mathbb{R}^2$$

is convex, but it follows from example 5 that the corresponding class of densities Φ is not convex.

To secure that $\tilde{\tilde{y}}^*$ exists and that $\tilde{\tilde{y}}^*$ and the associated certainty equivalent can easily be determined, it is sufficient to suppose Θ as compact and convex. From the convexity of Θ, however, the convexity of Φ does not at all follow. ■

Theorem 1:

Let the investor specify his preknowledge by a non-empty class Φ of normal distributions as possible prior distributions. Let the associated range of parameters Θ according to (19) be compact and convex. Then the following is true:

$$\tilde{\tilde{y}}^* = \frac{1}{\alpha}\tilde{\tilde{\Omega}}^{*-1}(\tilde{\tilde{\mu}}^* - (1+r)v) \qquad (20)$$

is an optimum portfolio decision concerning the MaxE_{min}-criterion with the associated certainty equivalent:

$$\min_{\varphi\in\Phi} v_\varphi(g(X,\tilde{\tilde{y}}^*)) = w(1+r) + \frac{1}{2\alpha}(\tilde{\tilde{\mu}}^*-(1+r)v)^T\,\tilde{\tilde{\Omega}}^{*-1}(\tilde{\tilde{\mu}}^*-(1+r)v) \qquad (21)$$

where $(\tilde{\tilde{\mu}}^*,\tilde{\tilde{\Omega}}^*) \in \Theta$ is a solution of the following optimization problem

$$(\tilde{\tilde{\mu}}^* - (1+r)v)^T\,\tilde{\tilde{\Omega}}^{*-1}(\tilde{\tilde{\mu}}^* - (1+r)v) \qquad (22)$$

$$= \min_{(\mu,\Omega)\in\Theta} (\mu - (1+r)v)^T\,\Omega^{-1}(\mu - (1+r)v) .$$

---

1) Again only positive definite covariance matrices are taken into account.

Proof:

We will start by recalling formula (5):

$$\upsilon_\varphi(g(X,y)) = w(1+r) + y^T(\mu - (1+r)v) - \frac{\alpha}{2} y^T \Omega y \ .$$

This expression is concave as function of y and linear, therefore convex, as function of (μ,Ω). Θ and $\mathbb{R}^n$ are closed and convex; therefore, the following is true (see for example Rockafellar[1970], p. 393):

$$\inf_{\varphi\in\Phi} \sup_{y\in\mathbb{R}^n} \upsilon_\varphi(g(X,y)) = \sup_{y\in\mathbb{R}^n} \inf_{\varphi\in\Phi} \upsilon_\varphi(g(X,y)) \ .$$

Obviously the first supremum and the two infima are attained, because the underlying functions are continuous:

$$\min_{\varphi\in\Phi} \max_{y\in\mathbb{R}^n} \upsilon_\varphi(g(X,y)) = \sup_{y\in\mathbb{R}^n} \min_{\varphi\in\Phi} \upsilon_\varphi(g(X,y)) \ .$$

For

$$\begin{aligned} Z(y) &:= \min_{\varphi\in\Phi} \upsilon_\varphi(g(X,y)) \\ &= \min_{(\mu,\Omega)\in\Theta} [w(1+r) + y^T(\mu - (1+r)v) - \frac{\alpha}{2} y^T \Omega y] \end{aligned}$$

it is easily shown that Z is continuous, $Z(0) = w(1+r)$ and $Z(y) < w(1+r)$ outside of a sufficiently big sphere with center 0. Therefore, also the second supremum is attained.

$$\min_{\varphi\in\Phi} \max_{y\in\mathbb{R}^n} \upsilon_\varphi(g(X,y)) = \max_{y\in\mathbb{R}^n} \min_{\varphi\in\Phi} \upsilon_\varphi(g(X,y)) =: V \tag{23}$$

Hence, the existence of an optimal decision relating to the $\text{MaxE}_{\min}$-criterion is shown and V is the associated certainty equivalent.

The optimizations on the left side of (23) can easily be performed. Let (see (5),(6))

$$y^*(\mu,\Omega) = \frac{1}{\alpha} \Omega^{-1}(\mu - (1+r)v)$$

then it holds (φ is identified with the associated parameters (μ,Ω)):

$$\begin{aligned} V &= \min_{\varphi\in\Phi} \max_{y\in\mathbb{R}^n} \upsilon_\varphi(g(X,y) \qquad (24) \\ &= \min_{(\mu,\Omega)\in\Theta} \upsilon_\varphi(g(X,y^*(\mu,\Omega))) \\ &= \min_{(\mu,\Omega)\in\Theta} [w(1+r) + \frac{1}{2\alpha}(\mu-(1+r)v)^T\Omega^{-1}(\mu-(1+r)v)] \\ &= w(1+r) + \frac{1}{2\alpha}(\tilde{\tilde{\mu}}^*-(1+r)v)^T\tilde{\tilde{\Omega}}^{*-1}(\tilde{\tilde{\mu}}^*-(1+r)v) \end{aligned}$$

and it is shown that (21) specifies the certainty equivalent of an optimal decision.

According to (23), $\upsilon_\varphi(g(X,y))$ has an equilibrium point (y^*,φ^*) (see for example Burger [1966], p. 58):

$$\upsilon_{\varphi^*}(g(X,y)) \le V = \upsilon_{\varphi^*}(g(X,y^*)) \le \upsilon_\varphi(g(X,y^*)) \quad \forall\varphi\in\Phi\ ,\ \forall y\in\mathbb{R}^n \tag{25}$$

According to (24), especially $\tilde{\tilde{\varphi}}^*$ - the density of an $N(\tilde{\tilde{\mu}}^*,\tilde{\tilde{\Omega}}^*)$ - distribution - is an equilibrium strategy:

$$\max_{y\in\mathbb{R}^n} \upsilon_{\tilde{\tilde{\varphi}}^*}(g(X,y)) = V\ .$$

For an equilibrium strategy y^*, (25) yields $(\varphi^* = \tilde{\tilde{\varphi}}^*)$:

$$\max_{y\in\mathbb{R}^n} \upsilon_{\tilde{\tilde{\varphi}}^*}(g(X,y)) = \upsilon_{\tilde{\tilde{\varphi}}^*}(g(X,y^*))\ . \tag{26}$$

As $\tilde{\tilde{\Omega}}^*$ is positive definite, the maximum in (26) is uniquely determined (see (20)):

$$y^* = y^*(\tilde{\tilde{\mu}}^*,\tilde{\tilde{\Omega}}^*) = \tilde{\tilde{y}}^*\ .$$

$(\tilde{\tilde{\varphi}}^*,\tilde{\tilde{y}}^*)$ is, therefore, an equilibrium point. (23),(25) result in:

$$\min_{\varphi\in\Phi} \upsilon_\varphi(g(X,\tilde{\tilde{y}}^*)) = V = \max_{y\in\mathbb{R}^n}\ \min_{\varphi\in\Phi} \upsilon_\varphi(g(X,y))\ ,$$

i.e. $y^* = y^*(\tilde{\tilde{\mu}}^*,\tilde{\tilde{\Omega}}^*)$ is an optimal portfolio decision. ■

If $((1+r)v,\Omega)\in\theta$ for one Ω, $\tilde{\tilde{y}}^* = 0$ is obviously true, i.e. the whole initial wealth is invested without any risk. Here, the pessimism shows which is characteristic for the MaxE_{min}-principle, similarly as for the Minimax-principle.

As the convex combination of positive definite matrices is again positive definite, the demand of convexity of θ can not only be fulfilled in special cases as for example knowing the covariance matrix.

Example 7:

Let $n=1$, $\mu_i\in\mathbb{R}$, $\sigma_i^2\in\mathbb{R}^+$ $(i=1,2)$ with $\mu_1\le\mu_2$, $\sigma_1^2\le\sigma_2^2$, and

$$\theta = \{(\mu,\sigma^2)\,|\,\mu\in[\mu_1,\mu_2],\sigma^2\in[\sigma_1^2,\sigma_2^2]\}\ .$$

θ is a cartesian product of two closed intervals, and is therefore compact and convex.

For the solution $(\tilde{\tilde{\mu}}^*,\tilde{\tilde{\Omega}}^*)$ of (22) results

$$\tilde{\tilde{\sigma}}^{2*} = \sigma_2^2$$

$$\tilde{\tilde{\mu}}^* = \begin{cases} \mu_2 & \text{if} \quad (1+r)v > \mu_2 \\ \mu_1 & \text{if} \quad (1+r)v < \mu_1 \\ (1+r)v & \text{if} \quad (1+r)v \in [\mu_1, \mu_2] \end{cases}$$

If $(1+r)v \in [\mu_1, \mu_2]$, then $((1+r)v, \sigma^2)$ is a solution of (22) for any $\sigma^2 \in [\sigma_1^2, \sigma_2^2]$.

The optimal portfolio decision is:

$$\tilde{\tilde{y}}^* = \begin{cases} \dfrac{\mu_2 - (1+r)v}{\alpha\ \sigma_2^2} & \text{if} \quad (1+r)v > \mu_2 \\ \dfrac{\mu_1 - (1+r)v}{\alpha\ \sigma_2^2} & \text{if} \quad (1+r)v < \mu_1 \\ 0 & \text{if} \quad (1+r)v \in [\mu_1, \mu_2] \end{cases}$$

The first line corresponds to short sales $(\tilde{\tilde{y}}^* < 0)$, and the third line to a risk free investment. The solution of (22) and the optimal portfolio decision are independent of σ_1^2 . The reason is that corresponding to the MaxE$_{min}$-principle the most unfavourable parameter values are relevant for evaluating a portfolio decision. Here the highest possible variance σ_2^2 is most unfavourable independent of the expectation value because the decision-maker is risk-averse. ■

Example 8:

Let $n = 1$, $\mu \in \mathbb{R}$, $\sigma^2 \in \mathbb{R}^+$, $k_i \in \mathbb{R}^+$ $(i = 1,2)$ with $k_1 \le k_2$, and

$$\theta = \{k\mu, k\sigma^2)) \quad k \in [k_1, k_2]\} .$$

θ is again compact and convex. According to (22), the function

$$\delta(k) = \frac{(k\mu - (1+r)v)^2}{k\ \sigma^2}$$

is to be minimized with respect to $k \in [k_1, k_2]$. If k^* is the optimal solution:

$$\delta(k^*) = \min_{k \in [k_1, k_2]} \delta(k)$$

then $(k^*\mu, k^*\sigma^2)$ is a solution of (22).

Differentiating δ gives the result

$$\delta'(k) = \frac{(k\mu - (1+r)v)(k\mu + (1+r)v)}{k^2\ \sigma^2} ,$$

and it follows for the realistic case $(1+r)v > 0$, $\mu > 0$:

$$k^* = \begin{cases} k_2 & \text{if} \quad (1+r)\frac{v}{\mu} > k_2 \\ k_1 & \text{if} \quad (1+r)\frac{v}{\mu} < k_1 \\ (1+r)\frac{v}{\mu} & \text{if} \quad (1+r)\frac{v}{\mu} \in [k_1,k_2] \end{cases}$$

Then the optimal portfolio decision is:

$$\tilde{\tilde{y}}^* = \begin{cases} \frac{k_2\mu - (1+r)v}{k_2\ \sigma^2} & \text{if} \quad (1+r)\frac{v}{\mu} > k_2 \\ \frac{k_1\mu - (1+r)v}{k_1\ \sigma^2} & \text{if} \quad (1+r)\frac{v}{\mu} < k_1 \\ 0 & \text{if} \quad (1+r)\frac{v}{\mu} \in [k_1,k_2] \end{cases}$$

Again the first line corresponds to short sales, and the third line to a risk-free investment. If $(1+r)\frac{v}{\mu} < k_1$ then $(\tilde{\tilde{\mu}}^*, \tilde{\tilde{\sigma}}^{2*}) = (k_1\mu, k_1\sigma^2)$, e.g. in opposition to the situation of example 7 now the smallest possible value of the variance of X is relevant for determining the optimal portfolio. ∎

5. Asset Pricing under Uncertainty

Now let the initial prices v not be given exogenously but to be determined as equilibrium prices. In the scope of the hybrid model, hence with knowledge of the prior data for each investor, this is possible for homogeneous as well as for non-homogeneous expectations without difficulties (see Lintner [1969] for example). The risk approaches presented in Sec. 2 and Sec. 3 for the prior parameters can also be treated in the same way because both finally lead to a single prior distribution.[1)]

In this final section the determination of the equilibrium prices in the case of partial uncertainty about the prior parameters treated in Sec. 4 is addressed. For simplicity it is assumed that all market participants have homogeneous partial information about the prior distribution according to (19).

According to that it is started from the following market model:

A group M of investors is considered, investor k owns an initial wealth $w_k \in \mathbb{R}$ and has a constant absolute risk aversion $\alpha_k > 0$, $k \in M$. Each investor describes his preknowledge about the distribution of the end-of-period values by the same class Φ of normal distributions or by the same set Θ of possible parameter values according to (19). Let Θ fulfill the assumptions of theorem 1 in Sec. 4. For given prices v the portfolio which is the optimal

---

1) or in the case of Sec. 3 to distributions that are equivalent in the sense that they create the same optimal portfolio.

one for investor k results from (20):

$$\tilde{\tilde{y}}_k^* = \frac{1}{\alpha_k} \tilde{\tilde{\Omega}}^{*-1} (\tilde{\tilde{\mu}}^* - (1+r)v) \quad , \; k \in M \tag{27}$$

where $(\tilde{\tilde{\mu}}^*, \tilde{\tilde{\Omega}}^*)$ is the solution of (22) which is the same for all investors.

Hence the equilibrium condition for the market is $(\mathbb{1} := (1,\ldots,1)^T \in \mathbb{R}^n)$:

$$\mathbb{1} = \sum_{k \in M} \tilde{\tilde{y}}_k^* \; , \tag{28}$$

or according to (27)

$$\mathbb{1} = \frac{1}{\alpha_M} \tilde{\tilde{\Omega}}^{*-1} (\tilde{\tilde{\mu}}^* - (1+r)v) \tag{29}$$

with

$$\frac{1}{\alpha_M} := \sum_{k \in M} \frac{1}{\alpha_k} \; .$$

The equilibrium prices v are obtained by resolving the value v in (29) where it has to be taken into account that $\tilde{\tilde{\mu}}^*$ and $\tilde{\tilde{\Omega}}^*$ depend on v. In the limiting case of perfect information about (μ, Ω) (i.e. $|\theta| = 1$) the usual evaluation formula results from (29).

If there is a solution v of (28), then from (27),(29) results

$$\tilde{\tilde{y}}_k^* = \frac{\alpha_M}{\alpha_k} \mathbb{1} \quad , \; k \in M$$

i.e. the separation theorem is true.

In the case of only one risky asset and if θ is a rectangular set, the situation can easily be analyzed:

Example 9:

The situation of example 7 is now supposed to be true for each investor. As homogeneous expectations are assumed, the cases (1) (short sales) and (2) (only risk-free investment) cannot lead to an equilibrium price. But for the case $(1+r)v < \mu_1$ which is left an equilibrium exist.

Let

$$v = \frac{\mu_1 - \alpha_M \sigma_1^2}{1+r} \; , \tag{30}$$

obviously $(1+r)v = \mu_1 - \alpha_M \sigma_2^2 < \mu_1$ and it follows from example 7 for this price v :

$$\tilde{\tilde{\sigma}}^{2*} = \sigma_2^2$$
$$\tilde{\tilde{\mu}}^* = \mu_1 \; .$$

Finally, (30) is the solution of (29) for this $(\tilde{\tilde{\mu}}^*, \tilde{\tilde{\sigma}}^{2*})$, and, therefore, (30) gives an equilibrium price. (30) shows that the equilibrium price declines with growing uncertainty. ■

For the situation of example 8 the equilibrium price can easily be determined, too.

Example 10:

In addition to the assumptions of example 8 (for each investor) let

$$\mu > \alpha_M \sigma^2 \quad , \qquad (31)$$

which is certainly realistic. Again the cases of short sales and of purely a risk-free investment cannot lead to an equilibrium but the remaining second case:

Let

$$v = k_1 \frac{\mu - \alpha_M \sigma^2}{1 + r} \quad , \qquad (32)$$

then it follows from (31):

$$(1+r)v > 0 \quad , \quad \mu > 0$$

and

$$(1+r)\frac{v}{\mu} = k_1 (1 - \frac{\alpha_M \sigma^2}{\mu}) < k_1 \quad .$$

Therefore,

$$\tilde{\tilde{\sigma}}^{2*} = k_1 \sigma^2$$

$$\tilde{\tilde{\mu}}^* = k_1 \mu$$

for this price v (see example 8). Finally, (32) is the solution of (29) for this $(\tilde{\tilde{\mu}}^*, \tilde{\tilde{\sigma}}^{2*})$, e.g. (32) gives an equilibrium price. Again the equilibrium price declines with growing uncertainty. ■

In general, e.g. for $n > 1$, resolving (29) is difficult,[1] neither is the existence of equilibrium prices secured. But for the situation of a known covariance matrix Ω , the situation mainly analyzed in Sec. 2 and 3, the equilibrium prices can easily be determined using the following theorem.

---

[1] possibly an iterative algorithm by means of (22), (29) could be used.

Theorem 2:

Let each investor specify his preknowledge by the same non-empty class Φ of normal distributions as possible prior distributions. Let the associated range of parameters according to (19) be

$$\theta = \{(\mu,\Omega) \mid \mu \in M\} \tag{33}$$

where $\Omega \in \mathbb{R}^{(n,n)}$ is positive definite, and $M \subset \mathbb{R}^n$ is compact and convex. Then the following is true:

$$v = \frac{\bar{\mu}^* - \alpha_M \Omega \, 1\!|}{1+r} \tag{34}$$

are equilibrium prices, if $\bar{\mu}^* \in M$ is a solution of

$$1\!|^T \bar{\mu}^* = \min_{\mu \in M} 1\!|^T \mu \ . \tag{35}$$

The corresponding solution of (22) is

$$\tilde{\tilde{\Omega}}^* = \Omega$$

$$\tilde{\tilde{\mu}}^* = \bar{\mu}^* \ .$$

Proof:

First, the following general assertion is shown: Let $y \in \mathbb{R}^n$, $N \subset \mathbb{R}^n$ be compact and convex, $\bar{\nu} \in N$ be a solution of

$$y^T \bar{\nu} = \min_{\nu \in N} y^T \nu \ , \tag{36}$$

and $w := \bar{\nu} - y$, then the following equations hold:

$$(\bar{\nu} - w)^T (\bar{\nu} - w) = \min_{\nu \in N} (\nu - w)^T (\nu - w) \tag{37}$$

$$\bar{\nu} - w = y \ . \tag{38}$$

(38) is obviously true. Supposed there exist a $\nu' \in N$ with

$$(\nu' - w)^T (\nu' - w) < (\bar{\nu} - w)^T (\bar{\nu} - w)$$

$$\Rightarrow (\nu' - \bar{\nu} + y)^T (\nu' - \bar{\nu} + y) < y^T y$$

$$\Rightarrow (\nu' - \bar{\nu})^T (\nu' - \bar{\nu}) + 2(\nu' - \bar{\nu})^T y < 0$$

$$\Rightarrow \nu'^T y < \bar{\nu}^T y$$

which is a contradiction to (36). Therefore, (37) is also shown.

Ω^{-1} is positive definite. Therefore, a nonsingular matrix $A \in \mathbb{R}^{(n,n)}$ exists which satisfies

$$\Omega^{-1} = A^T A \ .$$

Let

$$N := \{A\mu \mid \mu \in M\} \ ,$$

$$y := \alpha_M A^{T-1} 1\!\!| \ ,$$

$\bar{\nu}$ be a solution of (36) and $w := \bar{\nu} - y$.

Using the transformations

$$v := \frac{A^{-1} w}{1+r} \ ,$$

$$\bar{\mu} := A^{-1} \bar{\nu} \ ,$$

(37) gives the result

$$(\bar{\mu} - (1+r)v)^T \Omega^{-1} (\bar{\mu} - (1+r)v) = (\bar{\nu} - w)^T (\bar{\nu} - w)$$

$$= \min_{\nu \in N} (\nu - w)^T (\nu - w)$$

$$= \min_{\mu \in M} (\mu - (1+r)v)^T \Omega^{-1} (\mu - (1+r)v) \ ,$$

which corresponds to (22), eg. $\tilde{\bar{\mu}}^* = \bar{\mu}$, $\tilde{\tilde{\Omega}}^* = \Omega$. (38) results in

$$A\bar{\mu} - (1+r)Av = \alpha_M A^{T-1} 1\!\!|$$

or

$$\Omega^{-1} (\bar{\mu} - (1+r)v) = \alpha_M 1\!\!|$$

which is equivalent to the equilibrium condition (29). The equilibrium prices are

$$v = \frac{A^{-1} w}{1+r} = \frac{A^{-1} (\bar{\nu} - y)}{1+r}$$

$$= \frac{A^{-1} (A\bar{\mu} - \alpha_M A^{T-1} 1\!\!|)}{1+r}$$

$$= \frac{\bar{\mu} - \alpha_M \Omega 1\!\!|}{1+r} \ .$$

Finally, $y^T \bar{\nu} = \alpha_M 1\!\!|^T \bar{\mu}$, and $\min_{\nu \in N} y^T \nu = \min_{\mu \in M} \alpha_M 1\!\!|^T \mu$, and (36) is equivalent to the optimization problem (35), e.g. $\bar{\mu} = \bar{\mu}^*$. ■

It is remarkable that $\bar{\mu}^*$ only depends on M , not on Ω . As mentioned in Sec. 1, the prices v are the total values of the considered assets. The solution $\bar{\mu}^*$ of (35), therefore, is that prior expectation vector for which the total market value of all assets, e.g. $1\!\!|^T v$, is minimal:

$$1\!\!|^T v = \frac{1\!\!|^T \bar{\mu}^* - \alpha_M 1\!\!|^T \Omega 1\!\!|}{1+r}$$

$$= \min_{\mu \in M} \frac{1\!\!\mathrm{l}^T \mu - \alpha_M 1\!\!\mathrm{l}^T \Omega\, 1\!\!\mathrm{l}}{1+r}$$

An increasing uncertainty, therefore, leads to a decreasing total market value of all assets.

References

Bamberg, G.; Spremann, K. (1981): Implications of Constant Risk Aversion, Zeitschrift für Operations Research, 25, 205 - 224

Barry, C.B. (1974): Portfolio Analysis under Uncertain Means, Variances, and Covariances, Journal of Finance 29, 515 - 522

Bawa, V.S.; Brown, S.J.; Klein, R.W. (1979): Estimation Risk and Optimal Portfolio Choice, North-Holland Publishing Company, Amsterdam-New York-Oxford

Bierlein, D. (1963): Einheitliche Prinzipien für die Beurteilung statistischer Verfahren, Blätter der Deutschen Gesellschaft für Versicherungsmathematik 6, 442 - 456

Bühler, W. (1977): Portfeuilleplanung bei unvollkommen bekannten Mittelwerten und Varianzen, Proceedings in Operations Research 7, 158 - 167

Bühler, W. (1984): Capital Budgeting and Financial Planning under Qualitative Data Information, in: J.P. Brans (Ed.): Operational Research '84, 250 - 265

Burger, E. (1966): Einführung in die Theorie der Spiele, 2. Auflage, Walter de Gruyter, Berlin

Cohen, K.J.; Hawawini, G.A.; Maier, S.F.; Schwartz, R.A.; Whitcomb, D.K. (1983): Estimating and Adjusting for the Intervalling-Effect Bias in Beta, Management Science 29, 135 - 147

Goel, P.K. (1983): Information Measures and Bayesian Hierarchical Models, Journal of the American Statistical Association 78, 408 - 410

Goel, P.K.; DeGroot, M.H. (1981): Information about Hyperparameters in Hierarchical Models, Journal of the American Statistical Association 76, 140 - 147

Hsu, D.A. (1982): A Bayesian Robust Detection of Shift in the Risk Structure of Stock Market Returns, Journal of the American Statistical Association 77, 29 - 39

Jennings, R.H.; Barry, C.B. (1983): Information Dissemination and Portfolio Choice, Journal of Financial and Quantitative Analysis 18,1, 1 - 19

Jobson, J.D.; Korkie, B. (1980): Estimation for Markowitz Efficient Portfolios, Journal of the American Statistical Association 75, 544 - 554

Kalymon, B.A. (1971): Estimation Risk in the Portfolio Selection Model, Journal of Financial and Quantitative Analysis 6, 559 - 582

Kofler, E.; Menges, G. (1976): Entscheidungen bei unvollständiger Information, Springer-Verlag, Berlin-Heidelberg-New York

Kofler, E.; Menges, G.; Fahrion, R.; Huschens, S.; Kuss, U. (1980): Stochastische partielle Information, Statistische Hefte 21, 160 - 167

LaValle, I.H. (1970): An Introduction to Probability, Decision and Inference, International Series in Decision Processes, New York

Levy, H.; Kroll, Y. (1980): Sample vs. Population Mean-Variance Efficient Portfolios, Management Science 26,11, 1108 - 1116

Lin, W.T. (1981): A Minimum Bayes Risk Approach to Optimal Portfolio Choice, International Journal of Systems Science 12, 495 - 509

Lin, W.T.; Boot, J.C.G. (1982): A Linear Decision Analysis Model of Optimal Portfolio Investments, International Journal of Systems Sciences 13, 469 - 489

Lintner, J. (1969): The Aggregation of Investor's Diverse Judgement and Preferences in Purely Competitive Security Markets, Journal of Financial and Quantitative Analysis 4, 347 - 400

Maier, S.F.; Peterson, D.W.; Van der Weide, J.H. (1982): An Empirical Bayes Estimate of Market Risk, Management Science 28, 728 - 737

Mao, J.C.T.; Särndal, C.E. (1966): A Decision Theory Approach to Portfolio Selection, Management Science 12, B 323 -B 333

Morris, J.R. (1974): The Logarithmic Investor's Decision to Acquire Costly Information, Management Science 21, 383 - 391

Pratt, J.W.; Raiffa, H.; Schlaifer, R. (1965): Introduction to Statistical Decision Theory, McGraw-Hill, New York

Richter, H. (1963): Subjektive Wahrscheinlichkeit und multisubjektive Tests, Zeitschrift für Wahrscheinlichkeitstheorie 1, 271 - 277

Rockafellar, R.T. (1970): Convex Analysis, Princeton, University Press

Wilhelm, J. (1981): Zum Verhältnis von Capital Asset Pricing Model, Arbitrage Pricing Theory und Bedingungen der Arbitragefreiheit von Finanzmärkten, Zeitschrift für betriebswirtschaftliche Forschung 33, 891 - 905

Winkler, R.L.; Barry, C.B. (1975): A Bayesian Model for Portfolio Selection and Revision, Journal of Finance 30, 179 - 192.

Option Valuation: Theory and Empirical Evidence

Robert Geske and Siegfried Trautmann

Summary: This paper reviews option valuation theory and the empirical evidence. The rapid growth of interest in option theory is probably due to the abundance of relevant applications in the financial marketplace. The precision of the option valuation models relies primarily on preference-free, enforceable arbitrage conditions. First, these arbitrage conditions are reviewed, and the related partial equilibrium hedging models are discussed. Next, the more general equilibrium, non-hedging models are briefly surveyed. Then, the differences in options on equity, debt, currency, and futures are mentioned, along with other applications of option theory.

Most of the empirical work testing the arbitrage boundaries has been related to equities, where the market data originated. Empirical tests of the boundaries and tests comparing various option models are reviewed for options on a variety of underlying assets. The estimation problems most relevant to option pricing are also discussed.

Table of Contents:

Capital Market Equilibria. Ed. by G. Bamberg and K. Spremann

1. Introduction

The history of trading options is very long, and it is also rather checkered. Stories in the Bible describe both the terms and the exchange of options, as do historical accounts of Medieval and Renaissance periods. Usually, these tales attribute great risk and often much ruin to those foolish enough to trade options. No doubt, the wisdom of the times is reflected in the tales. However, today the wisdom of the times is greater, at least with respect to options. In the last fifteen years, we have learned to regard the trading, the pricing, and the uses of options as a precise science. Today, we know exactly why past predictions of the great risk involved with trading options were correct, but we have further learned how to use options to control risk. As we will see, the most widely used model for valuing options is the European model developed by Black and Scholes (1973). However, almost all options traded in the world market place are American options. The distinction between European and American options is somewhat misleading, because it has nothing to do with geography, but instead describes the differences between the exercise properties of two options. The European option can only be exercised at one specific point in time, the expiration date of the option. On the other hand, an American option can be exercised at any point in time between the origination date and the expiration date of the options.

This paper reviews the development of modern option pricing theory (section 2) and the results of the corresponding empirical tests (section 3). In section 2.1, we discuss the preference and distribution-free results. Here, bounds on the range of feasible prices are implied by arbitrage conditions. Subsection 2.2 discusses distributional assumptions and hedging models. This approach is popular with traders because hedging specifies a technique for reducing risk while making markets in options. The preference assumptions of non-hedging models, new option instruments, and applications of option theory to other financial valuation problems are discussed in the remaining subsections of the theoretical part. Section 3 starts with a discussion of the problems of testing model validity and market efficiency. Subsections 3.1 and 3.2 report results of boundary condition tests. These boundary tests avoid confounding joint hypotheses of both model validity and market efficiency. The empirical evidence on different option pricing models is discussed subsequently, and estimation problems relevant to option pricing are briefly reviewed.

2. Option Valuation Theory

2.1 Preference and Distribution-Free Results

The choice of whether to buy or sell one risky asset or another is an example of a decision problem under uncertainty. Expected utility theory has been developed and refined for many uncertainty problems since its advent during World War II. There, it drew attention for many important investment decisions, such as the inventory stock-out problem of supplying bullets to a machine-gun nest. The theory focuses on the tastes (or preferences) and beliefs (or probability distributions) of individuals, subject to a variety of possible constraints. In finance today, many decision problems under uncertainty are about optimal investment decisions, subject to the constraint of no margin, taxes, or being fully invested. Another major research topic in financial theory is asset valuation under uncertainty.

Most valuation models in modern financial economics, such as the capital asset pricing model (CAPM), the option pricing models (OPM), and the arbitrage pricing models (APM), impose restrictions on the individual's tastes (for example quadratic utility), or beliefs (normal or lognormal distributions) in order to simplify the problem. However, in option pricing theory, Merton (1973a) has shown that merely by assuming individuals which prefer more to less (i.e., are rational), arbitrage will place restrictions on the values of put and call options. This section discusses these arbitrage restrictions. The arbitrage results will be stated but not proven.

We assume that markets are perfect, which allows us to ignore short sale restrictions, margin requirements, transaction costs, taxes, differences in borrowing and lending rates, illiquidity, and price pressures. All of these effects can be introduced, some more easily than others. Interest rates can be random, but they must always be positive. The arbitrages will be between options differing only in time to expiration, options differing only in exercise price, or between options, the underlying stock, and default-free zero-coupon bonds.

2.1.1 Call Options

A call option gives its owner the right to buy a specified asset for a specified price within a specified time period. The specified price of the underlying asset is termed the exercise or strike price K .

The specified expiration date T of the option implies a time premium which is wasting. An option (put or call) differs from a futures contract where the holder must take delivery of the underlying asset at expiration, or buy back the future to avoid that obligation. By definition, the optionholder has the option to take delivery, and it is the theory of this option value which is the focus of much discussion. The following paragraphs begin the review of the valuation theory.

The value C of a call option will never be less than zero. This is because limited liability of the stock restricts the stock price S to be positive. Also, the value of a call will never be worth less than either zero or its exercise value $S - K$. Furthermore, the value of a European call will be greater than the exercise value by the difference between the exercise price and the present value of the exercise price. In fact, if dividends are paid over the life of the option and the call is dividend unprotected, the call value will be greater than the difference between the stock price and the present value of the exercise price, less the present values of any stock dividends to be paid prior to expiration. Finally, the call will never sell for more than the stock. These conditions can be expressed by the following inequality:

$$S \geq C \geq \max(0, S - Ke^{-rT} - \sum_j D_j \, e^{-rt_j}) \tag{1}$$

where r is the riskless interest rate, and D_j denotes the amount of dividend paid at date t_j.

Arbitrage also forces restrictions on the relation between changes in the call prices as the exercise price changes. Given two calls which differ only in exercise price, the one with the lower exercise price, K_1, must be at least as valuable as the other. Furthermore, the difference in value between these two calls must never be greater than the difference in their exercise prices. This can be expressed by the following inequality:

$$-1 \leq [C(K_2) - C(K_1)]/(K_2 - K_1) \leq 0 \ . \tag{2}$$

Finally, given three calls (butterfly spreads) differing only in exercise prices, the value of the call with the middle exercise price can never be greater than a weighted average of the two extreme calls (convexity). This can be expressed as:

$$C(K_2) \leq w_1 C(K_1) + w_2 C(K_3) \ , \tag{3}$$

where the weights (w_1 and w_2) are the ratios of the partial to the total difference in the exercise prices:

$$w_1 = \frac{K_3 - K_2}{K_3 - K_1}, \quad w_2 = \frac{K_2 - K_1}{K_3 - K_1} \tag{3a}$$

The time value of an American option is always positive. Given two calls which differ only in time to expiration, the one with more time to expiration must be at least as valuable as the other. When T_2 is greater than T_1, this relation can be expressed as follows:

$$C(T_2) \geq C(T_1) \; . \tag{4}$$

Since American calls can be exercised prior to their expiration date, arbitrage imposes restrictions on the optimal exercise policies. Merton (1973a) showed that an American call will sell for the same price as a European call when the underlying stock does not pay dividends. In this instance, the option to exercise early has no value. The logic is as follows: The owner of an American call can take one of three choices: (i) hold it; (ii) exercise it; or (iii) sell it. Since the premium above (i.e., exercise value) is always positive prior to expiration, selling the call dominates exercising it, except when the underlying stock pays dividends. Then, it may be rational to give up the premium above parity to get the dividend. Thus, an American call should only be exercised just before an ex-dividend date or at expiration. If it is ever optimal to exercise a particular call option, then all other calls with either smaller exercise prices or less time to expiration should also be exercised at that time. However, it will never be optimal to exercise an American call early if the present value of the dividends to be paid over the life of the call are less than the possible interest that can be earned on the exercise price during the same time period.

2.1.2 Put Options

A put option gives its owner the right to sell the specified asset for a specified price within a specified time period. Thus, a put seems to be the opposite of a call, since semantically, the right to sell is the opposite of the right to buy. However, in option valuation theory, such simple reasoning can lead to confusion. Both the right to buy and the right to sell have unique value, which we will see depend on the allowable range of the underlying asset price. The following paragraphs discuss this theory of value for puts.

Similar to call options, arbitrage restrictions exist for unprotected American put options. An American put will never sell for less than either zero or the difference between the exercise price and the stock price, $K - S$. The maximum value a put can achieve is its exercise price, because of the limited liability of the stock. The relations can be summarized by the following inequality:

$$K \geq P \geq \max(0, K-S) \quad , \tag{5}$$

where P denotes the put value.

Arbitrage also forces restrictions on the relation between changes in put prices for different exercise prices. Given two puts which differ only in exercise price, the one with the higher exercise price must be at least as valuable as the other. Furthermore, the difference in value between these two puts must never be greater than the difference in their exercise prices. This can be expressed by the following inequality:

$$1 \geq [P(K_2) - P(K_1)] / (K_2 - K_1) \geq 0 \tag{6}$$

Finally, given three puts (butterfly spread) differing only in exercise price, the value of the put with the middle exercise price can never be greater than a specific weighted average of the values of the two extreme puts. This can be expressed as follows:

$$P(K_2) \leq w_1 P(K_1) + w_2 P(K_3) \tag{7}$$

where the weights (3a) are ratios of the partial to the total differences in the exercise prices (convexity).

Since the time value of an American put is always positive, given two puts which differ only in time to expiration, the one with more life remaining will be more valuable. If T_2 is greater than T_1 , this can be expressed as:

$$P(T_2) \geq P(T_1) \tag{8}$$

However, for a European put, more time to expiration can sometimes reduce value. The intuition is, if it is optimal for the putholder to exercise early, then more time to expiration only prolongs the agony of not being able to exercise an option. Merton (1973a) also demonstrated that an American put always has a positive probability of premature exercise. This occurs because the limited liability of the stock bounds the stock price below at zero. Thus, for some (low) stock price, it is better to take the exercise proceeds and invest them at the risk-free rate rather than wait for the additional option value. At this critical stock price where the put is exercised early, the premium above parity has gone to zero and the put is worth its exercise value. Dividends paid on the underlying stock increase put values because theyreduce the stock price, and thus, dividends reduce the probability of early exercise. In fact, the put should never be exercised prematurely if the present value of the dividends to be paid prior to expiration of the put exceed the present value of interest that could be earned on the exercise price during the same time period. Finally, if it is ever optimal to exercise a particular put, then all other puts with either a larger exercise price or less time to expiration should also be exercised at that time.

2.1.3 Relations Between Puts and Calls

Converters, reverse converters, and box spreaders make a business of converting calls into puts, puts into calls, and calls, puts, and the underlying stock into risk-free bonds. These conversions or replications hold exactly for European options, and the relation between these securities is termed put-call parity. The following arbitrage condition describes this relation for European options having the same exercise price and expiration date:

$$P = C - S + Ke^{-rT} . \tag{9}$$

This implies that a bought put can be duplicated by a bought call, short stock, and lending the present value of the exercise price.

American options complicate these conversion and replication strategies. The package of securities necessary to replicate the American option's countable but infinite set of exercise contingencies, is itself infinite (see Geske and Johnson, 1984) . The simple equality of European put-call parity does not hold, and only a pair of inequalities hold for either payout-protected American options or for options written on non-dividend paying stock:

$$C - S + K \geq P \geq C - S + Ke^{-rT} \tag{10}$$

When dividends are paid and the option is not payout-protected, these bounds must include the dividends. Uncertainty about interest rates and about dividends further complicate these bounds. Transactions costs, margin requirement, and differential borrowing and lending rates widen the inequality bands bounding the American put value.

2.1.4 Additional Arbitrage Restrictions

In all of the above arbitrage relations, no assumption about the distribution of stock price changes was necessary. However, in order to discuss even weak restrictions with respect to stock price, it is necessary to assume that the distribution of stock price changes is independent of the level of the stock price. Although this is generally not valid, as even casual empiricism would reveal, it may not be a bad assumption. Given this assumption, the value of one call can never be greater than the value of an otherwise identical call with a higher stock price. If S_2 is greater than S_1, this can be expressed as:

$$C(S_2) \geq C(S_1) \tag{11}$$

Also, given three calls which are identical, except for different stock prices, the value of the call on the middle stock price can never be greater than a weighted average of the values of the calls on the two extreme stock prices.

$$C(S_2) \leq w_1 C(S_1) + w_2 C(S_3) \tag{12}$$

where the weights (comp. (3a)) are ratios of the partial to the total differences in the stock prices (convexity).

2.2 Distributional Assumptions and Hedging Models

2.2.1 Hedge Portfolios

In the last section, we were able to learn something about rational option pricing by studying the restrictions placed on option values by arbitrage. Most of the arbitrage results did not require very specific assumptions about individual preferences (i.e., utility) or beliefs (i.e., distribution of stock price changes). It was only necessary to assume that investors are rational, and for the arbitrage restrictions with respect to the stock price, that the distribution of stock price changes be independent of the level of the stock price. In order to be more specific about the price process for options in a securities market where individuals allocate their wealth to select optimal investments, we need to be more specific about either their preferences, their beliefs, or both. Here, we will make stronger assumptions about investors' beliefs regarding the distribution of stock price changes in order to present the hedging models for option values. The European option models will be discussed first because they are simpler than the American option hedging models.

First, assume that investors believe that the distribution of stock price changes follows a lognormal (proportional) diffusion process. The lognormal is empirically preferred to a normal (absolute) diffusion because the probability of price changes appears to be a constant proportion of the level of the stock price rather than a constant absolute amount. Now, if investors can trade continuously for this price process, and if the option's price evolution is derived entirely from stock price changes so that the option and the stock are perfectly correlated, then investors can form perfect, self-financing, riskless hedges between the option and underlying stock. This hedge portfolio contains two risky securities, the option and the stock. Earlier work in finance taught us that in order to efficiently diversify risk in a two-security portfolio, the higher the correlation among the two securities, the better the diversification. If the two risky securities are perfectly correlated, then by buying one and selling (writing) the other in the correct proportions all the risk can be eliminated.

In order to demonstrate this concept, consider the following hedge portfolio, H, consisting of n_S shares of stock and n_C calls:

$$H = n_S S + n_C C . \tag{13}$$

Now, if the stock price changes, inducing a change in the call price, and assuming all else is (approximately) constant, what proportion of shares of stock to calls can the investor hold so that the value of the hedge will not change? To derive this "hedge ratio", set the change in the value of the hedge, dH, induced by changes in the stock price, dS, and call price, dC, to zero, and solve for the number of calls to write (buy) per share of stock long (short). This yields

$$dH = n_S\, dS + n_C\, dC = 0 . \tag{14}$$

If we take $n_S = 1$ we have

$$n_C = -1/(dC/dS)$$

where dC/dS is the hedge ratio. This simple example is illustrative, but is only approximate because as the stock price and call price change, so must the ratio of calls per share of stock in order to remain risk-free. Furthermore, when the investor sells out of one position in order to obtain the required new riskless hedge ratio, the hedging transaction must be self-financing. Fortunately, this is exactly what happens. In order to make this hedge an enforceable arbitrage, a third security, riskless bonds, should be added to the hedge portfolio. When riskless bonds are included, it is immediately evident that the option investment can be exactly replicated by a levered position in the underlying stock. This replication is the forcing mechanism of the arbitrage between the option, the stock, and riskless bonds. The riskless bonds also facilitate the self-financing.

The solution to the European call option pricing problem will depend on the assumption made to describe the distribution of stock price changes, dS . Before stating the various assumptions leading to different hedging models, consider the notable implications of the hedging approach. First, any investor who is perfectly hedged does not care whether the stock price goes up or down, since the value of the hedge is independent of the direction of stock price movements. This intuition implies that the option value may be independent of the expected return on the stock. Second, the arbitrage conditions necessary to maintain the hedge only require that investors be greedy, but not risk-averse. Investors could prefer risk and still the above riskless arbitrage portfolio would place restrictions on the relation between the option price and the stock price. Third, if the stock price is the only variable assumed to be random in the hedge, then the call value will only depend on one random variable. Fourth, the ability to create riskless hedges does not imply that investments in call options are riskless, or that investors only earn the risk-free rate on their investment. In fact, if an investor correctly feels that an option is over or underpriced, the proper establishment of this arbitrage portfolio will yield returns in excess of the risk-free rate, at no risk.

Now, return to the consideration of the relevant assumption for the distribution of stock price changes, dS . The origin of the alternatives discussed here stems primarily from empirical observations of stock price movements. The models are simple attempts to capture the observed phenomena. There are two main differences in these models of stock price changes:

(i) whether the price changes are continuous
(ii) whether the variance of price changes is constant.

The seminal model in modern option pricing theory (Black and Scholes 1973) assumes that the stock price changes are continuous with a constant variance of price changes. The other models vary these assumptions in an attempt to capture differences in the way information induces stock price changes. Several models are catalogued in Table 1. Some motivation of the assumptions is contained in Sec. 2.2.3. The equations resulting from the models are given in the Appendix.

Table 1: Assumptions of Models for Pricing Options

Model	Price Change	Variance	Motion Equation
1. Diffusion (Black-Scholes)	Continuous	Constant	$dS = \mu Sdt + vSdz$, where dz is the increment of a standard Gauss-Wiener process and μ is the expected instantaneous rate of return
2. Binomial (Cox, Ross, Rubinstein)	Discrete	Constant	$S(t+1) - S(t) = f(u,d)S(t)$
3. CEV (Cox-Ross)	Continuous	Changing	$dS = \mu Sdt + vS^{\rho}dz$
4. Compound (Geske)	Continuous	Changing	$dS = \mu Sdt + (\partial S/\partial V)(V/S)v'Sdz$
5. Displaced (Rubinstein)	Continuous	Changing	$dS = \mu Sdt + v'Sdz$
6. Jump (Cox-Ross)	Discontinuous	Constant	$dS = (\mu-\lambda k)Sdt + Sdq$ (dq = increment of a Poisson process with parameter λ)
7. Diffusion-Jump (Merton)	Continuous/ Discontinuous	Constant	$dS = (\mu-\lambda k)Sdt + vSdz + Sdq$

2.2.2 The Classical Black-Scholes Model

In the partial equilibrium diffusion model of Black and Scholes (1973), the hedge between the stock, the option, and the riskless bond is maintained continuously. The arbitrage relation between the call and its replication by a unique position in the stock and riskless bond implies that the resultant valuation equation for the option does not depend on whether the stock price is in equilibrium. In other words, all information may not be reflected in the stock price which therefore may be over or undervalued, and still the option valuation equation must hold. The Black-Scholes equation is only for European options, and is given by:

$$C = SN(d_1) - Ke^{-rT} N(d_2)$$

where

S = stock price at current date

K = exercise price

T = time to expiration

v^2 = variance of the stock's rates of return

r = riskless interest rate

$N(\cdot)$ = the cumulative standard normal distribution

$$d_1 = \frac{\ln(\frac{S}{K}) + rT + \frac{1}{2} v^2T}{v\sqrt{T}}$$

$$d_2 = d_1 - v\sqrt{T}$$

First, note that the expected return on the stock does not directly enter this equation. It only enters indirectly through the stock price, which is observable. As predicted in hedging models, the expected direction of stock price movements is not important to the value of the option. This is the primary reason why hedging models are so accurate relative to other financial valuation models, and probably the reason they have gathered the attention of so many academics and practitioners.

Although this formula appears complex, it has at least two intuitive interpretations. The first is that it represents the present value of the probability of receiving the exercise value, if and only if, $S(^{T})$, the stock price at expiration, is greater than K, the exercise price. The first term, $SN(d_1)$, is the present value of receiving the stock, and the second term, $-Ke^{-rT}N(d_2)$, is the present value of paying the exercise price, if and only if the option is exercised. Another interpretation is based on the arbitrage idea that the call can be replicated by a levered position in the stock. Then the first term is the amount invested in the stock, and the second term is the amount borrowed.

2.2.3 A Brief Description of Other Option Valuation Models

The binomial hedging model (Cox, Ross, Rubinstein, 1979) is based on a discrete process where the stock price can move to only one of two positions in a finite time interval. The size of the up and down (u and d) movements is a constant proportion of the stock price, and this implies a constant variance of stock price movements. The primary advantage of the binomial model is simplicity. In the limit, as the discrete time interval is reduced to zero, the binomial model can be made to converge to the Black-Scholes model. In addition, the binomial process is flexible, and depending on how the limits are taken and what is assumed about the up and down movements, the binomial process can incorporate the changing variance and jump process models. While this flexibility is useful pedagogically, empirically, the limiting parameters of each model must be estimated and then converted into the proper up and down jumps.

CEV means constant elasticity of variance models (Cox-Ross, 1976b). In these models, the stock price process is continuous, and the variance of stock price changes is dependent on the level of the stock price. The volatility of the stock's rate of return is $\hat{v} = vS^{\rho-1}$. The elasticity of this olatility with respect to the stock price, $(\partial\hat{v}/\partial S)(S/\hat{v})$, is a constant, namely $\rho-1$. For these processes, if $\rho < 1$, the variance of the rate of return varies inversely with the stock price. This property has been empirically established by many researchers. If $\rho > 1$, the opposite (direct) relation holds between the volatility and the stock price. When $\rho = 1$, the CEV corresponds to the Black-Scholes constant variance model. Thus, the CEV model is also flexible since it can handle a variety of relations between the stock price and the volatility, and it contains the Black-Scholes model as a special case.

The compound option model (Geske, 1979a) offers an economic rationale for the inverse relation observed between the volatility of stock price changes and the stock price. It is a capital structure argument, based on the observation that as the stock price changes with a fixed amount of corporate debt outstanding, the firm's leverage ratio will vary inversely with the stock price. This will induce the observed inverse relation between stock return volatility and stock price. To keep the problem simple, the firm is assumed to consist of only pure discount bonds maturing at T and stock. The stock is then considered to be an option on the assets of the firm, and an option on the stock is an option on an option.

In the compound option model, the volatility of the stock rate of return is nonstationary, changing randomly as the leverage changes. Although the resultant formula appears complex (see Appendix for definitions of terms), it has in intuitive interpretation. The first two terms of the formula, $VN_2(h, k; \rho) - Me^{-rT}N_2(h', k'; \rho)$, represent the present value of receiving the stock if the stock price at the option expiration date T is greater than the exercise price ($S(T) > K$, or if $V > \bar{V}$), just as in the Black-Scholes formula, only now the stock is itself an option on the firm. The third term in the formula is identical to the Black-Scholes second term $(-Ke^{-rT}N(h))$, and represents the present value of paying the exercise price, if and only if $V > \bar{V}$ (or $S(T) > K$). The compound option model contains the Black-Scholes model as a special case when there is no effective leverage in the firm (i.e., $M = 0$ or $T_M = \infty$).

The displaced diffusion model (Rubinstein, 1983) is a third changing variance model for which the simple Black-Scholes equation is again a special case. This model is motivated from the asset side of the balance sheet, while the compound option model is motivated by the liabilities. In the compound option model, the changing liabilities of stocks and bonds induces the nonstationarity in the stocks' variance. In the displaced diffusion model, a portfolio of risky and riskless assets is the source of the changing variance. To keep the problem simple, the firm is assumed to own two types of assets, one risky and one riskless. If the value of the firm rises at greater than the riskless rate, it must be due to the return on the risky asset. This shifts the portfolio composition toward the risky asset, and since the volatility of both assets is assumed constant, the volatility of the firm and also of the stock will rise. Thus, there is a direct relation between the stock price and its volatility, which is opposite to the relation in the compound option model.

In diffusion models, price changes are small and continuous, whereas empirically, we sometimes notice large and discontinuous price changes. This difference in price changes can be conceptualized as alternative models of the rate of arrival of unexpected, important information. An example would be the discovery of a new mine or a tender offer for the firm. To construct a hedging model of discontinuous price changes, the discontinuity must be deterministic. This is one example of a pure jump process, where the price is constant between jumps, and very infrequently a jump of constant amplitude occurs. The resulting jump model (Cox-Ross, 1976b) has two terms as in the Black-Scholes equation, and the interpretation of them is similar to before. However, the probability terms indicative of whether the stock price is greater than the exercise price are complementary Poisson, rather than cumulative normal. Although this model allows for the empirically observed discontinuous price changes, the assumption that in between infrequent jumps the price remains constant, and at the jumps the size of the price move is constant seems unrealistic.

The diffusion-jump model (Merton, 1976a) is an attempt to incorporate a more realistic distribution than the pure jump process. If the amplitude of the jump is allowed to be random, and if between jumps small random (diffusion) price changes are allowed, then the resultant model will no longer be a pure hedging model. No arbitrage portfolio can be constructed to remove this generalized uncertainty. However, if the jumps of individual stocks are assumed to be uncorrelated with the market, then all of the jump risk is nonsystematic and thus diversifiable. The intuition of the solution to this problem is that a hedger must hold a well-diversified portfolio to eliminate the jump risk, and then continuously adjust the portfolio to hedge the diffusion risk. Thus, the resulting formula contains the sum of infinitely many Black-Scholes type calls weighted by the Poisson probabilities reflecting the likelihood of the jumps. The variance of the jump-diffusion differs from the pure diffusion, but it is stationary.

2.2.4 Analytic Models for American Calls and Puts

All of the above hedging models listed in Table 1 were developed for valuing European options, but listed options are American and can be optimally exercised at any time prior to expiration. As previously discussed, puts always have a positive probability of early exercise, while calls may only be exercised just before a dividend payment or at expiration. Many approximations exist which accurately price American options. In discrete time, the binomial model can be modified to check for exercise at all relevant instants. In the case of listed call options on stock which currently have at most a nine-month life in the U.S. (in Germany nine and one half months), there would be a maximum of three dividends and one expiration, or four exercise times during the life or the option. For currently listed puts, approximately 150 exercise checks are necessary for penny accuracy (Geske-Shastri, 1985). In continuous time, when approximating the partial differential equation subject to the relevant exercise boundaries, a similar number of critical stock price computations are required for accurate valuation of both puts and calls. However, when evaluating an analytic solution to the continuous time problem, only three or four exercise checks are necessary for accuracy.

These analytic models of American calls (Roll, 1977, Geske, 1979b, and Whaley, 1981) and puts (Geske-Johnson, 1984) are based on the compound option model. At each relevant exercise instant, the investor has an option on an option, and the choice is either to exercise or to take the next option. The solutions are differentiable, and thus provide analytic formulae for hedge ratios and other sensitivities. Furthermore, this compound option approach can be used to value American options on currencies and futures, where both calls and puts have a positive probability of premature exercise at every instant. Shastri-Tandon (1984a), Whaley (1984a), Bodurtha-Courtadon (1984) model American options on currencies, while Shastri-Tandon (1984b), Whaley (1984b), Brenner, Courtadon, Subrahmanyan(1984), Ramaswamy and Sundaresan (1984), and Ball-Torous (1985b)model American options on futures.

The hedging models based on arbitrage provide unique insights about preference-free valuation. In fact, since preferences do not enter the problem, the solutions should be consistent with any set of preferences.[1] Thus, if we assume risk neutrality, we should be able to discount the expected value of the option at expiration by the riskless interest rate to find the option's current value. In order to compute the expected value of the option at expiration, if we can find the terminal distribution of stock price changes conditional on the current stock price, then we can solve the option valuation problem by conventional discounting of cash flows. Cox-Ross (1976b) demonstrated this solution technique. However, if we cannot create self-financing, riskless hedges, then preferences will enter the valuation process. If trading is not continuous, possibly because of transaction costs, or if other sources of risk enter the option problem, possibly through random interest rates or payouts, or if the jumps are correlated with the market, then perfect hedging may not be feasible, and preferences may enter the problem. The next section discusses preference-based option models.

2.3 Preference Assumptions and Non-Hedging Models

Prior to the growth of interest in option models, most valuation theory in financial economic approached the valuation problem from the demand, or preference side. In the recent tradition of solving choice problems under uncertainty by assuming individuals maximize expected utility of terminal wealth, much effort has been placed on investigating the conditions where individual demand equations can be aggregated to arrive at a market clearing valuation equation. The work of Wilson (1968) and Rubinstein (1974) documents the sets of assumptions on preferences (i.e., utility functions) and beliefs (i.e., distributions) which will allow aggregation yielding equilibrium valuation equations. The difficulty with most of these solutions is that they involve the estimation of parameters such as the

---

[1] See Harrison and Kreps (1979) and Kreps (1981) for details regarding preference requirement in arbitrage pricing.

expected return on the market, or a market risk aversion parameter where the measurement error is large.

Rubinstein (1976) was the first to demonstrate that the continuous trading assumption could be relaxed in a preference-based setting, and yet a preference-free option model would result. If utility functions are of the constant proportional risk averse (CPRA) family, and stock returns are lognormally distributed, then the resultant option valuation equation is identical to Black-Scholes. At first, this seemed to be a paradox, since riskless hedging appeared to be the key ingredient necessary for a valuation expression independent of an expected return. However, recall that investors who possess the class of constant absolute and constant proportional risk averse utility functions behave myopically (i.e.,are shortsighted). Myopia implies that investors today act as if they will not value the opportunity to revise their portfolios tomorrow (Mossin, 1968), even if they ultimately do revise tomorrow.

Brennan (1979) extended these preference-based results by showing that with constant absolute risk averse utility functions, and normal distributions of security returns, risk neutral valuation results also occur. These risk neutral valuation relations may provide valuable insights to our understanding of more complex option valuation problems where riskless hedging does not appear feasible. Rubinstein's (1976) result is based on a familiar "arbitrage" condition termed the "law of one price". The idea is that any two securities with identical cash flows in every state must sell for the same price. Brennan's (1979) basic valuation equation follows from the first order conditions of the portfolio optimization problem for the representative investor. Egle and Trautmann (1981) confirmed these results by using an alternative, more basic, "no-arbitrage" condition.

2.4 New Option Instruments

Since the advent of the equity option market in April, 1973, new options have been proposed and listed on many other instruments. Although some of the proposals are still pending by the Securities and Exchange Commission (SEC), today, options are listed on currencies, on stock indices, on debt instruments and on futures trading on these underlying instruments. Many of the earlier option results will apply to these new contracts, but there are some differences. For example, call options on futures and currencies will always possess a positive probability of premature exercise, and like the American put, will be more difficult to value. The empirical investigation of these new option instruments is just beginning, and some results will be presented later in this paper.

The concept of early exercise for an American call on a future can be seen immediately by considering a European call. Black (1976) showed that since arbitrage relates the futures price, F, to the current spot price S by the riskless cost of carry (i.e., $S = Fe^{-rT}$), the Black-Scholes European option pricing model will apply to European futures options simply by substituting Fe^{-rT} for the stock price S in equation (15). Now, as the futures price becomes large relative to the exercise price, the value of a European call on a future converges to $(F - K)e^{-rT}$ as a lower bound. Since the American call can be exercised immediately for $(F - K)$, early exercise is always possible. The reasoning is similar for American currency options, where the differential interest rate between domestic and foreign countries is similar to a stock paying a continuous dividend. Since call options on dividend-paying stocks can be exercised early, American call options on currencies will be more valuable than European calls.

Options on government securities (i.e., debt options) are more difficult to value because of the interest rate sensitivity of the fixed payout, and because the bond price converges to the amount of the terminal payout (i.e, face value). The fact that each fixed (cf., semiannual) payout is sensitive to a different interest rate implies that debt option values depend on many correlated random variables. Originally, most papers in this area assumed a specific stochastic process for the interest rate(s) which determined bond prices. For example, Brennan-Schwartz (1982) derived an equilibrium model of the term structure which implied equilibrium bond prices, and then options were priced off these bond prices. Geske (1981) pointed out that a hedging approach between the optioned bond, a financing bond, and the option might yield a better model because bond market prices could be used directly, regardless of whether the bond price was an equilibrium price.

While Brennan-Schwartz' equilibrium approach and Geske's hedging approach both required two random variables, Courtadon (1982) and Cox, Ingersoll, Ross (1985) presented a model based on only one random interest rate. Ball and Torous (1983) assumed a stochastic process for the bond price (Brownian bridge) which accommodated its convergence to a terminal value. The empirical work is slowly accumulating, while the theoretical work on this difficult problem continues.

2.5 Applications of Option Theory

As was first noted by Black-Scholes (1973) and Merton (1973a), option theory can be used to value corporate securities. Merton (1974) showed that the stock and pure discount bonds of a firm that has no other payouts can be valued directly by application of option theory. This leads to insights about the risk structure of interest rates. Black-Cox (1976), Geske (1977), and Cox-Ross (1976b) extended the analysis to consider junior debt, securities of arbitrary maturity, and general corporate payouts. Ingersoll (1976) and Brennan and Schwartz (1977) applied the theory to problems of dual funds and callable, convertible debt and preferred stock. Option theory has also been applied to interpretations of the firm's financing and investment decisions by Galai and Masulis (1976), insurance concepts, such as deposit insurance by Merton (1977b) portfolio insurance by Leland (1980) to warrant valuation (Galai-Schneller, 1978), and Emanuel (1983), leasing problems, rights offerings, and employee stock options (Smith-Zimmerman, 1976). The list of applications is already long and still growing. The empirical evidence collected to date on a variety of option concepts is the topic of the next section.

3. Empirical Tests of Option Valuation

The primary goal of this chapter is to present the main results of the empirical work in option valuation. After a discussion of the problems of testing model validity and market efficiency, the analysis concentrates on the empirical examination of the theoretical results discussed in Section 2. To begin, a few useful terms will be defined and explained:

1. *Value vs. Price:* The distinction is the market prices an asset while a model values the asset. An asset will be considered underpriced (overpriced) when the market price is below (above) the model value. Underpriced (overpriced) assets are considered to be good buys (sells).
2. *Efficient market:* A market (or a set of markets) will be termed efficient if no single trader can consistently make above-normal,

risk-adjusted profits on an after-transaction cost and after-tax basis.

3. *Synchronous markets:* Synchronous markets are markets in which (1) trading in related assets takes place simultaneously in time (trading synchronization) and, (2) the technology for registration of trades accurately reflects the transaction time and the time the price information is made available to market participants (data sychronization). Market synchronization is required in order to test for arbitrage profits, although it is not a necessary condition for market efficiency.

4. *Above-normal profits:* For a riskless portfolio strategy (e.g., buying one option and selling the appropriate number of underlying shares), above-normal profits mean profits in excess of the risk-free rate of interest (i.e., on a government bond with the same maturity as the strategy). An uncertain yield is considered above-normal, if, after adjusting for risk, it is in excess of the expected return. The expected return is determined by an asset pricing model (c.f., the capital-asset-pricing model (CAPM) or the arbitrage-pricing model (APM)).

5. *Ex-post tests:* Based on information at time t, a trading strategy is devised and, by assumption, a position is established based on prices at time t. The position will be liquidated one period later at $t+1$, based on prices available at that time. Such a test procedure ignores the time lag in acting upon a profit opportunity indicated by the date, t, mispricing signal.

6. *Ex-ante tests:* Based on information at time t, a trading strategy is devised, but the position is established at time $t+1$ at prices that are unknown at time t. The position will be liquidated one period later at $t+2$, based on prices available at that time.

The statistical inference based on empirical studies of option valuation is complicated by the fact that usually some or all of the hypotheses about model validity (and its correct parameter estimation), market efficiency, market synchronization and data accuracy are tested jointly. In order to gain clearer insights from these confounding joint tests, empirical analysis of option valuation can be classified in the following way:

1. Test of boundary conditions between an individual option and the underlying asset.
2. Tests of boundary conditions between different options and the underlying asset.
3. Tests of absolute price levels for options.

From Section 2, it is clear that most boundary conditions are model independent and, therefore, the corresponding tests are more rigorous than those of the third class. But even boundary condition tests are joint tests of market efficiency, market synchronization, and data accuracy if market synchronization cannot be guaranteed, and the tests are conducted as ex-post tests. Given accurate data and correct risk adjustment, above-normal profits from an ex-post test may indicate either market inefficiency or nonsynchronous markets. It is a definite indication of market inefficiency only if above-normal profits are revealed from an ex-ante test. Table 2 summarizes the expected results for the different permutations of the joint hypotheses regarding model validity, market efficiency, and market synchronization, given accurate (market) data.

Empirical tests of option valuation models may be further complicated by market imperfections. Besides ignoring commissions costs and taxes, most option models also ignore the bid-ask spread. The latter should be considered in an efficiency test, since a listed security is generally bought at its (higher) ask price and sold at its (lower) bid price. The observed bid-ask spread is the most important component of the transaction costs, whenever market efficiency is measured in terms of a lowest cost trader, such as a market maker on the trading floor paying negligible commissions and no brokerage fees (c.f.,Phillips and Smith, 1980). Other sources of problems are insufficient depth (i.e., number of option contracts traded at a given price) or the virtual illiquidity of some option contracts and markets (out-of-the-money options near expiration or the German stock option market before the 1983 changes in trading rules), or finally, the discreteness of trading with minimum price changes will affect the results (e.g., in the U.S. markets, one-eighth $ for options, and in the German stock option markets, one-twentieth DM for stocks and options).

Table 2

Joint Hypotheses and Expected Results

(Adapted from Galai, 1983)

Model is Correct and its Parameters are Correctly Estimated	Option Market is Efficient	Markets are Synchronous	Expected Results
Yes	Yes	Yes	Good predictions of option prices by the option pricing model for given stock prices. But, there is not way to make above-normal profits.
Yes	Yes	No	"Paper" ex-post profits, but no above-normal profits can be expected ex-ante.
Yes	No	Yes	Ex-ante above-normal profits are expected. No alternative model is expected to yield more.
Yes	No	No	Both "paper" and realized profits are expected.
No	Yes	Yes	Less than (risk-adjusted) expected profits, though normal.
No	Yes	No	Less than (risk-adjusted) expected profits, may be ex-post profits.
No	No	Yes	Potential for above-normal profits, but an alternative model may yield more.
No	No	No	Poor predictions of option prices; an alternative model may show higher ex-post and ex-ante profits.

3.1 Test of Boundary Conditions Among an Individual Equity Option and the Underlying Stock

Rational boundaries for the price of a simple call or put option are described by relations (1) and (5), respectively. Of these upper and lower boundary conditions, only the lower boundary condition for a call option has been empirically tested. Galai (1978) and Bhattacharya (1983) performed tests of dividend unprotected call options traded on the Chicago Board Options Exchange (CBOE) during the exchange's first eight months of operation (April 1973 to November 1973), and during the period August 1976 to June 1977, respectively. While Galai's (1978) early data ignores the depth of the market, the bid-ask spread, and transactions costs, Bhattacharya's (1983) better data does closely approximate the market's operational constraints. Both studies consider the time lag in acting upon a profit opportunity indicated by a mispricing signal. That is, market efficiency is tested by means of Galai's ex-ante test.

Table 3 presents the observed frequency and average size of three types of call option lower bound violations defined in the following equations characterizing (1) immediate exercise, (2) European lower bound, and (3) pseudo-American lower bound, respectively:

$$\varepsilon_1 = S - K - C \leq 0 \tag{16}$$

$$\varepsilon_2 = S - Ke^{-rT} - \sum_{j=1}^{n} D_j e^{-rt_j} - C \leq 0 \tag{17}$$

$$\varepsilon_3 = \max_{i \in I}(S - Ke^{-rt_i} - \sum_{j<i} D_j e^{-rt_j}) - C \leq 0 , \tag{18}$$

where $I = \{1,...,n+1\}$, $t_0 = 0$ (the current date), $t_{n+1} = T$, and D_j denotes the amount of dividend paid at date t_j $(j = 1,2,...,n)$.

Table 3

Tests of Call Option Boundary Violations

(Results of Bhattacharya, 1983)

	Immediate exercise test $H_0 : \varepsilon_1 \leq 0$	European lower bound test $H_0 : \varepsilon_2 \leq 0$	Pseudo-American lower bound test $H_0 : \varepsilon_3 \leq 0$
Sample size	86,137	54,735	32,432
Mispricing frequency	1,120	1,304	442
Average mispricing per contract ($)	12.57	9.88	10.85
Number of positions executed	759	670	139
Average profit per contract ($)			
• for a zero transaction cost trader	4.91	5.17	8.20
• for a member of the NYSE	- 0.59	- 6.98	- 8.26
• for a member of the CBOE	- 7.00	-13.14	- 8.63

The first type of mispricing occurs if the immediate exercise value of the option is greater than its current market value (i.e., $\varepsilon_1 > 0$). The second type of mispricing takes into consideration the European lower bound for a dividend unprotected call option that is expected to be held to its maturity. That is, if $\varepsilon_2 > 0$, then the European call dominance condition is violated. Finally, if the expression defined as ε_3 is positive, then the pseudo-American lower bound is violated. As distinguished from the European lower bound, this lower bound considers the possibility of exercising the unprotected American call at any time t_j, just before the stock goes ex-dividend.

A comparison of Galai's and Bhattacharya's ex-post test results shows that the relative mispricing frequencies (mispricing frequency divided by sample size) observed in both studies are similar. The average dollar mispricing magnitudes per contract, however, are significantly smaller in the study of Bhattacharya (1983). This result is due to the consideration of bid-ask spreads in the calculation of the mispricing magnitude. A second reason for the smaller ex-post inefficiency in the later sample period might be "learning" as CBOE traders became more experienced. On the other hand, both studies have the following in common: mispricing occurs most frequently for deep-in-the-money options with a short time to maturity. This leads Bhattacharya (1983, p. 177) to conclude that if these options were held by (average) investors, "they may have sold the calls at a discount so as to avoid having to exercise them and incur a round-trip transaction cost in the stock." Thus, some of the mispricing may be due to the existence of different transaction costs for different market participants.

More importantly, the last three rows of Table 3 demonstrate that only in the zero transaction cost case, the observed mispricing could have been translated into above-normal profits on an average basis. Furthermore, by trying to simulate a trading strategy based on mispricing signals, Bhattacharya (1983), like Galai (1978) for his earlier sample period, observes a "substantial reduction in the mean profit opportunities coupled with their transformation into uncertain outcomes" (Galai 1978, p. 209). In summary, for the largest option market in the world, no evidence contrary to option market efficiency was found when transaction costs were taken into account.

In a recent paper, Trautmann (1985a) reports violations of the European lower bound for call options traded on the Frankfurt Option Exchange (FOE) during the first eighteen months after the 1983 trading rule changes (April 1983 to September 1984). Compared with the European lower bound test in Table 3, in this study the violation is defined by

$$\varepsilon_2' = \varepsilon_2 + \left(\sum_{j=1}^{n} D_j \right) e^{-rT} \tag{19}$$

because stock options traded in Germany are (partially) payout protected (i.e., similar to Over-the-Counter (OTC) options in the United States). That is, when a stock pays a dividend, the exercise price of the option is reduced by the amount of the dividend. Also, when a company issues rights to purchase additional shares of stock at less than the market price, the exercise price is reduced by the market price of the right, if the rights expire before the options.

There were 891 violations of the bound, or about 1.4 % of the sample size of 63,391, when the transaction costs of the lowest cost trader were taken into account. The average mispricing magnitude was DM 59.96 per contract (comprising rights to 50 shares in the case of German stocks). When a strategy based on observed mispricing was adopted, the resulting executed positions averages losses of DM 60.58 net of the transactions costs for the lowest cost trader (e.g., the floor broker). Recall that such a trading strategy consists of buying the call, shorting or selling the stock, lending an amount equal to the sum of the present values of the exercise price and the expected dividends, and holding this portfolio until expiration. Since short selling is not permitted legally in Germany, however, this strategy could have been pursued only by owners of the underlying stock.

Tests concerning the immediate exercise lower bound and the pseudo-American lower bound have not been conducted in Trautmann's study because Geske, Roll and Shastri (1983) demonstrated that this payout protection completely inhibits the early exercise of American call options. Therefore, for the payout protected call options traded in Germany, the pseudo-American lower boundary test parallels exactly the European lower boundary test. On the other hand, violations of the immediate exercise lower bound may not have been observed in Germany for two simple institutional reasons: first, in Germany, a call option cannot be bought and exercised on the same day. Second, the German board-brokers who trade stock options have reportedly prevented call transactions from violating this condition.

3.2 Test of Boundary Conditions Among Different Equity Options and the Underlying Stock

Among all boundary conditions involving more than one option written on the same underlying stock, most interest has been devoted to the relations between the prices of a put and a call option having the same exercise price and expiration date. This relation, termed put-call parity was first proposed and tested by Stoll (1969). By transforming equation (9) into a least-squares regression model, he empirically investigated put-call parity among Over-the-Counter (OTC) options written during 1967 in the U.S. Even though the estimated intercept was significantly higher than the expected value (zero), Stoll (1969, p. 823) reasons that his results are consistent with his model.

Later, Gould and Galai (1974) argued that regression analysis is not an appropriate tool for investigating arbitrage opportunities. Following Merton's (1973b) extension of put-call parity to American options, they claimed that, in the absence of transaction costs, any market violation of relation (10) may indicate market inefficiency. Again, using OTC options data from 1967 to 1969, Gould and Galai observed many violations where the right side of condition (10) exceeded the price of the put. Taking into account transaction costs, these mispricing signals disappeared for nonmembers of the exchange, while members could have made above-normal profits. However, no ex-ante test has been conducted to examine the extent to which the remaining mispricing signals would translate into above-normal profits.

Klemkosky and Resnick (1979) were the first to test the put-call parity relation for American options traded on the CBOE, the American, and the Philadelphia Stock Exchanges. Transactions data for one day each month from July 1977 to June 1978 for fifteen stocks and their dividend unprotected options were used in testing relation (10), modified for dividend payments. Also, the data was screened to eliminate those options which were likely to be prematurely exercised. Violations of the lower and upper boundary (in terms of a call) for a dividend unprotected American put are expressed by the gross terminal profit, ε_4, from engaging in a long hedge position:

$$\varepsilon_4 = (C - P - S)e^{rT} + K + \sum_{j=1}^{n} D_j e^{r(T-t_j)} \tag{20}$$

and by the gross terminal profit, ε_5, from engaging in a short hedge position:

$$\varepsilon_5 = (S + P - C)e^{rT} - K - \sum_{j=1}^{n} D_j e^{r(T-t_j)} \qquad (21)$$

A long hedge position can be established by selling (writing) a call and purchasing an equivalent position obtained by a long position in the underlying stock, buying a put, and financing the purchase in part by borrowing at the riskless interest rate r the amount $Ke^{-rT} + \Sigma_{j=1}^{n} D_j e^{-rt_j}$, where D_j is the dividend payment at date t_j.

In order to approximate the required simultaneity of option and stock prices, Klemkosky and Resnick (1979) considered only those positions whose hedge securities were traded within one minute of each other. From these 606 positions, 66 violated the sufficient condition for no premature exercise of the call option and were eliminated. Of the remaining 540 long hedge positions, 243 guaranteed a non-negative, riskless terminal profit $(\varepsilon_4 > 0)$. But, after introducing transaction costs of $20 per trade for a member of the exchange and $60 for a non-member, it was found that only 147 member observations and 38 non-member observations of the 540 acceptable observations, respectively, were still profitable.

In perfect capital markets, a short hedge position is obtained by selling a long hedge position (i.e., $\varepsilon_4 = -\varepsilon_5$). The corresponding terminal profit, ε_5, however, equals $-\varepsilon_4$ only if neither the put nor the call option will be prematurely exercised. For a call option, there exists a sufficient condition for not premature exercise, but without sufficient dividends paid exactly at expiration, there is no condition which assures that the put will not be exercised early. Hence, the return on a short hedge where an American put is written is potentially more risky to the hedger than the return on a long hedge where the put is bought. Using the same data set, Klemkosky and Resnick (1979) found that of the original 606 short hedge positions, 240 (127) indicated positive terminal profits, ε_5, in excess of the $20 ($60) transaction cost. However, the extent to which retional premature exercise of the put would reduce profits was not examined.

In their 1979 paper, the ex-post analysis was not followed by ex-ante tests. Consequently, the detected "paper" profits may have been solely a result of asynchronous markets. Therefore, in 1980, Klemkosky and Resnick extended the previous work by conducting an ex-ante analysis with the same data set. Hedges constructed five and fifteen minutes after mispricing signals indicated terminal profits in excess of transaction costs of $20 per hedge. Although the long hedge results indicate that only for high ex-post profitability levels the corresponding ex-ante level is significantly lower, the market efficiency hypothesis was not rejected by the authors. This conclusion is not surprising given the results of Phillips-Smith (1980), who showed that even for a member of both the stock and options exchanges, the total level of transaction costs (including opportunity costs of membership on the exchanges and the bid-ask spread differentials) exceeds $70 per contract. Furthermore, for the ex-ante results of the short hedge, profits were significantly lower than the ex-post results on the long hedge investments, but higher than the ex-ante returns. This might be expected, since these higher returns may be regarded as a compensation for the risk associated with the written put in the short hedge position.

Trautmann (1985a) also examines the profitability of long hedge positions consisting of stock and dividend protected options traded on the Frankfurt Stock Exchange and Frankfurt Option Exchange, respectively, during the period April, 1983 to September, 1984. Because of the protection of German stock options against dividend payments, the gross terminal profit from engaging in a long hedge position,

$$\varepsilon_4' = (C - P - S)e^{rT} + K + \sum_{j=1}^{n} D_j(e^{r(T-t_j)} - 1) \; , \qquad (22)$$

is slightly different from equation (20). Unfortunately, the required simultaneity of option and stock prices could not be guaranteed in the German market. Alghough trading in the related assets takes place (almost) simultaneously on the same trading floor, there was no information available about the exact time of each transaction or bid/ask price quotations. For a certain option series at most one transaction price or bid/ask quote is registered per trading day. These prices together with the odd-lot prices (Kassakurse) of the underlying stocks have been used to establish a single long hedge position per trading day and option series.

In the ex-post analysis, 8,714 of 15,507 positions revealed a mispricing magnitude ε_4', which exceeded the explicit transaction costs of the lowest cost traders. These net terminal profits were used as the signal to trigger the ex-ante establishment of the long hedge.

The thinness of the option market, however, caused serious problems in completing such a position within the next trading day. The long hedge was attempted only when it was possible to buy the put option (the least liquid asset) within the next trading day. Depite this non-simultaneous long hedge construction, there remained some open positions which could not be hedged (even within the next 20 trading days). Nevertheless, 5,802 long hedge positions could be established, and more than 75 % yielded a positive net terminal profit for an exchange member. Major parts of these positive returns, however, may be regarded as a compensation for the risk associated with the nonsimultaneous construction of the ex-ante long hedge position and for the opportunity costs of an exchange membership.

The convexity rule (3), which involves three call options differing only in their exercise prices has been empirically examined by Galai (1979) and Bhattacharya (1983). In the latter study, which takes into account transactions costs, only one violation of this boundary condition was found among the 1,006 triplets of CBOE options observed from August, 1976 to June, 1977. For a comparable sample size, but earlier sample period, Galai (1979) detected twenty-four violations for the zero transaction cost case. The results offer strong support for the market efficiency hypothesis.

3.3 Tests of Equity Option Pricing Models

Option pricing models are constructed in part to explain or predict the absolute price levels of options trading in synchronized, efficient capital markets. The inablility of a model to explain observed market prices may be due to one or more of the following facts:

(1) the mathematical structure of the model is incorrect, or
(2) model parameters have been incorrectly measured, or
(3) the options market is inefficient, or
(4) the markets for the related assets are nonsynchronous.

Although most models fail strict predictability tests, other criteria for judging the model's validity are available. To date, four major approaches for testing an option model's validity have been distinguished:

(1) tests of robustness
(2) tests of predictability
(3) tests of unbiasedness
(4) tests of hedge return behavior

Among these tests, perhaps the most intuitive is to predict market prices with model values using parameters based on historical data. Since casual empiricism indicates that the standard deviation of the stock's rate of return is not constant over time, the historical volatility may not be a good estimate of future volatility. Following an idea of Latané and Rendleman (1976), more sophisticated tests of predictability use the pricing model itself to improve the estimation techniques. By equating the option's actual market price to the model value, and solving (numerically) for the only unobservable parameter, the standard deviation of the stock's return, one obtains the model implied standard deviation (ISD). Provided that (1) the model is correct, (2) option and stock markets are efficient and synchronous, and (3) the ISDs are derived from actual market prices, then the prediction error should approach zero. Nevertheless, sufficient differences between observed prices and model values could exist to permit trading profits. However, a hedging test would have to be conducted to detect systematic market inefficiency since a predictability test only compares accuracy.

Tests of unbiasedness focus on identifying systematic behavior in the prediction error of the valuation models. For some biases (with respect to time and striking price), the concept of ISD has served as the main workhorse, since it helps to isolate the hypothesis of the model's validity. For bias with respect to the volatility, the ISD is not appropriate, as will be emphasized later. Assuming the model to be tested is valid, it is expected that the ISD will be stationary across maturities and striking prices. Deviations from this expectation may be due to the model being misspecified. Furthermore, if volatilities are constant over time, the ISD is also expected to be approximately equal to the historical time-series standard deviation. However, nonstationarity, market inefficiency or lack of synchronous data may cause the deviations from this expectation which are difficult to isolate.

Tests of hedge return behavior empirically examine whether the return on an (almost) riskless hedge position is above-normal. In their pioneering test, Black and Scholes (1972) created a riskless hedge position by buying (selling) one option, and at the same time selling (buying) an appropriate fraction (more precisely, the hedge ratio $N(d_1)$) of the underlying stock. Alternatively, Whaley (1982) formed a hedge position by buying underpriced and selling overpriced options in proportions such that the net investment is zero and no risk is assumed. As long as the hedge return is computed by using market prices, both approaches jointly test the propositions that:

(1) the mathematical structure of the model is correct, and
(2) the model parameters have been correctly measured, and
(3) the options market is efficient, and
(4) the markets for the related assets are sychronous.

Tests of robustness investigate how the results predicted by a model change when its basic assumption are violated or when its input parameters are incorrectly measured. Typically, such a test involves the direct comparison of alternative model values, or the examination of hedge returns calculated (partly or totally) from simulated data. The (not exhaustive) survey of the literature presented in Table 4 indicates that most of the purely empirical studies on option pricing models involve more than a single test. It is, therefore, not possible to unambiguously classify these studies with respect to the testing approach applied. In the following paragraphs, the main results of the empirical testing approaches (1) - (4) are briefly reviewed. Since tests of robustness are useful in interpreting the other test results, these are summarized first.

3.3.1 Results of Robustness Tests

In a recent paper, Ball and Torous (1985a, p. 155) "provide statistical evidence consistent with the existence of lognormally distributed jumps in a majority of the daily returns of a sample of NYSE listed common stocks." However, they find no "operationally significant differences between the Black-Scholes and Merton model prices of the call options written on the sampled stock." Ball and Torous confirm Merton's (1976b) prediction that only for short-maturity and out-of-the-money calls do the jump model prices deviate significantly (up to 100 %). Thus, although most optioned stocks exhibit statistically significant jumps, the jumps are both too small and too frequent to cause option values to differ much from the diffusion model.

Black and Scholes (1972) and Bhattacharya (1980) test whether the deviation of the empirical distribution of stock price changes from the assumed stationary, lognormal distribution affects the expected hedge returns. To isolate this effect, Bhattacharya modifies the empirical hedge return test in two ways. First, as in Black-Scholes original study, instead of an estimate of the stock return volatility, its realization during the option's life was used in the hedge ratio

Table 4

Survey of Empirical Testing Approaches

Empirical and simulative studies on option pricing models (not exhaustive!). The type of testing approach is marked in the following way:
1 = test of robustness, 2 = test of predictability, 3 = test of unbiasedness, 4 = test of hedge return behavior.

Note: OTC = Over-The-Counter Market, SIM = SIMulated Sample Market or period, CBOE = Chicago Board of Options Exchange, AOE = American Options Exchange, FOE = Frankfurt Options Exchange.

Year of Public.	Name of Authors	Sample Market	Sample Period (Year/Month)	Testing Approach 1	2	3	4
1972	Black/Scholes	OTC	66/01-69/12	x		x	x
1975	Black	CBOE	73/04-74/12		x	x	
1976	Merton	SIM	SIM	x			
1976	Boyle/Ananthanarayanan	SIM	SIM			x	
1976	Latané/Rendleman	CBOE	73/10-74/06		x	x	x
1977	Galai	CBOE	73/04-73/11				x
1977	Trippi	CBOE	74/08-75/03		x		
1978	Chiras/Manaster	CBOE	73/06-75/04		x	x	x
1978	Finnerty	CBOE	73/04-74/12				x
1978	Schmalensee/Trippi	CBOE	74/04-75/05		x	x	
1979	MacBeth/Merville	CBOE	75/12-76/12		x	x	
1980	Boyle/Emanuel	SIM	SIM	x			
1980	MacBeth/Merville	CBOE	75/12-76/12		x	x	
1980	Bhattacharya	CBOE	76/05-77/10	x			
1982	Whaley	CBOE	75/01-78/03		x	x	x
1982	Gultekin/Rogalski/Tinic	CBOE/AOE	75/01-76/01		x	x	
1982	Emanuel/MacBeth	CBOE	76/01-78/12		x	x	
1983	Blomeyer/Klemkosky	CBOE	77/07-78/06			x	x
1983	Galai	CBOE	73/04-73/11				x
1983	Geske/Roll/Shastri	SIM	SIM			x	
1983	Trautmann	FOE	79/01-83/03		x	x	
1984	Geske/Roll	SIM	SIM			x	
1984	Geske/Roll	CBOE	76/08/24	x	x	x	
1984	Blomeyer/Johnson	CBOE	78/06-78/08		x	x	
1985	Ball/Torous	CBOE	83/01	x			
1985	Rubinstein	CBOE	76/08-78/08			x	
1985	Trautmann	FOE	83/04-85/06		x	x	x

calculation. Second, in the hedge return calculation, the option's market price is replaced by its corresponding model price. This analysis of the hedge returns led Bhattacharya (1980, p. 1,094) to conclude that "if stationarity of the return distributions is assumed and hedge positions are revised daily, then the Black-Scholes formula exhibits no operationally significant mispricing except for at-the-money options with one day to maturity."

While the above-mentioned robustness tests considered empirical stock price movements, in Boyle and Emanuel (1980), stock returns were randomly generated to simulate the assumed lognormal distribution. Their aim is to analyze the deviations from the assumed distribution of continuously hedged returns, when the portfolio is rebalanced at discrete time intervals. They demonstrate that the discrete hedge distribution is particularly skew, and some consequences of this skewness for empirical hedge return tests are explored.

3.3.2 Results of Predictability Tests

Since listed options are American and the Black-Scholes formula is for European options, it is realistic to expect a prediction error attributable to the early exercise component of the price. There are American formulae that can price the early exercise component of option value. These American models which model the early exercise feature as compound options are based on the compound option model of Geske (1979a). Whaley (1982) examines the pricing performance of Roll's (1977) model for American call options on dividend-paying stocks (as modified by Geske (1979b) and Whaley (1981)), and compares it with two suggested approximation methods based on the Black-Scholes model. To analyse each model's power, he uses the model-specific ISDs calculated from the closing stock prices of week $t-1$ and the closing stock prices of week t to predict closing option prices of week t.

For this one-week prediction interval, all three formulas yielded prices which are, on average, within three and a half cents of the observed market price of $4.1388. For each of the 160 weeks in the sample period observed market prices C_j from 91 option classes were regressed on each model's price estimates $\hat{C}_j$, as follows

$$C_j = \alpha_0 + \alpha_1 \hat{C}_j + \varepsilon_j \tag{23}$$

where ε_j is a disturbance term. With perfect prediction, the values of the coefficients α_0 and α_1 in this regression would be indistinguishable form zero and one, respectively. The average values of the weekly parameter estimates $\bar{\hat{\alpha}}_0$ and $\bar{\hat{\alpha}}_1$, ranged from -0.0508 to -0.0300 and 1.0088 to 1.0091, respectively. Whaley (1982, p. 44) concludes that "all of the models seem to perform extremely well, with the explained variation being greater than 98 percent in all cases (i.e., the average of the coefficients of determination from the regressions $\bar{R}^2$ is ≥ 0.98 for each model). However, all models demonstrate a slight tendency to overprice high-priced options (i.e., $\bar{\hat{\alpha}}_1 > 1$).

Although the mispricing errors were small on average, the Black-Scholes model exhibited previously documented systematic biases. The Black-Scholes model tends to undervalue (relative to the market) near maturity call options (i.e., one month to expiration), deep out-of-the-money call options (i.e., $S/K < .75$), and call options on stocks with relatively low historical volatility. The model overvalues call options that are deep in-the-money (i.e., $S/K > 1.25$), and call options on stocks with relatively high historical volatility. Furthermore, MacBeth and Merville (1979) and Rubinstein (1985) have noted that the money bias tends to reverse itself in different time periods, and Geske and Roll (1984a) showed that this reversal of the money bias may be partially attributable to improper treatment of early exercise.

Trautmann (1983b) tested the pricing performance of the Black-Scholes model using dividend-protected FOE options written in the 222-week period before the 1983 changes in trading rules. In this sample period, no organized secondary market for stock options existed. Thus, trading was illiquid, and an option's price could only be consistently observed on the day the contract was written. An observed option price was only considered if within the preceding five trading days at least two contracts have been written on the same underlying stock with the same maturity. All prices observed within this five-day period for options of the same maturity were used to calculate the ISDs are predictors of the future return volatility. The average values of the weekly parameter estimates, $\bar{\hat{\alpha}}_0$ and $\bar{\hat{\alpha}}_1$ ranged from 0.072 to 0.121 and 0.981 to 0.993, respectively, depending on the option's maturity. The average of the coefficients of determination from the cross-sectional regressions $\bar{R}^2$, ranged from 0.915 for 2-month options to 0.953 for 6-month options.

Emanuel and MacBeth (1982) extended the previous research of MacBeth and Merville (1980) in comparing the predictability of the Black-Scholes and CEV model. The root-mean-squared forecast errors indicate that for short-term predictions, the CEV model yields more accurate predictions that the Black-Scholes model. However, "the superiority of the constant elasticity of variance model diminishes as the prediction interval increases. In general, for prediction intervals of one month or longer, the Black-Scholes model does as well as the constant elasticity of variance model" (p. 541). The explanation of this result may be found in the nonstationary behavior of the estimated elasticity parameter ρ in the CEV model.

The American put valuation problem has been addressed by Brennan-Schwartz (1977), Parkinson (1977), Cox, Ross, and Rubinstein (1979), and Geske and Johnson (1984). The empirical work on valuing American puts is less advanced than for American calls, in part because puts werde not listed until June, 1977. Brennan-Schwartz find that putholders do not seem to optimally exercise the put. Farkas and Hoskin (1979), using Parkinson's model on weekly CBOE data from June to December, 1977, find the model to undervalue the puts on average, especially the out-of-the-money options.

In a direct comparison between a European and an American valuation model, using 10,295 CBOE transaction observations from June through August, 1978, Blomeyer and Johnson (1984) establish that the Geske-Johnson American model dominates the Black-Scholes European model. Although the Geske-Johnson American put model will yield the same value as the above alternatives, it is an order of magnitude faster. The fact that the American value is significantly closer to the market price in more than the majority of cases indicates that the early exercise is an important component of the put price.

In summary, it must be concluded that in the case of the most widely traded dividend-unprotected American call options, Roll's (1977) American formula did yield consistently better predictions of market prices than the Black-Scholes European model. Also, the Geske-Johnson American put model appears to dominate the Black-Scholes European model.

3.3.3 Results of Unbiasedness Tests

The Black-Scholes model values do not consistently give unbiased predictions of market prices. The reported biases have occurred with respect to

- the stock's volatility
- the exercise price
- the time until expiration.

Black and Scholes (1972) and MacBeth and Merville (1979) document the phenomenon that options on low-risk stocks are undervalued and options on high-risk stocks are overvalued by the model. Black (1975) reports that in the early years of trading on the CBOE, the model systematically undervalued deep out-of-the money options and near-maturity options while it overvalued deep in-the-money options. However, MacBeth and Merville (1979) and Rubinstein (1985) document a reversal of this striking price bias for the years 1976 and 1977, respectively. That is, the authors conclude that the Black-Scholes model undervalues (overvalues) the prices for in-the-money (out-of-the money) options. This bias acts as if the ISD, the stock volatility implied by an observed option price, were inversely related to the exercise price. But, Emanuel and MacBeth (1982) found that the original striking price bias observed by Black (1975) (which exhibits a direct relation between ISDs and exercise prices) had reestablished itself in late 1977 and 1978.

Geske and Roll (1984a) offered an explanation of these biases based on the dividend-induced early exercise feature of American call options. In fact, Whaley (1982) does demonstrate empirically that these biases are reduced when Roll's (1977) American call option formula is employed. For each model Whaley tested, the following cross-sectional regressions were estimated for each week during the 160-week sample period to regress the relative prediction error on the stock's volatility, the extent to which the option is in- or out-of-the-money, and the time until expiration:

$$\frac{C_j - \hat{C}_j}{\hat{C}_j} = \alpha_0 + \alpha_1 \hat{\sigma}_j + \varepsilon_j \tag{24}$$

$$\frac{C_j - \hat{C}_j}{\hat{C}_j} = \alpha_0 + \alpha_1 \left(\frac{S_j - K_j e^{-r_j T_j}}{K_j e^{-r_j T_j}} \right) + \varepsilon_j \tag{25}$$

$$\frac{C_j - \hat{C}_j}{\hat{C}_j} = \alpha_0 + \alpha_1 T_j + \varepsilon_j \quad . \tag{26}$$

Roll's (1977) corrected formula serves to reduce the magnitude of the slope coefficient α_1 and the coefficient of determination in the cross-sectional regressions (24),(25), and (26), but the hypothesis that there is no relationship between the relative prediction error $(C_j - \hat{C}_j)/\hat{C}_j$ and the volatility estimate $\hat{\sigma}_j$ is soundly rejected. Contrary to previous evidence, for each of the three models compared, the extent to which the option is in-the-money or out-of-the-money apparently does not significantly affect the model's prediction error. The results of regression (26) show that while there exists a significantly negative relationship for the valuation method based on the Black-Scholes formula (i.e., it undervalues near maturity options and overvalues longer maturity options), it virtually disappears when Roll's model is used.

Geske and Roll (1984a) suggest that dividend uncertainty may explain a small component of the variance bias exhibited by both the Black-Scholes European and Roll's American model. Trautmann (1983b), however, demonstrates empirically with FOE data that the consideration of this aspect does not remove this bias. By constructing a subsample of 19,040 call options with no dividend payments expected prior to expiration, it was found that in this subsample the variance bias is even more significant than in the total sample comprising 28,299 options.

Rubinstein (1985) examines whether one of the alternatives to the Black-Scholes model listed in Table 1 can explain the observed striking price and time-to-maturity biases of the Black-Scholes values. The null hypothesis is that the Black-Scholes formula produces unbiased values and hence ISDs should be constant for options on the same underlying stock with different maturities and striking prices. By comparing simulated and observed ISDs across maturities and striking prices, he tries to distinguish which pricing formula seems to better explain the observed biases from Black-Scholes values. This methodology avoids the difficult task of estimating the stock volatility. Furthermore, to circumvent possible objections of regression analysis with data that is not normally distributed, nonparametric tests were conducted since they require no assumptions about the population from which the observed sample is drawn. According to this test design, Rubinstein argues that the main measurement problem is the simultaneity of the market prices for the option and the underlying stock. To surmount these problems, the data are taken from Berkeley Options Transactions Data Base. This is a time-stamped record (to the nearest second) of all reported trades, quotes, and volume on the CBOE during the day.

Examination of the observed ISDs from August 23, 1976 to August 31, 1978, confirms the previous finding that, for an out-of-the-money call, the shorter the time to expiration, the higher its ISD which means it was relatively overpriced. This is the only result which is consistent over the whole sample period. The other conclusions depend on the subperiod considered (first subperiod: August 23, 1976 to October 21, 1977, second subperiod: October 24, 1977 to August 31, 1978), and reveal reversals in both the time and money bias observed in each subperiod.

These conclusions confirm the previous findings of MacBeth and Merville (1979) that the direction of the striking price bias changes from time to time. More importantly, Rubinstein concludes that no one alternative model seems to remove all the observed Black-Scholes biases. His proposal is to build a composite model which might, in addition, depend on some macroeconomic variables, such as the level of stock market prices, the level of stock market volatility and the level of interest rates.

Geske and Roll (1984b) repeat Whaley's tests using the Berkeley Options Transaction Data for all options traded at midday on August 24, 1976, resulting in a sample of 667 different options on 85 stocks. Options on the same stock differed by exercise price, expiration dates, and scheduled dividend payments prior to expiration. A subsample of 119 options in 28 different stocks with zero scheduled dividends during their remaining life was identified within the main sample. Using regression analysis, Geske and Roll demonstrate the original time, money, and volatility biases are present in the entire sample. Next, they show that in the nondividend subsample, the time and money biases are significantly reduced, but the volatility bias remains large. However, by correcting the volatility estimates of all stocks for errors in variables by "shrinking" the volatility of each stock in their sample toward the mean of the sample in a manner suggested by Stein (see Effron and Morris, 1975) the volatility bias is reduced. Thus, Geske and Roll conclude that the time and money biases may be more related to improper model treatment of early exercise while the volatility bias may be more related to estimation problems than to model assumptions (see Section 3.5).

3.3.4 Results of Hedge Return Behavior Tests

Most of the studies using option valuation models to identify overvalued/undervalued call options and then testing for market efficiency are based on the hedging technique of Black and Scholes (1972). That is, if the model value C^M is higher (lower) than the market price C, the call is underpriced (overpriced), and a long (short) position is taken in the call with a corresponding short (long) position is in the stock. If, in an ex-post test, the hedge position is established at time t and liquidated at $t+1$, the ex-post hedge return is

$$R_{H,t+1} = \begin{cases} (C_{t+1} - C_t) - N(d_{1,t})(S_{t+1} - S_t) & \text{if } C_t < C_t^M \\ N(d_{1,t})(S_{t+1} - S_t) - (C_{t+1} - C_t) & \text{if } C_t > C_t^M \end{cases} \tag{27}$$

The hedge return minus the opportunity cost $(e^{r\Delta t}-1)I_{H,t}$ on the investment

$$I_{H,t} = \begin{cases} C_t - N(d_{1,t})S_t & \text{if } C_t < C_t^M \\ N(d_{1,t})S_t - C_t & \text{if } C_t > C_t^M \end{cases} \tag{28}$$

will give the excess return for the hedged position.

Working with OTC data, Black and Scholes (1972) adjusted the hedge position daily by buying or selling shares of the underlying stock, assuming no transaction costs. Since a secondary market in OTC options was virtually nonexistent, they use their model to simulate the market prices needed for the calculation of daily hedge returns. When regressing the observed positive excess returns against a market index, no significant systematic risk was detected. When transactions costs were included, the substantial positive excess returns detected in the zero transaction cost case vanished.

Galai (1977) repeated this ex-post test with CBOE options by adjusting the options' positions. The hedge return averaged over all option contracts considered was \$9.80 per option contract (on 100 shares) per day. Furthermore, he performed an ex-ante test where, on day $t-1$, it is decided whether the option was over or underpriced, and the hedge ratio was calculated. The hedge position, however, is established and liquidated on day t and $t+1$, respectively. As expected, the average of the hedge returns fell from \$9.80 to \$5.00 per option contract per day for the ex-ante test. While in the ex-post test for 71 option series out of 202, the average of the time-series hedge return was significantly different from zero (at the 5 percent level of significance), this number dropped from 71 to 12 in the ex-ante test. Since the average opportunity costs for the hedge investment (about \$0.30 per contract per day) were found to be negligible, only the inclusion of transaction costs might eliminate the remaining positive hedge returns.

Similar magnitudes of excess hedge returns were observed when a spreading strategy was simulated. A spreading strategy consists of a long position in an undervalued option on the same underlying stock. Galai (1977, p. 195) concludes that "the market did not seem perfectly efficient to market makers" but,... "it does not seem that a non-member of the CBOE can expect to achieve above-normal profits consistently."

Chiras and Manaster (1978), in a similar study, use ISDs instead of historical volatilities to identify over or underpriced CBOE options with respect to the Black-Scholes values. A spread position is established for those options whose theoretical values deviate by at least 10 percent from the market price. The amount of each option included in the hedged position is determined by its hedge ratio and all established positions are liquidated one month later. This spreading strategy is used to eliminate the effect of stock price movements on the hedge returns. Unfortunately, the requisite of being able to identify both an underpriced and an overpriced option on the same stock restricts the number of options that may be included in the sample. Although they are careful to realize the ex-post nature of their tests, the positive excess hedge returns led them to conclude that even non-members of the CBOE could have made above-normal profits in the sample period. Using the data of Chiras and Manaster, Bookstaber (1981) and Phillips and Smith (1980) demonstrate, however, that the paper profits observed by Chiras and Manaster disappear when the nonsimultaneity of option prices and the bid-ask spread is considered, respectively.

In Whaley (1982), the validity of Roll's (1977) American call option model is tested jointly with the propositions that the previous week's ISD is an accurate reflection of the expected volatility and that the related markets are efficient. Roll's model is used to identify underpriced/overpriced options, and then a hedge portfolio is created by buying underpriced and selling overpriced CBOE options, such that the portfolio's net investment and its systematic risk is zero. Whaley rebalances the portfolio weekly, and thus the sample includes 160 weekly hedge returns. At the 0.0115 percent significance level, the null hypothesis of a zero hedge return was rejected. However, a proportional transaction cost rate of 0.616 percent was sufficient to eliminate all the profits that could be realized by following the cost-less trading strategy. Since the Phillips and Smith (1980) estimate of the bid-ask spread transaction cost component exceeds this critical rate, option market efficiency is soundly supported.

Blomeyer and Klemkosky (1983) also compare the ability of the Black-Scholes and Roll option pricing models to identify overpriced and underpriced call option contracts by using the hedging technique suggested by Black and Scholes (1972). The option positions in the hedge portfolio are adjusted for each new option transaction price, and the returns are calculated over the intervals between successive transactions. Since the Roll model allows for the early exercise of CBOE options, it is expected that the Roll model should outperform the Black-Scholes model for options written on high-dividend-yield stocks. However, the model-specific hedge results do not differ significantly. For both models, the ex-post excess hedge returns are significantly positive over most trading days and underlying securities. Even the ex-ante analysis produced significant positive returns on a before-transaction cost basis. But, these average profits disappear after the returns are adjusted for transaction costs.

3.4 Tests of New Option Instruments

In the 1980s, the Securities and Exchange Commission (SEC) granted permission to begin trading put and call options on foreign currency exchange rates, on futures on stock indices, currencies, and commodities, and on short-term Treasury Bills, and long-term Treasury Bonds. The volume in these markets is expected to increase as more investors become aware of their potential. The previously discussed theory of pricing options on equities applies to these new option instruments, with some changes.

For example, call option on currencies and futures have a positive probability of early exercise. The intuition regarding early exercise of American calls on currencies and futures can be attributed to an implied dividend effect with reasoning similar to the equity case. The implied dividend for currencies is the differential risk-free interest rate in the foreign and domestic countries, and is the cost of carry in the futures market. The debt options are more difficult to value than equity options because of the fixed maturity and fixed payout, and because it is not sensible to assume constant interest rates. There are several empirical papers testing valuation models for the new options.

For the currency options, Bodurtha and Courtadon (1984) test the efficiency of the Philadelphia Stock Exchange Foreign Currency Options Market using transactions data during the time period from February, 1983 to September, 1984. They find violations of the early exercise boundaries and of the put-call parity condition. However, when bid-ask spread transaction costs and simultaneous prices are used, most of the violations disappear. Shastri and Tandon (1984a) test a version of the Geske-Johnson American Options model applied to currency options for both puts and calls using the same Philadelphia data. They find systematic deviations between market prices and model values with respect to the time to expiration and the amount in or out-of-the-money. The model tends to undervalue out-of-the-money options, long maturity puts and short maturity calls, while it overvalues in-the-money options, short maturity puts, and long maturity calls. A hedging strategy returns abnormal profits, but these are eliminated when the bid-ask spread is properly considered.

Whaley (1984b) examines the prices of options on futures using transactions data from the Chicago Mercantile Exchange (CME) on the S & P 500 futures options from January to December, 1983. He compares the Black European futures option model to a version of the Geske-Johnson American model using about 15,000 observations for calls and 14,000 for puts. Whaley shows that both models undervalue in-the-money options and options with a long time to maturity. He demonstrates that the European model's bias is larger and more statistically significant than the American model. Finally, he shows that the market is efficient for retail customers who pay the bid-ask spread. Shastri and Tandon (1984b) also examine options transactions data from the CME on S & P 500 and Deutsche Mark futures during the time period of February, 1983 to December, 1984. Like Whaley, they use a version of the Geske-Johnson American option model adjusted for futures options. They demonstrate that biases exist with respect to the exercise price and time to expiration. They also confirm market efficiency by showing that hedging profits vanish when the bid-ask spread is considered.

Dietrich-Campbell and Schwartz (1984) test the Brennan/Schwartz debt option model on Treasury bill and bond option data collected from closing prices reported in The Wall Street Journal, for the year from November, 1982 through October, 1983. They report that the Brennan/ Schwartz model overvalues put and call options on long maturity bonds. The calls and overvalued by 33 cents and the puts by 30 cents, on average. This is better than an application of Black-Scholes, which is shown to overvalue the same options by 57 and 55 cents, respectively. For Treasury Bill options, the Brennan/Schwartz model misvalues the puts and calls by 4.3 and 3.1 cents, respectively. The errors are catalogued with respect to striking price and time to maturity. (It would be useful to know the percent error, but this work is preliminary.) Their paper also supports efficiency in the debt options market by showing that profits disappear when bid-ask spreads are considered.

3.5 Estimation Problems

A theoretical option value is a function of several variables which must be observed or estimated. As we have seen, this includes the price of the underlying asset, the exercise price, time to expiration of the option, the interest rate over the life of the option, the volatility of the underlying asset, and any payouts to the underlying assetholder scheduled during the option life. Typically, the exercise price and the option expiration date are contracted and known with certainty, and have no estimation problems.

The price of the underlying asset can be observed, albeit imperfectly, if it is trading in a market. This measurement error regarding the exact location of the underlying asset price (at or within the bid-ask spread) is further complicated by the lack of simultaneous trading in the option and the stock markets (or currency, futures, or bond markets). Transactions data, time stamped in both markets, with recorded trades indicating at the bid or ask, are the best data financial economists can get to alleviate this measurement problem. The interest rate is generally assumed constant over the option life. For short-lived options (less than one year) this assumption may be the best way to treat an otherwise difficult problem. Which interest rate is used in the hedge process, and differential borrowing and lending rates further complicate this estimation problem. However, estimation of the interest rate does not appear to be a serious problem for equity options since their values are not very sensitive to changes in interest rates (debt options are obviously an exception). Also, scheduled dividend payments over the life of the option are uncertain, but for short-lived options, this uncertainty is small. The option value is most sensitive to the volatility of the underlying asset. Since volatility is not directly observable, it must be measured. Measurement of volatility is probably the most important estimation problem in valuing options, and it will be the focus of this brief subsection.

It is well-known that an unbiased estimate of the volatility will produce a biased estimate of an option value (Thorpe, 1976). The bias in the option value arises because the option formula (Black-Scholes, et al.) are nonlinear functions of the volatility, and unbiasedness is not preserved under nonlinear transformations. However, this source of bias in the option price is not large, as Boyle/Ananthanarayanan (1977) document. Furthermore, Butler/Schachter (1985) demonstrate how this transformation bias can be eliminated.

A more serious potential problem in variance estimation is errors in variables. It is well-known that the Black-Scholes model undervalues options on low variance stocks and overvalues options on high variance stocks. Geske and Roll (1984b) point out that the variance-related mispricing always arises in the context of an inter-stock comparison, in contrast to the striking price and time-to-exiration biases, which are detected in an inter-option comparison. Unlike the striking price and time until expiration, the true variance is identical for all options on the same stock on a given date. Thus, investigations of variance-related mispricing cannot rely on the implied variance (Latané and Rendleman, 1976), but must instead be based on historical estimates of actual stock return volatility.

There are many techniques to improve the volatility estimate for a single stock. Parkinson (1980), Garman and Klass (1980), and Beckers (1983), use more information (high, low, open, and close for the day) in the estimate. But, the essence of the present problem is that a number of variances are estimated simultaneously, one for each stock, and then option mispricing is related cross-sectionally to these several estimates. Geske-Roll (1984b) demonstrate that by optimally "shrinking" each individual stock variance estimate to the grand mean of all estimates, the observed volatility bias is eliminated.

4. Appendix: Formulae for the Evaluation of European Calls

In this Appendix, formulae are given for the evaluation of a variety of European option pricing models subject to the motion equations listed in Table 1. For a more detailed explanation of each model the reader is referred to the original paper mentioned in Sec. 2.2.3. We start with model number 2 of Table 1, the binomial model, since the Black-Scholes diffusion model was already given in Sec. 2.2.2.

Binomial Model

According as the unit of time is chosen there are two different ways to present the model and the resulting valuation formula.

- Alternative 1: Unit of time is the interval between two successive jumps (for instance one day). The time T to the expiration of the call is an integer number of such units of time. Of course, the risk-free rate of interest r has to refer to this small unit too.
- Alternative 2: Unit of time is - as usual - one year. If the number of jumps occurring up to the expiration of the call is denoted by n, an evaluation formula results which depends on the number n fixed beforehand.

Alternative 2 is more appropriate to analyze the limiting behavior $(n \to \infty)$ provided that the jump size is suitably related to n, whereas alternative 1 is the natural extension of the simple two-state one-period model to the T period case. The following description is based on alternative 1.

$$C = S \cdot B(a;T,p') - K \cdot R^{-T} \cdot B(a;T,p) = \text{call value} ,$$

where

S = stock price at current date

K = exercise price

T = time to expiration

$R = 1 + r$ = one plus the risk-free rate of interest

$p = \frac{R-d}{u-d}$ (sometimes denoted as 'hedging probability')

$p' = \frac{u}{R} p$

u = multiplicative factor of up jump (i.e. the jump is from S to $u \cdot S$) ; $u > R$

d = multiplicative factor of down jump; $d < R$

$B(a;T,p) = \sum_{j=a}^{T} \binom{T}{j} p^j (1-p)^{T-j}$ = complementary binomial distribution function

a = smallest non negative integer greater than

$$\ln\left(\frac{K}{Sd^T}\right)/\ln\left(\frac{u}{d}\right),$$

if a happens to be greater than T, the call value C turns out to be zero.

Constant Elasticity of Variance (CEV) Model

$$C = S \cdot \sum_{n=1}^{\infty} g(n,x)G(n+\lambda,y) - K \cdot e^{-rT} \sum_{n=1}^{\infty} g(n+\lambda,x)G(n,y),$$

where the (new) symbols have the meaning:

$\lambda = \frac{1}{2(1-\rho)}$ ($\rho \neq 1$ is the exponent of the motion equation in Tab. 1)

$x = \frac{2\lambda r}{v^2(e^{rT/\lambda} - 1)} S^{1/\lambda} e^{rT/\lambda}$ (v is the coefficient of the motion equation in Tab. 1)

$$y = \frac{2\lambda r}{v^2(e^{rT/\lambda} - 1)} K^{1/\lambda}$$

and

$g(n,z) = \frac{e^{-z} z^{n-1}}{\Gamma(n)}$ = gamma density function

$G(n,w) = \int_w^{\infty} g(n,z)dz$ = complementary standard gamma density function.

Compound Option Model

$$C = V \cdot N_2(h,k;\rho) - M \cdot e^{-rT_M} N_2(h-v'\sqrt{T},k-v'\sqrt{T_M};\rho) - K \cdot e^{-rT} N(h) ,$$

where

V = current market value of the firm

M = maturity value of the firm's zero coupon debt

T = time to expiration of the option

T_M = time to maturity of the zero coupon debt (where $T < T_M$)

$\rho = \sqrt{T/T_M}$

and

$$h = \left[\ell n\left(\frac{V}{\bar{V}}\right) + rT + \frac{1}{2}v'^2T\right]\frac{1}{v'\sqrt{T}}$$

$$k = \left[\ell n\left(\frac{V}{M}\right) + rT_M + \frac{1}{2}v'^2T_M\right]\frac{1}{v'\sqrt{T_M}}$$

v' = standard deviation of rate of return on the firm's asset

$\bar{V}$ is the value of V defined by the equation:

$$V \cdot N(k) - M \cdot e^{r\tau} N(k - v'\sqrt{\tau}) - K = 0 \quad (\text{where } \tau = T_M - T) .$$

Finally,

$$N_2(h,k;\rho) = \frac{1}{2\pi\sqrt{1-\rho^2}} \int_{-\infty}^{h}\int_{-\infty}^{k} \exp\left\{-\frac{1}{2}\,\frac{x^2 - 2\rho xy + y^2}{1-\rho^2}\right\} dy\, dx$$

= bivariate normal distribution function with mean vector = (0,0) and variances = 1 .

$$N(k) = \frac{1}{\sqrt{2\pi}} \int_{-\infty}^{k} e^{-\frac{x^2}{2}} dx$$ = univariate standard normal distribution function.

Displaced Diffusion Model

(Special Case: No dividend payments)

$$C = a \cdot S \cdot N(x) - (K - bS)e^{-rT} N(x - v'\sqrt{T}) = \text{call value} ,$$

where

$$x = \frac{\ell n\left(\frac{aS\,e^{rT}}{K-bS}\right)}{v'\sqrt{T}} + \frac{1}{2}v'\sqrt{T}$$

$a = \alpha(1+\beta)$

$b = (1-\alpha-\alpha\beta)e^{-rT}$

v' = standard deviation of rate of return on the firm's risky asset

α = fraction of the total firm value currently invested in the risky asset; accordingly, $1-\alpha$ is the fraction invested in the riskless asset.

β = firm's debt-equity ratio.

Jump Process Model

$$C = S \cdot P(x;\lambda) - K \cdot e^{-rT} P(x;\lambda/k) = \text{call value},$$

where

λ = expected jump frequency per unit time

k = expected jump amplitude

x = nonnegative integer representing the smallest number of Poisson stock price jumps, such that the option is in-the-money at the expiration date (i.e. $S(T) > K$)

$P(x;\lambda) = \sum_{i=x}^{\infty} \frac{e^{-\lambda}\lambda^i}{i!}$ = complementary Poisson distribution function with argument x and parameter λ.

Diffusion-Jump Model

(Special case: The jump amplitude has a lognormal distribution)
Assuming the jumps have no market component and are thus completely diversifiable, then

$$C = \sum_{i=0}^{\infty} \frac{e^{-\lambda' T}(\lambda' T)^i}{i!} C_i(S,K,T,\sigma_i,r_i) = \text{call value},$$

where

C_i = Black-Scholes value of a European call with time to expiration T and striking price K on a stock with current price S and volatility σ_i, conditional on knowing that exactly i Poisson jumps occur during the life of the option.

$\sigma_i = \sqrt{v^2 + \delta^2 \frac{i}{T}}$

δ^2 = variance of the jump component

$\lambda' = \lambda(1+k)$

λ = expected jump frequency per unit time

k = expected jump amplitude

$r_i = r - \lambda k + \frac{i \,\ell n\,(1+k)}{T}$.

References:

Ball, C.A.; Torous, W.N. (1983): Bond Price Dynamics and Options, Journal of Financial and Quantitative Analysis 18, 517-531

Ball, C.A.; Torous, W.N. (1985a):On Jumps in Common Stock Prices and Their Impact on Call Option Pricing, Journal of Finance 40, 155-173

Ball, C.A.; Torous, W.N. (1985b):Futures Options and the Volatility of Futures Prices, Working Paper, University of Michigan

Beckers, S. (1980): The Constant Elasticity of Variance Model and Its Implications for Option Pricing, Journal of Finance 35, 661-673

Beckers, S. (1981): Standard Deviations Implied in Option Prices as Predictors of Futures Stock Price Variability, Journal of Banking and Finance 5, 363-381

Beckers, S. (1983): Variance of Security Price Returns Based on High, Low, and Closing Prices, Journal of Business 56, 97-112

Bhattacharya, M. (1980): Empirical Properties of the Black-Scholes Formula under Ideal Conditions, Journal of Financial and Quantitative Analysis, 1081-1105

Bhattacharya, M. (1983): Transactions Data Tests of Efficiency of the Chicago Board Options Exchange, Journal of Financial Economics 12, 161-185

Bhattacharya, M.; Rubinstein, M. (1978): Berkeley Options Data Base, Mimeographed, University of California, Berkeley

Black, F. (1975): Facts and Fantasy in the Use of Options, Financial Analysts Journal 31, 35-72

Black, F. (1976): The Pricing of Commodity Contracts, Journal of Financial Economics 3, 167-179

Black, F.; Cox, J.C. (1976): Valuing Corporate Securities: Some Effects of Bond Indenture Provisions, Journal of Finance 31, 351-368

Black, F.; Scholes, M. (1972): The Valuation of Option Contracts and a Test of Market Efficiency, Journal of Finance 27, 399-417

Black, F.; Scholes, M. (1973): The Pricing of Options and Corporate Liabilities, Journal of Political Economy 81, 637-659

Blomeyer, E.C.; Resnick, B.G. (1982): An Empirical Investigation of the Compound Option Pricing Model, Unpublished Manucript

Blomeyer, E.C.; Johnson, U. (1984): An Empirical Testing of American Put Pricing, Unpublished Working Paper, Louisiana State University

Blomeyer, E.C.; Klemkosky, R.C. (1983): Tests of Market Efficiency for American Call Options, in: Brenner, M. (ed.): Option Pricing: Theory and Applications, Lexington Books, Lexington, 101-121

Bodurtha, J.; Courtadon, G. (1963): Efficiency Tests of the Foreign Currency Option Market, Ohio State University, Working Paper

Bookstaber, R.M. (1981): Observed Option Mispricing and the Non-simultaneity of Stock and Option Quotations, Journal of Business 54, 141-155

Boyle, P.P.; Ananthanarayanan, A.C. (1977): The Impact of Variance Estimation in Option Valuation Models, Journal of Financial Economics 5, 375-387

Boyle, P.P.; Emanuel D.C. (1980): Discretely Adjusted Option Hedges, Journal of Financial Economics 8, 259-282

Brennan, M.J. (1979): The Pricing of Contingent Claims in Discrete Time Models, Journal of Finance 34, 53-68

Brennan, M.J.; Schwartz, E.S. (1977a): The Valuation of American Put Options, Journal of Finance 32, 449-464

Brennan, M.J.; Schwartz, E.S. (1977b): Convertible Bonds: Valuation and Optimal Strategies for Call and Conversion, Journal of Finance 32, 1699-1716

Brennan, M.J.; Schwartz, E.S. (1980): Analysing Convertible Bonds, Journal of Financial and Quantitative Analysis, 907-929

Brennan, M.J.; Schwartz, E.S. (1982): An Equilibrium Model of Bond Pricing and a Test of Market Efficiency, Journal of Financial and Quantitative Analysis 17, 301-329

Brenner, M. (ed.) (1983): Option Pricing - Theory and Applications, Lexington Books, Lexington Mass.

Brenner, M.; Galai, D. (1981): The Properties of the Estimated Risk of Common Stocks Implied by Options Prices, Working Paper, University of California, Berkeley

Brenner, M.; Courtadon, G.; Subrahmanyan, M. (1984): Options on Stock Indices and Stock Index Futures, Working Paper, New York University

Butler, J.S.; Schachter, B. (1985) Unbiased Estimation of the Black-Scholes Formula, Journal of Financial Economics, forthcoming

Chiras, D.P.; Manaster, S. (1978): The Information Content of Option Prices and a Test of Market Efficiency, Journal of Financial Economics 6, 213-234

Courtadon, G. (1982): The Pricing of Options on Default-Free Bonds, The Journal of Financial and Quantitative Analysis 17, 75-100

Cox, J.C.; Ingersoll, J.; Ross, S. (1985): A Theory of the Term Structure of Interest Rates, Econometrica 53, 385-407

Cox, J.C. (1975): Notes on Option Pricing I: Constant Elasticity of Variance Diffusions, Mimeographed, Stanford University

Cox, J.C.; Ross, S.A. (1976a): A Survey of Some New Results in Financial Option Pricing Theory, Journal of Finance 31, 383-402

Cox, J.C.; Ross, S.A. (1976b): The Valuation of Options for Alternative Stochastic Processes, Journal of Financial Economics 3, 145-166

Cox, J.C.; Rubinstein, M. (1983): A Survey of Alternative Option Pricing Models, in: Brenner, M. (ed.): Option Pricing: Theory and Applications, Lexington, Lexington Books, 3-33

Cox, J.C.; Rubinstein, M. (1985): Options Markets, Englewood Cliffs, N.J., Prentice-Hall

Cox, J.C.; Ross, S.A.; Rubinstein, M. (1979): Option Pricing: A Simplified Approach, Journal of Financial Economics 7, 229-263

Dietrich-Campbell, B.; Schwartz, E.S. (1984): Valuing Debt Options: Empirical Evidence, University of British Columbia, Working Paper, November

Dothan, U.L. (1978): On the Term Structure of Interest Rates, Journal of Financial Economics 6, 59-69

Effron, B.; Morris, C. (1975): Data Analysis Using Stein's Estimation and Its Generalization, Journal of the American Statistical Association 70, 311-319

Egle, K.; Trautmann, S. (1981): On Preference-Dependent Pricing of Contingent Claims, in: H. Göppl and R. Henn (eds.): Money, Banking and Insurance, Königstein/Ts., 400-416

Emanuel, D.C. (1983): Warrant Valuation and Exercise Strategy, Journal of Financial Economics 12, 211-236

Emanuel, D.C.; MacBeth, J.D. (1982): Further Results on the Constant Elasticity of Variance Call Option Pricing Model, Journal of Financial and Quantitative Analysis 17, 533-554

Farkas, K.L; Hoskin , R.E. (1979): Testing a Valuation Model for American Puts, Financial Management 8, 51-56

Finnerty, J.E. (1978): The CBOE and Market Efficiency, Journal of Financial and Quantitative Analysis 13, 29-38

Fischer,E.O.; Zechner, R. (1984): Diffusion Process Specifications for Interest Rates: An Empirical Investigation for the RFG, in: Bamberg, G.; Spremann, K. (eds.): Risk and Capital, Springer Publ. Company, Berlin-Heidelberg-New York-Tokyo, 64-73

Fuller, R.J. (1977-1978): Factors which Influence Listed Call Option Prices, Review of Business and Economic Research 13, 21-34

Galai, D. (1977): Tests of Market Efficiency of the Chicago Board Options Exchange, Journal of Business 50, 167-197

Galai, D. (1978): Empirical Test of Boundary Conditions for CBOE Options, Journal of Financial Economics 6, 187-211

Galai, D. (1979): A Convexity Test for Traded Options, Quarterly Review of Business and Economics 19, 83-90

Galai, D. (1983a): The Components of the Return from Hedging Options Against Stocks, Journal of Business 56, 45-54

Galai, D. (1983b): A Survey of Empirical Tests of Option Pricing Models, in: Brenner, M. (ed.): Option Pricing: Theory and Applications, Lexington Books, 45-85

Galai, D.; Masulis, R.W. (1976): The Option Pricing Model and the Risk Factor of Stock, Journal of Financial Economics 3, 53-81

Galai, D.; Schneller, M.I. (1978): Pricing Warrants and the Value of the Firm, Journal of Finance 33, 1333-1342

Garman, M.B.; Klass, M.J. (1980): On the Estimation of Security Price Volatilities from Historical Data, Journal of Business 53, 67-78

Geske, R. (1977): The Valuation of Corporate Liabilities as Compound Options, Journal of Financial and Quantitative Analysis 12, 541-552

Geske, R. (1979a): The Valuation of Compound Options, Journal of Financial Economics 7, 63-81

Geske, R. (1979b): A Note on an Analytic Valuation Formula for Unprotected American Call Options on Stocks with Known Dividends, Journal of Financial Economics 7, 375-380

Geske, R. (1981): Notes on the Pricing of Bond Options, University of California, Los Angeles, Manuscript

Geske, R.; Johnson, H.E. (1984): The American Put Option Valued Analytically, Journal of Finance 39, 1511-1524

Geske, R.; Roll, R. (1984a): On Valuing American Call Options with the Black-Scholes European Formula, Journal of Finance 39, 443-455

Geske, R.; Roll, R. (1984b): Isolating the Observed Biases in American Call Pricing: An Alternative Variance Estimator, UCLA Working Paper, 4-84, February

Geske, R. ; Shastri, K. (1985): Valuation by Approximation: A Comparison of Alternative Valuation Techniques, Journal of Financial and Quantitative Analysis 20, 45-71

Geske, R. ; Roll, R.; Shastri, K. (1983): Over-the-Counter Option Market Dividend Protection and "Biases" in the Black-Scholes Model: A Note, Journal of Finance 38, 1271-1277

Gombola, M.J.; Roenfeldt, R.L.; Cooley, P.L. (1978): Spreading Strategies in CBOE Options: Evidence on Market Performance, Journal of Financial Research 1, 35-44

Gould, J.; Galai, D. (1974): Transactions Costs and the Relationship Between Put and Call Prices, Journal of Financial Economics 1, 105-129

Gultekin, N.B.; Rogalski, R.J.; Tinic, S.M. (1982): Option Pricing Model Estimates: Some Empirical Results, Financial Management, 58-69

Harrison, J.M.; Kreps, D.M. (1979): Martingales and Arbitrage in Multiperiod Security Markets, Journal of Economic Theory 20, 381-408

Ingersoll, J.E. (1976): A Theoretical and Empirical Investigation of Dual Purpose Funds, Journal of Financial Economics 3, 83-123

Klemkosky, R.C.; Resnick, B.G. (1979): Put-Call Parity and Market Efficiency, Journal of Finance 34, 1141-1155

Klemkosky, R.C.; Resnick, B.G. (1980): An Ex-Ante Analysis of Put-Call Parity, Journal of Financial Economics 8, 363-378

Kreps, D.M. (1981): Arbitrage and Equilibrium in Economics with Infinitely Many Commodities, Journal of Mathematical Economics 8, 15-35

Latané, H.A.; Rendleman, R.J. (1976): Standard Deviations of Stock Price Ratios Implied in Option Prices, Journal of Finance 31, 369-381

Leland, H.E. (1980): Who Should Buy Portfolio Insurance, Journal of Finance 35, 581-596

MacBeth, J.D.; Merville, L.J. (1979): An Empirical Examination of the Black-Scholes Call Option Pricing Model, Journal of Finance 34, 1173-1186

MacBeth, J.D.; Merville, L.J. (1980): Test of Black-Scholes and Cox Call Option Valuation Models, Journal of Finance 35, 285-303

Madansky, A. (1977): Some Comparisons of the Case of Empirical and Lognormal Distributions in Option Evaluation, Proceedings of the Seminar on the Analysis of Securities Prices, Chicago: Center for Research in Securities Prices, University of Chicago, 155-168

Merton, R.C. (1973a): Theory of Rational Option Pricing, Bell Journal of Economics and Management Science 4, 141-183

Merton, R.C. (1973b): The Relationship Between Put and Call Option Prices: Comment, Journal of Finance 28, 183-184

Merton, R.C. (1974): On the Pricing of Corporate Debt: The Risk Structure of Interest Rates, Journal of Finance 29, 449-470

Merton, R.C. (1976a): Option Pricing when Underlying Stock Returns are Discontinuous, Journal of Financial Economics 3, 125-144

Merton, R.C. (1976b): The Impact on Option Pricing of Specification Error in the Underlying Stock Price Returns, Journal of Finance 31, 333-350

Merton, R.C. (1977a): On The Pricing of Contingent Claims and the Modigliani-Miller Theorem, Journal of Financial Economics 5, 241-250

Merton, R.C. (1977b): An Analytic Derivation of the Cost of Deposit Insurance and Loan Guarantees: An Application of Modern Option Pricing Theory, Journal of Banking and Finance 1, 3-11

Merton, R.C.; Scholes, M.S.; Gladstein, M.L. (1982): The Returns and Risks of Alternative Put-Option Portfolio Investment Strategies, Journal of Business 49, 1-55

Mossin, J. (1968): Optimal Multiperiod Portfolio Policies, Journal of Business 41, 215-229

Parkinson, M. (1977): Option Pricing: The American Put, Journal of Business 50, 21-36

Parkinson, M. (1980): The Extreme Value Method for Estimating the Variance of the Rate of Return, Journal of Business 53, 61-65

Patell, J.M.; Wolfson, M.A. (1979): Anticipated Information Releases Reflected in Call Option Prices, Journal of Accounting Research 1, 117-140

Phillips, S.M.; Smith, C.W. (1980): Trading Costs for Listed Options: The Implications for Market Efficiency, Journal of Financial Economics 8, 179-201

Ramaswamy, K.; Sundaresan, S.M. (1984): The Valuation of Options on Futures Contracts, Working Paper, Columbia University

Roll, R. (1977): An Analytic Valuation Formula for Unprotected American Call Options on Stocks with Known Dividends, Journal of Financial Economics 5, 251-258

Rubinstein, M. (1974): An Aggregation Theorem for Security Markets, Journal of Financial Economics 1, 225-244

Rubinstein, M. (1976): The Valuation of Uncertain Income Streams and the Pricing of Options, Bell Journal of Economics 7, 407-425

Rubinstein, M. (1977): The Strong Case for the Generalized Logarithmic Utility Model as the Premier Model of Financial Markets, in: Levy and M. Sarnat (eds.): Financial Decision Making Under Uncertainty, New York, 11-62

Rubinstein, M. (1983): Displaced Diffusion Option Pricing, Journal of Finance 38, 213-217

Rubinstein, M. (1985): Nonparametric Tests of Alternative Option Pricing Models Using All Reported Trades and Quotes on the 30 Most Active CBOE Option Classes from August 23, 1976 through August 3, 1978, Journal of Finance 40, 455-480

Schmalensee, R.; Trippi, R.R. (1978): Common Stock Volatility Expectations Implied by Option Premia, Journal of Finance 32, 129-147

Shastri, K.; Tandon, K. (1984a): Valuation of American Options on Foreign Currency, University of Pittsburgh, Working Paper

Shastri, K.; Tandon, K. (1984b): Valuation of American Options on Futures Contracts, University of Pittsburgh, Working Paper

Smith, C.; Zimmerman, J. (1976): Valuing Employee Stock Option Plans Using Option Pricing Models, Journal of Accounting Research 14, 357-364

Stoll, H.R. (1969): The Relationship Between Put and Call Option Prices, Journal of Finance 24, 801-824

Stoll, H.R. (1973): The Relationship Between Put and Call Prices: Reply, Journal of Finance 28, 185-187

Thorpe, E. (1976): Common Stock Volatilities in Option Formulas, Proceedings of the Seminar on the Analysis of Security Prices, 2, 235-276

Trautmann, S. (1983a): Tests of Two Call Options Pricing Models Using German Stock Options Market Data from January 1979 - March 1983, in: H. Göppl and R. Henn (eds.), Geld, Banken und Versicherungen, Verlag Versicherungswirtschaft, Karlsruhe, 619-639

Trautmann, S. (1983b): An Alternative Derivation of the Black/ Scholes Formula and Its Empirical Examination with German Stock Options Market Data, Discussion Paper No. 54, Institut für Entscheidungstheorie und Unternehmensforschung, Universität Karlsruhe

Trautmann, S. (1985a): Distribution-Free Tests of the Efficiency of the Frankfurt Options Exchange from April 5, 1983 through September 28, 1984, in: H. Göppl and R. Henn (eds.), Geld, Banken und Versicherungen, 1087-1094

Trautmann, S. (1985b): Die Bewertung von Finanztitel mit Wahlrechten - Theoretische Analyse sowie empirische Überprüfung für den deutschen Kapitalmarkt, Unpublished Manuscript, forthcoming

Trippi, R. (1977): A Test of Option Market Efficiency Using a Random-Walk Valuation Model, Journal of Economics and Business 29, 93-98

Vasicek, O. (1977): Equilibrium and Term Structure, Journal of Financial Economics 5, 177-188

Whaley, R.E. (1981): On the Valuation of American Call Options on Stocks with Known Dividends, Journal of Financial Economics 9, 207-212

Whaley, R.E. (1982): Valuation of American Call Option on Dividend-Paying Stocks - Empirical Tests, Journal of Financial Economics 10, 29-58

Whaley, R.E. (1984a): On Valuing American Futures Options, Financial Analysts Journal, forthcoming

Whaley, R.E. (1984b): Valuation of American Futures Options: Empirical Tests, University of Alberta, Working Paper, April

Wilson, R. (1968): The Theory of Syndicates, Econometrica 36, 119-132.

The Value of Security Agreements

Bernd Rudolph

Summary: The purpose of this paper is to examine security agreements in the light of some well known models of financial theory. In section 1 a survey of common credit support decision models is given and the role of collateralization is examined in the context of these models. Section 2 seeks to prove that the neoclassical theory of finance fails to explain the empirical evidence of security agreements in credit-contracts. Section 3 examines a rather new approach and it is shown on the basis of this approach that security agreements can be interpreted in a rather satisfactoring manner. Collaterals and credit covenants are realized as instruments of influencing the trustworthiness of the borrower. In sections 4 and 5 finally several types of credit contract covenants are structurized and discussed with respect to their practical efficiency. In the appendix some main results of the neoclassical approach are proved in a more general way.

Table of Contents:

Capital Market Equilibria. Ed. by G. Bamberg and K. Spremann

1. A Survey of Credit Support Decision Models

1.1 Credit Decisions in a Restricted Capital Market

To discuss the comprehension of secured debt in the several approaches of financial theory it is useful to classify the assumptions about the expectations of the creditors in the different models of credit support decision, as shown in figure 1.

First of all one can distinguish credit support decisions when lenders have secure expectations from such decisions under risk or uncertainty. Credit support decisions with secure expectations are strictly spoken trivial decisions, but often discussed in connection with imperfect capital markets with credit restrictions and therefore this case is included in the scheme of figure 1. On restricted capital markets credit rationing is a characteristic feature. Credit rationing itself can be interpreted as a reaction of the lender on the uncertainty about the future financial result of his investments. This uncertainty is only implicitly treated in the lender's calculation, above all in the form of fixed credit lines. Collaterization in such an approach is to be seen as a different tool to limit the creditor's commitment.

1.2 Market Uncertainty

As Hirshleifer and Riley (1979) made clear in their remarkable expository survey on the economics of uncertainty and information that the analytical decision theory has to deal with two kinds of uncertainty: the market uncertainty and the technological or event uncertainty. Although the financial literature considers almost exclusively event uncertainty, there is the remarkable exception of Milde's (1980, 1981) approach which is of interest for our survey because of comprehending the phenomenon of securing debt explicity.

We discuss this approach separated from other approaches of individual credit support decision, because the assumptions about the expectations of the creditors are not unique. Milde wants to explain why the credit market is characterized by a variety of different interest rates, a phenomenon called 'interest rate dispersion'.

Interest rate dispersion is not only evoked by different interest rates which relate to the different rating-classes of debtors, but furthermore because debtors do not know the specific security requirements of the banks. To prevent high costs of searching for the

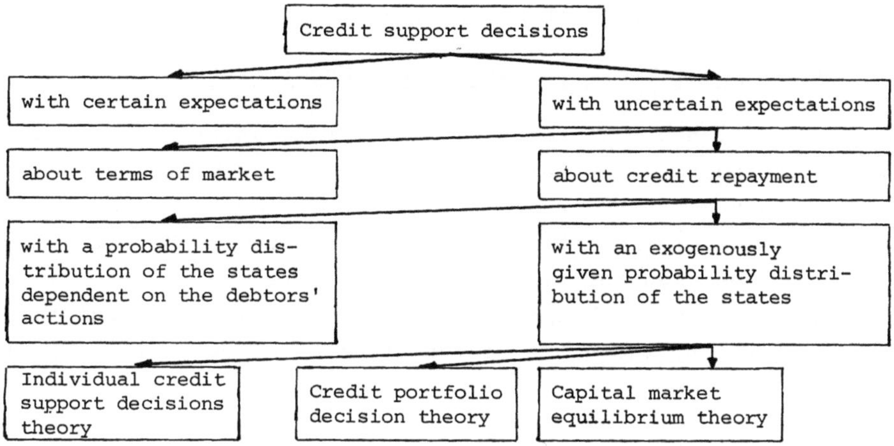

figure 1

debtor's specific risk class specialized bank, the borrowers accept interest rates too high in relation to their standing. The costs of searching are difficult to specify and thus one hardly expect prescriptive statements of this approach. But it is a convincing idea to explain interest dispersion with the prevention of searching costs.

Until now we did not specify Milde's definition of 'secured debt'. In his model the debtor pays his loan back with the proceeds $X(s)$ of the investment project, and, under certain circumstances with the liquidation proceeds $Y(s)$ of the collateral. $X(s)$ and $Y(s)$ are random numbers which are dependent on the state of the world s. If K is the amount of the credit, and r is the loan's interest rate at the end of the period, the bank will get:

$$Z = \min[(1+r)K, X(s) + Y(s)]$$

If there is no doubt about the borrower's willing to repay the credit, each asset of the debtor is liable to the bank even without a claim on a collateral security, and therefore the bank will not need a collateral Y to secure the debt claim. Securities in Milde's approach define the firm's level of solvency, which is measured by the amount of net property before credit support.

Therefore the results of the model do <u>not</u> refer to the collateral policy of the bank, but to the bank's solvency policy specifying the minimum solvency requirements for the customer. A similar argumentation can be shown to hold for the definition of secured debt in the credit rationing approach of Stiglitz and Weiss (1981).

1.3 Credit Support Decisions with Event Uncertainty

We already mentioned that comprehending market uncertainty is the exception of the rule in credit support theory. Usually one regards event uncertainty, where an uncertainty about the future states is assumed which determine the repayment of the credit. Decision theory distinguishes between the risk situation, where the future states of the world will occur with specified given probabilities, and the gambling situation, where the states are the various acting possibilities of the opponent.

It the states of the world occur independently of the borrower's behavior, then the risk of the credit position is to be seen as the risk on the lacking credit standing of the debtor. If the states depend on the acting possibilities of the debtor, then the credit risk is a credit reliability risk. But one should assume that credit standing and credit reliability risk do not occur isolated but in combination.

The most elaborated neoclassical approach of the credit support theory considers the risk of a decreasing credit standing of the borrower exclusively. We will discuss the main models of the neoclassical approach in the next section.

2. Neoclassical Theory and Secured Debt

2.1 The Basic Approach

This theory assumes that a bank decides about an individual credit support at the time the customer asks for this loan. Each credit decision is made exclusively without considering the total credit engagement of the bank. The need of an individual decision is caused in default of information about the future credit demand, and by the organization of decentralized bank decisions, which is characteristic for branch bank systems (Rudolph 1974).

The bank's decisions about credit supports depend on the net profit of the credit positions. Let us define K as the demanded loan amount, and r as the interest rate. Furtheron i is the interest rate the bank has to pay for the refinancement of its credit support. Thus the mean of the interest excess G of a credit position will be

$$E(G) = (1+r)K\,\alpha(r,K) - (1+i)K ,$$

where α is the mean credit repayment quota. For $\alpha = 1$ the bank expects the repayment at the end of the period with certainty, for $\alpha < 1$ the bank expects with a certain probability which among others depends on the interest rate r and on the credit amount K that the credit will not be paid back in the whole amount.

Given this very easy approach, one can specify collateral as an instrument to raise the mean repayment quota α. But notice that such a reduction of the creditfailment is only imaginable if several creditors share the chances and the risk of the debtor's assets. Only then it is possible for one creditor to shift risk to the others, if his individual debt contract contains collateral covenants. If the bank is the sole creditor the debtor's total property is liable and an additional collateral agreement can't improve the creditor's position.

Concerning credit collateral policy we do not get new fundamental results of the theory of credit portfolio decisions except the now necessary consideration of the correlation of expected future values of the collateral security with the expected future values of the firm's total assets.

2.2 Secured Debt and Capital Market Equilibrium

The theory of capital market equilibrium investigates among others whether a shift of default risks from one creditor to other creditors can cause any advantages for the debtor. In a corporation with outstanding debt these advantages would result in a rise of the market value of the debt and therefore in an increased market value of the firm.

If the creditors act rationally and on the presumptions usually summarized for the assumption of a perfect capital market one can show that the collateral policy of a levered firm is irrelevant for its market value. One could call this statement analogous to the irrelevance hypothesis of Modigliani and Miller (1958) the collateral irrelevance hypothesis: Given perfect capital markets possible risk differences between credit positions are fully reflected in their market values with the consequence that risk transfers between creditors will cause an altogether equally high total market value of the outstanding debt.

This result of capital market equilibrium theory (which will be proved in a more general way in the appendix) can be explained by a simple example. To that end we inspect a company with the invested capital containing only two assets. At the end of the period the liquidation proceeds of the two assets X and Y will depend on three states of the world s_1, s_2 and s_3. The contingent proceeds are shown in table 1.

The firm incurs debt from bank A and bank B and has to redeem the amount of $T_A = 55$ and $T_B = 55$ at the end of the period. Presumed the default free interest rate is 10 % and the market is risk neutral so that the present market value of financial claims is the discounted mean, the debt claims of bank A and B both have the value:

$$F_A = F_B = \frac{1}{2 \cdot 1.1} [0.3 \cdot 88 + 0.7 \cdot 110] = 47$$

liquidation proceeds \ state / probability	s_1 0.3	s_2 0.4	s_3 0.3	mean
X	60	60	60	60
Y	28	105	72	72
X + Y	88	165	132	132

table 1

The value of the equity of the firm amounts to

$$E = \frac{1}{1.1} [0.4 \cdot 55 + 0.3 \cdot 22] = 26$$

and the total value of the firm is

$$W = F_A + F_B + E = 120 \ .$$

Consider now bank A insisting on a collateral to secure its credit. The debt contract is secured if the firm pledges the asset X or Y or both assets to the bank with the provision that should the firm default the bank has the right to seize and sell the collateralized asset. Should the proceeds from the sale exceed the outstanding amount, the excess is returned to the firm. If the proceeds are insufficient to meet the outstanding amount, the bank retains all of the proceeds and becomes an unsecured creditor for the remaining debt.

Assume the firm offers the asset with the liquidation proceeds X as a security to the bank A. Because $X = 60$ for all states the credit position of A is riskless and the value of claim A now is

$$F_A = \frac{55}{1.1} = 50 .$$

Because of Bank A's exploitation right on the security the paying schedule for bank B changes in the state s_1 and B's claim now has a value of

$$F_B = \frac{1}{1.1}(0.3 \cdot 33 + 0.7 \cdot 55) = 44 .$$

The value of the total debt, which is $F = 47 + 47 = 94$ without collateral, does not change with securing the debt position of bank A. The claim A's value gains 3 units, but this rise is exactly compensated for by the 3 units decrease of the value of claim B.

2.3 Collateral Policy and Non-Market-Value Debt Claims

Contrary to the just discussed collateral irrelevance hypothesis Scott (1977) has shown that a firm can maximize its value when it uses all its assets as collateral for the creditors. Scott is arguing that in the case of the debtor's default some debt has to be paid before distributing the bankruptcy estate to the creditors. These costs are especially sales taxes, property taxes, excise taxes, the administrative costs of bankruptcy and legal damages claims. Typically, these claims have to be paid only under certain circumstances and they are not considered in the calculation of the value of the debt. Therefore they do not incur the value of the firm. Thus, if all the debtor's assets are transferred as collateral to the creditors with claims traded on the capital market, they outrank the mentioned non-market valued claims in case of default. The market value of the firm reaches its maximum when the claims with lacking market values have the lowest priority compared to the claims of the market participants.

One can easily confirm this result with the help of the former example. Look again at table 1 to see the distribution of the value of the firm's securities. Beside the payable debt of $T_A = 55$ and $T_B = 55$ consider now also some tax costs of $U = 33$, which have to be paid independent of the state of the world in $t = 1$. It is assumed that in a default of the firm the tax costs outrank the claims T_A and T_B.

Presumed furtheron a default free interest rate of 10 % and a risk neutral capital market, the value of the debt claims is

$$F_A = F_B = \frac{1}{2\cdot 1.1}\,[0.3\,(88-33) + 0.4\cdot 110 + 0.3\,(132-33)] = 41$$

and the market value of equity is

$$E = \frac{1}{1.1}\,[0.4\,(165-110-33)] = 8\ .$$

Thus the market value of the firm amounts to

$$W = F_A + F_B + E = 90\ .$$

In a first step we will now secure the debt of bank A with the liquidation proceeds X , then in addition we will also secure the debt of bank B with the liquidation proceeds of Y to observe the altering of the firm value when different securing strategies are applied.

If bank A gets title on the asset with the liquidation proceeds X , its credit position is riskless and the market value has the amount of

$$F_A = \frac{55}{1.1} = 50\ .$$

Bank B has to consider that in states s_1 and s_3 tax costs have a higher priority and the value of its claim thus will be only

$$F_B = \frac{1}{1.1}\,[0.4\cdot 55 + 0.3\cdot 44] = 32\ .$$

The collaterization of bank A does not change the total market value of the debt $F = 82$ because the risk transfer fully diminishes the claim of bank B : the tax costs $U = 33$ outrank claim B in the case of default.

But if the claim of bank B is secured by exploitation rights of the liquidations proceeds Y (while bank A keeps its collateral), the market value of debt F will rise. In this case $F_A = 50$ again, but bank B receives the liquidation proceeds Y in the states s_1 and s_3 <u>before</u> the tax costs are paid and this will increase the value of its claim to

$$F_B = \frac{1}{1.1}\,[0.3\cdot 28 + 0.7\cdot 55] = 42.64\ .$$

If bank B would have also a subordinate exploitation right on the collateral of bank A , it could obtain a 5 unit raised liquidation profit in the state s_1 , and the debt value would be:

$$F_B = \frac{1}{1.1}\,[0.3\cdot 33 + 0.7\cdot 55] = 44\ .$$

The just described collateral policy can create the maximum value of the debt $F = 94$ because the creditors A and B are able to shift the utmost risk on the claim U which does not possess a market value.

3. The Theory of Credit Support Decisions in the Light of the Economics of Information

3.1 Collaterals as a Tool to Limit the Creditability Risk

Our previous considerations about collateral policy in the scope of the neoclassical theory of credit support decisions focus in the following results of the theory of the credit market equilibrium:

- On a perfect and complete capital market the collateral policy of a firm is irrelevant for its market value (collateral irrelevance hypothesis).
- Considering insufficiencies of the capital market, i.e. market exogenous claims on the corporate's securities, a collateral policy shifting the utmost risk from the market creditors to the non-market creditors will cause the maximum market value of the firm (fully collateral policy).

We are not satisfied with these results of the neoclassical theory: Although securing debt causes high private and public costs (monitoring costs, contract costs, administrative costs, law costs etc.) this instrument is still of great importance on real financial markets. The neoclassical theory can explain this discrepancy only with the total collateral policy. But on real capital markets full collaterization is rather the exception than the rule.

On the other hand it is not unusual that debt contracts imply collateral-agreements even if the covenantee presumptively is and remains the sole creditor, so that in this case a risk transfer to other creditors is of no importance because secured and unsecured credit positions are equivalent.

Including the reasoning of the economics of information in the neoclassical theory of credit support decisions will disclose us a theoretical base to explain the practice of collateralization in creditor/debtor relations. But notice that the ideas of the economics of information are to <u>complete</u> our previous thoughts in such a way that deciding about credit support the bank has to consider the risk of credit standing and of credit reliability combined.

To concrete the idea of the economics of information in this context it is useful to investigate in the first stage the isolated risk of credit reliability. It will be shown that collateral can bound or even eliminate that risk. In the next section we will examine the situation where both risks have to be considered conjointly.

The well known model of Jaffee and Russell (1976) is a first approach to investigate the isolated risk of credit reliability. The topic of the model is the phenomenon of credit rationing: "Credit rationing occurs when lenders quote an interest rate on loans and then proceed to supply a smaller loan size than that demanded by the borrowers".

The neoclassical solution of this gap proposes that the unsatisfied borrowers will offer a higher interest rate, which will motivate the bank to rise the loan supply for an increased risk premium; this process finally will end when credit supply and demand are in equilibrium at a certain interest rate.

Credit rationing is an instrument of the banks to influence the average solidity of their customership. A decrease of the mean credit supply can reduce the number of "dishonest" debtors, because the incentive to breach the contract is smaller if it is a paltry credit amount. Therefore credit reliability is not a permanent (fixed) unchangeable condition of the borrower, but a consequence of an economical reasoning.

The borrower will fulfill the contract (i.e. repay the loan) if it is economical advantageous and on the other side he will breach the contract if this behavior is profitable. Through its debt-policy the bank can influence the lucrativeness of repayment for the debtor. If not paying involves certain costs for the borrower (cost to default) the bank can reduce the numbers of borrowers which have an advantage if they fail to repay. These costs are given exogenously in the Jaffee and Russell model, whereas the exogenously given amount can be different for each borrower.

In contrast to this assumption of an exogenous cost factor Rudolph (1982) showed the ability of the banks to influence the cost of default. Banks could especially increase these costs if they enclose collateral convenants in loan contracts so that in case of the borrower's nonpayment he will lose part of his securities to the bank. Collaterals therefore can increase the probability of repayment.

With the inclusion of collateral in the model of Jaffee and Russell one gets a common price equilibrium instead of the rationing equilibrium, because with a given credit standing of the borrower the repayment of the loan is only a question of the debtor's will.

Since the assumption of a given credit standing is not realistic, we have to examine in the next section the decisions of a bank in the face of a credit standing risk and a credit reliability risk. We will discuss the problems of this situation with the help of our former numerical example.

3.2 Contemporaneous Examination of Credit Standing Risk and Credit Reliability Risk

Let us take again the probability distributions of X and Y , as shown in table 1 to demonstrate the simultaneous analysis of the credit-standing and credit-reliability risk of a firm. The distributions determine the debtor's credit standing for given loan quantities.

The credit reliability risk on the other hand is to be seen in the fact that the creditor does not know whether the firm will keep the assets with the liquidation proceeds X and Y until the end of the period to serve the bank's receivables or if the firm sells the assets and disposes of the proceeds in another way. Creditors are faced with uncertain expectations which of the alternatively possible plans of the firm will be realized after the credit is placed at the firm's disposition.

Swoboda (1975) calls these risks as distribution risks: "We'll call the risk that a position of a creditor alters caused by subsequent decisions of the firm distribution risk" (as e.g. issuing additional debt which will dilute the claim of the original creditor). Later on several articles of the financial literature focused on this problem and summarized the main post-credit strategies of debtors (Smith and Warner 1979b, Smith 1980). We will discuss these strategies based on the numerical example of table 1 and examine whether creditors could diminish the distribution risk with the help of collateral.

3.2.1 Changing the Dividend Policy

After the issue of the credit, the firm can raiseits dividend rate, in spite of a former declared lower rate, and thus increase the default risk for the creditors. The dividend payments can be financed by reduced investment (balance sheet cut) or financed by issuing additional debt (change of liabilities).

Dividend payments evoke a higher risk for the initial creditor, because liable capital (equity) is substituted by unliable capital (debt).

Let us consider the firm of our example adding a new loan with a receivable of $T_C = 22$ in $t = 1$ to its senior debt (with receivables of $T_A = 55$ and $T_B = 55$).

After the additional loan is issued, the market value of the whole debt will be

$$F = \frac{1}{1.1} (0.3 \cdot 88 + 0.7 \cdot 132) = 108$$

compared to 94 before the junior debt. The corresponding equity values are $120 - 108 = 12$ (with new debt) and 26 (before new debt). The debt value gained 14 unities, while the equity value lost these 14 unities. Since the market value of Bank C's claim is:

$$F_C = \frac{22}{132} \cdot 108 = 18 ,$$

the firm did not get 14 but 18 unities by raising the additional loan.

Since the transaction changed the values of bank A's and bank B's claims from 47 to 45, the loan quantity should be divided in such a manner, that the capital owner would get 14 unities and each of the banks A and B would get 2 unities. This distribution would keep the old market value relation of the debt/equity claims. But distributing the whole loan amount of 18 to the capital owners, the stockholder's wealth is increased to the detriment of the original creditors.

A wealth-shifting on account of the creditors caused by a credit financed dividend payment can be limited (in special cases even eliminated) if the debt of the initial creditors is secured.

Let us consider the case that creditors A and B have property rights (claims) of the firm's assets, which are united in a security pool and consist of the liquidation proceeds X and Y . Under these assumptions the market value of the total debt and the value of the unsecured debt are corresponding as demonstrated in section 2.2, and $F = 47 + 47 = 94$.

If the senior debt is fully secured and the firm issues junior debt with the principal of $T_C = 22$, its value will be:

$$F_C = \frac{1}{1.1} \cdot 0.7 \cdot 22 = 14 .$$

If the firm gets the disposal of this loan quantity and pays it instantly to the equity owners, the claims of the creditors A and B are not diluted. Since their debt is secured, they are protected against distribution risks caused by credit financed dividend payments to the equity owners.

As far as it concerns dividend payments by desinvestment (balance sheet cut), they too can be prevented by securing the debt. Secured debt gives the creditor the exploitation right on the security such that the management of the firm cannot arbitrarily dispose of the asset. Therefore the possibility of a dividend payment, financed with proceeds of sold assets, is reduced.

However, a total prevention of desinvestment financed payments is rather impossible. Creditors would have to use all the firm's assets as collateral to transfer the right to dispose over the firm's estate totally from the management to the lenders. Still, by securing debt, one can install upper bounds for dividend payments and protect those assets which may not be sold in order to use the proceeds for dividend payments (real estate, notworking assets).

3.2.2 Changing the Credit Policy

The levered firm can repay its debt to some creditors premature or it can secure some creditor's debt. Both policies are disadvantageous for the other creditors because their claims' value decreases. In the case of a premature repayment all the risk is transferred to the residual debt, while in the case of secured debt the amount of shifted risk from secured to unsecured debt depends on the quality of the collateral. Creditors with contracts including collateral covenants usually do not have to fear these forms of the distribution risk.

3.2.3 Changing the Investment Policy

Finally the firm has a third opportunity to transfer risk investing in projects with higher risk than declared to the creditors. Such an altered investment policy can increase the value of equity, because although the default risk rises, the firm realizes higher yields for the benefit of the shareholders in default-free states (Swoboda 1982).

Let us assume again a firm with two assets with the liquidation proceeds X and Y and in addition the opportunity of the firm to keep two other assets with the liquidation proceeds Z and Y in its estate without any technical difficulties. Table 2 describes the yields of the alternative plans x and z .

Though the mean of the receipts distribution is similar for plan x and z creditors A and B with receivables of $T_A = 55$ and $T_B = 55$ have every reason to fear the realization of plan z instead of plan x . While the value of debt is $F = 94$ and the value of equity is $E = 26$ if plan x is chosen, plan z will produce an equity value of $E \approx 42,4$ and a debt value of only $F \approx 77,6$. Thus the firm's management can cause an essential increase of the value of equity by preferring projects with higher risk.

Collateral can be seen as a tool to prevent (or limit) distribution risk, caused by a change of investment policy, because the investment policy of the firm would be determined if bank A or B put the security with the yield X in pledge.

To prevent an investment policy change, it would even be sufficient in this case, that one of the creditors put pledge on asset X . Conditional of the given credit reliability risk, securing one bank's debt will also improve the unsecured claim, because the raised default risk, which the unsecured creditor has to face after the other creditors claim, can be more than compensated by the reduction of the credit reliability risk.

To prove these market value rising effects of collateral, we will presume that banks A and B expect with an a priori probability of 50 % the realization of plan x or z . In this case the debt's value will be

$$F = 0.5 \cdot 94 + 0.5 \cdot 77.6 = 85.8$$

and the values of the claims A and B are 42.9 for each of the claims.

liquidation proceeds \ state / probability		s_1 0,3	s_2 0,4	s_3 0,3	mean
plan x	X	60	60	60	60
	Y	28	105	72	72
	X + Y	88	165	132	132
plan z	Z	0	105	60	60
	Y	28	105	72	72
	Z + y	28	210	132	132

table 2

Now A gets the security with the liquidation proceeds X as collateral with the result of a raised value of F = 94 caused by the dropped credit reliability risk. The collateral of A produces a risk shifting on account of B and favouring A .

The value of the secured claim A is 50 and the value of the unsecured debt B is only 44, thus inspite of the risk transfer on account of B the collateralization increases B's claim from 42.9 to 44 .

4. A Scheme of Credit Contract Covenants

4.1 Credit Contract Covenants

The previous sections should have made clear that collateralization can cause a risk transfer between the creditors, and collateralization can influence the behavior of the debtors during the period of credit. Especially, collateral can induce leveraged firms or other economic subjects to run a decent dividend, credit, and investment policy.

One can ascertain that securing debt with pledged assets is a rather strong policy to influence the behavior of the equity owners. Credit markets have developed also other and weaker instruments to lower the risk-shifting possibilities of the corporation. These strategies are documented in the several types of credit contract covenants in figure 2.

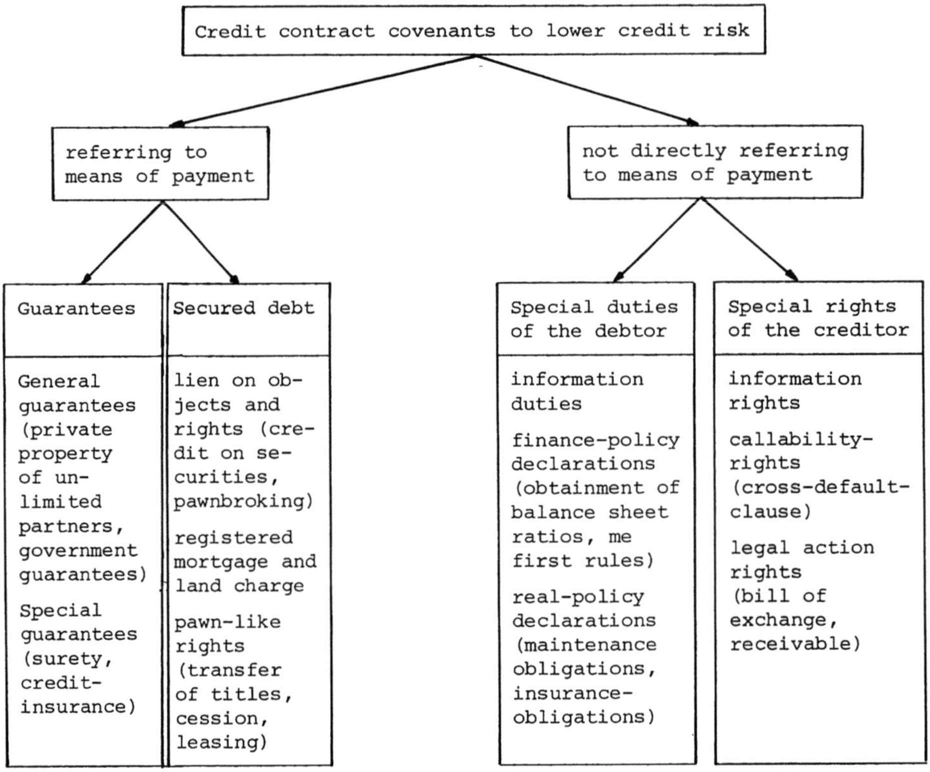

figure 2

Credit contract covenants are provisions included in debt contracts which either endow the creditors with special rights or bind the debtors to special obligations. These covenants in contrast to guarantee- or collateral-agreements, refer only indirectly to means of payment by influencing the probability distributions which determine the amount of repayment of the debtor.

Before discussing the cases in which the lenders should use the stronger or the weaker policy to control the debtor's behavior, we will give a short survey of the different types of covenants.

4.2 Covenants Referring Indirectly to Means of Payment

4.2.1 Special Obligations of the Debtors

Special obligations are duties which are not generally requested by the codes of civil law. A firm, for example, can be obliged to supply financial and other information for the credit period. The information about the economic status of the firm can be general (balance sheets, financial statements, reports etc.) or refer to special situations as changes in mortgage rights or in management. Additionally, the borrower can bind himself to obtain certain balance sheet relations, liquidity ratios or capital structure relations as long as the debt is outstanding.

Of great importance are the so called 'me first' rules. By including a me first rule in his debt contract a creditor wants to protect his position against dilution, which can be evoked if the firm issues additional debt. We can differ between three types of me first rules:

- The debtor can assure that he will not issue debt with a higher priority or doing so the existing debt will be upgraded (dept-priority-equality).
- Secured debt is often endowed with the obligation of the debtor that the will not sell, lease or pawn the security, with other words, the debtor 'reserves' the pledged asset to the creditor.
- The most restrictive type of me first rules binds the debtor not to sell, lease or pawn his assets, not to secure any other debt, or in the extreme case even not to issue any additional debt at all.

This last type leads us to a group of restrictions which binds the debtor to a specific maintenance of this assets. These obligations include for example the duty to treat real estate, machines or raw material in an orderly manner, or to insure these items. All these provisions interfere with the real-sphere of the firm and usually generate costs.

4.2.2 Special Rights of the Creditors

According to the special duties of the debtors we will first refer to the information rights of the lenders which are not installed in civil law. Banks often include in their general credit requirements the right of an insight in the economic situation of the borrower at any time wanted. Another right of the general requirement is the callability clause: the creditor can request the immediate repayment of the credit, if the debtor does not fulfill his special obligations.

Euro Bond contracts for example often include the so called 'cross default clause' which gives the creditor the right to call the credit if the debtor fails to fulfill his payment-obligations punctually to any other creditor.

The creditors can also be endowed with special rights to call in their due receivables. The creditor, whose claim is based on a bill of exchange does not need to remind the debtor and has to take no account of any terms if the debtor does not repay punctually. The bill credit endows the creditor with the right of the billprotest: the creditor gets a day of court hearing at an early date and he gets in the declaratory suit an enforceable title against the bill debtor. Thus the bill of exchange facilitates the action for payment, and therefore endows the bill creditor with extra rights compared to the usual civil law regulations of credit contracts.

4.3 Claims of Creditors which Refer to Means of Payment

While the just described covenants refer only indirectly to means of payment by influencing the probability distribution, we now discuss the claim of creditors which do refer to means of payment directly. This type of covenants can be divided in collateral-agreements (secured debt) and in guarantee-agreements.

Secured debt endows the lender with the right to seize a pledged asset of the firm's estate in case of default and to sell it. If a bank for example secures a corporation credit with the seized deposit of securities of the firm and the corporation defaults, the bank can sell the securities. Should the proceeds from the sale exceed the receivables of the bank, the excess is returned to the debtor or his estate; if the proceeds are insufficient, the bank retains all of the proceeds and becomes an unsecured creditor for the remainder due to him.

Depending on the legal classification of secured debt one can distinguish between lien on objects and rights, registered mortgage and land charge and pawn-like rights like cession and the transfer of titles for the purpose of securing debt.

Guarantees are claims of the lenders on means of payment of a third party. If the original borrower cannot repay the credit, the guarantor is obliged to fulfill the debtor's liabilities.

If guarantees serve to improve the position of all creditors, they are said to be general guarantees. General guarantees increase the liable property of the company. Examples are government guarantees or the private property of unlimited partners. If guarantees refer to an individual debt contract (which is to a certain creditor or a group of creditors) they are said to be special guarantees.

5. The Efficiency of Securing Debt

One cannot answer generally the question if creditors should use a strong instrument as collateralization to influence the owner's policy, or if a weaker policy (covenants) is sufficient, because it depends on the specific credit situation. The interbank market for example can do without collateralization, because the market participants know each other well, and the market participants are in steady commercial intercourse. If a borrowing bank undertook a business policy on the creditor's detriment, it could very easily lose its standing and could be excluded from the market. Therefore it seems to be dispensable on such a market to influence the debtor's policy explicitly.

On the commercial credit market, where longterm creditor/debtor relations are ascertainable, one can observe collateralization and nonpecuniary covenants to regulate the behavior of the debtor. Actually these nonpecuniary covenants are extremely important (as me first rules). Concerning smaller firms, collateralization is regular, whereas the crediting banks request especially real estate as securities.

If firms issue only small loan quantities and are relatively unknown to the crediting bank (because the credit contract is the sole relation between customer and bank) the bank will secure its debt with collateral-agreements to influence (although indirectly) the firm's business policy during the period of credit. In this case, collateral is an efficient and cheap instrument of debtor's self binding, which can save the creditor/debtor relation costly planning- and monitoring costs (Drukarczyk 1983, 1984).

6. Appendix: Secured Debt and Uncertainty

6.1 The Firm's Position

The financial effects of securing debt shall be derived in a single period model of a stock company. The firm's estate contains two assets, each of which can be values independently of the other asset's value. The market valued of the securities at the end of the period are given by $X(s) \geq 0$ and $Y(s) \geq 0$, where $s(s=1,2,\ldots,\bar{s})$ is the occuring state in $t=1$. If $q(\hat{s})$ is the present value of a financial claim which will pay its owner one unity of money if state $\hat{s}$ occurs, the market value V of the firm in $t=0$ is given by:

$$V = \sum_{s=1}^{\bar{s}} q(s)[X(s)+Y(s)] . \tag{1}$$

The firm has issued credit from bank A and B with the quantities K_A and K_B . The debt has to be repaid in $t=1$ in the amount of T_A and T_B (the repayment includes the interest).

Furtheron we assume that during the period liabilities in the amount of U will evoke which are not priced on the capital market, and which in case of default outrank the receivables T_A and T_B . To keep the analysis simple, let us assume $U < X(s)+Y(s)$ holds for all s such that the market value of the firm's securities in $t=1$ is in no case lower than the amount of the liability U . Given the total claim of the creditors on the firm is $T = T_A + T_B$ in $t=1$, debt's value in $t=0$ will be:

$$F = \sum_{s=1}^{\bar{s}} q(s) \min[T, X(s)+Y(s)-U] , \tag{2}$$

because the banks will get their receivable T or in case of default the residual of the firm's value minus the amount of U , since U has the higher priority. This residual amount will be smaller than the value of T , but since we assumed $U < X(s)+Y(s)$, the repayment to the banks cannot be negative.

Given $X+Y \geq U+T$ holds for each state s , where $s=1,2,\ldots,k-1$ and $X+Y < U+T$ holds for each state s , where $s=k,k+1,\ldots,\bar{s}$, we deliver a rule of distribution of the firm's estate to the creditors which corresponds to the Act of Bankruptcy. If the states of the world are divided in the described way, the value of the debt will be:

$$F = T \sum_{s=1}^{k-1} q(s) + \sum_{s=k}^{\bar{s}} q(s)[X(s) + Y(s) - U] . \qquad (3)$$

In the case of default the residual amount of the firm's estate minus U will be shared between creditors proportional to their original receivables T_A and T_B. Thus the market value of bank A's part of the debt will be (on account of a clearer presentation we will stop indicating X and Y furtheron):

$$\begin{aligned} F_A &= \sum_{s=1}^{\bar{s}} q(s) \min\left[T_A, \frac{T_A}{T}(X + Y - U)\right] \qquad (4) \\ &= \frac{T_A}{T} \sum_{s=1}^{\bar{s}} q(s) \min[T, X + Y - U] \\ &= \frac{T_A}{T} F , \end{aligned}$$

and the market value of bank B's receivable is:

$$\begin{aligned} F_B &= \sum_{s=1}^{\bar{s}} q(s) \min\left[T_B, \frac{T_B}{T}(X + Y - U)\right] \qquad (5) \\ &= \frac{T_B}{T} \sum_{s=1}^{\bar{s}} q(s) \min[T, X + Y - U] \\ &= \frac{T_B}{T} F . \end{aligned}$$

Since the shareholders have claim on the firm's assets minus the sum of liabilities in $t = 1$, and because of the limited liability of common stock, the value of the equity will be:

$$\begin{aligned} E &= \sum_{s=1}^{\bar{s}} q(s) \max[X + Y - U - T, 0] \qquad (6) \\ &= \sum_{s=1}^{k-1} q(s) [X + Y - U - T] \end{aligned}$$

Since the market value of the firm is the sum of the values of equity and debt and at the same time the market value V of the asset minus the present values of the non market valued liabilities, one can write:

$$\begin{aligned} W &= E + F \qquad (7) \\ &= \sum_{s=1}^{\bar{s}} q(s) [X + Y - U] \\ &= V - U \sum_{s=1}^{\bar{s}} q(s) . \end{aligned}$$

6.2 Derivation of the Value of Secured Debt

Let us assume now that bank A gets the asset with the market value X as a collateral for its credit. In the case of default A has a claim on the asset with value X ; thus the market value of bank A's receivable is:

$$F_A = T_A \sum_{s=1}^{k-1} q(s) + \sum_{s=k}^{\bar{s}} q(s) \min\left[T_A, X + \max\left\{\frac{T_A - X}{T - X}(Y - U), 0\right\}\right] . \qquad (8)$$

The first sum of (8) considers that if the firm does not default A will get the entire amount of its receivable T_A , while the second sum of (8) describes the payoff to A in case of default (all states where $U + T > X + Y$ holds), where A makes use of the collateral and receives its market value $X(s)$. If the proceeds $X(s)$ exceed T_A , the surplus is given back to the bankrupt's estate, because the repayment to A may not excess its receivable T_A . But if the receivable T_A exceeds the proceeds of X $(T_A > X)$, bank A has a residual claim on the bankrupt's estate in the amount of the excess $T_A - X$, which is outranked by the tax costs U , but is on equal priority with the receivables of bank B . In the case of $Y > U$, the residual claim of bank A will yield the positive ratio $(T_A - X) / (T - X)$, whereas otherwise the ratio will be zero, because the residual assets are used to pay the liability U .

Let us additionally divide the states of the world $(k, k+1, \ldots, \bar{s})$ in the states $(k, k+1, \ldots, l-1)$, where $X \geq T_A$ holds, and in the states $(l, l+1, \ldots, \bar{s})$, where $X < T_A$ holds, and we can change (8) to:

$$F_A = T_A \sum_{s=1}^{l-1} q(s) + \sum_{s=l}^{\bar{s}} q(s) \left[X + \max\left\{\frac{T_A - X}{T - X}(Y - U), 0\right\}\right] . \qquad (9)$$

The first sum of equation (9) shows that A will get the whole amount of its receivable if the firm does not default $(s = 1, 2, \ldots, k-1)$, or if default does occur, the liquidation proceeds of the collateral are sufficient to pay T_A completely $(s = k, k+1, \ldots, l-1)$. The second sum includes the present value of bankrupt's estate if the receivable T_A exceeds the yields of the collateral. In this case the bank will get the value X of the collateral and its part of the redundancy $Y - U$, if this margin is positive.

Comparing equation (9) to (4), whereas equation (4) values the unsecured credit of A, and (9) the secured claim, one can see that collateralization

- has raised the probability of a total repayment to bank A, unless none of the states $s = (k,k+1,...,l-1)$ occurs.
- has diminished the amount of an eventual lack of payment to bank A, unless $X = 0$ holds for $s = (l,l+1,...,\bar{s})$.

If one excludes the extreme case where $X = 0$ holds for $s = (k,k+1,....,\bar{s})$, the market value of the secured debt quantified by (9) is higher than the one of the unsecured debt in equation (4). And finally it is possible that, although a positive default risk occurs, bank A can construct a riskless credit position by collateralization. If $X \geq T_A$ holds for all states $s = (k,k+1,...,\bar{s})$ bank A's claim is free of any credit risk and its value is:

$$F_A = T_A \sum_{s=1}^{\bar{s}} q(s)$$

6.3 Market Value of the Debt in Dependence of its Collateral Policy

Now we have to examine the influence of collateralization on the value of the debt and of the firm. If securing bank A's debt raises not only the value of its receivable but also the market value of the debt, the market value of the firm can also be increased. To prove these relations, we will first inspect the interdependency of the value of bank A's receivable with the collateralization of its debt.

We can express the value of the unsecured debt by:

$$F_B = T_B \sum_{s=1}^{k-1} q(s) + \sum_{s=k}^{l-1} q(s) \max\{(X - T_A) + (Y - U), 0\} \tag{10}$$
$$+ \sum_{s=l}^{\bar{s}} q(s) \max\left\{\frac{T_B}{T-X}(Y - U), 0\right\} .$$

The first sum stands for the market value of the receivable in those states where default does not occur. The second sum indicates the market value in the case that the proceeds of security X in excess of the receivable T_A of bank A along with the proceeds of security Y serve to pay the liability U. After this liability is paid too, bank B can dispose over the residual bankrupt's estate.

The third sum refers to the situation, where the collateral-proceeds cannot satisfy bank A's receivable entirely, such that A and B have to share out $Y - U$ proportional to the quantity of their claim after the liability U is paid.

If you add the market values of (9) and (10) you will get the market value F_0 of the debt under the assumption that creditor A gets the asset with the value X as a collateral for its credit.

$$F_0 = T \sum_{s=1}^{k-1} q(s) + \sum_{s=k}^{l-1} q(s) \max\{X+Y-U, T_A\} + \sum_{s=1}^{\bar{s}} q(s) \max\{X+Y-U, X\} \,. \tag{11}$$

We will now compare this market value F_0 with the market value given in (3) which indicates the value of the unsecured debt. For an easier demonstration equation (3) is rewritten as:

$$F = T \sum_{s=1}^{k-1} q(s) + \sum_{s=k}^{l-1} q(s)[X+Y-U] + \sum_{s=1}^{\bar{s}} q(s)[X+Y-U] \,. \tag{3'}$$

Formulas (3') and (11) yield

$$F_0 = F + \sum_{s=k}^{l-1} q(s) \max\{0, (T_A - X) + (U-Y)\} + \sum_{s=1}^{\bar{s}} q(s) \max\{0, (U-Y)\} \geq F \tag{12}$$

whereby the inequality $F_0 \geq F$ can be strict since some states could occur where creditors will receive liquidation proceeds on account of the receivables U. From (12) we see that this is the case if $T_A > X+Y-U$ holds for at least one of the states $s = k,\dots,l-1$ or if $Y < U$ holds for at least one of the states $s = 1,\dots,\bar{s}$.

The size of the increase of F_0 depends on the amount of the default risk which is transferred to the creditor with receivable U, caused by securing the debt of A.

6.4 The Maximization of the Market Value with Total Collateral Policy

If bank A would not get only proceeds X, but also Y as a collateral, the market value of its claim would be:

$$F_A = T_A \sum_{s=1}^{m-1} q(s) + \sum_{m}^{\bar{s}} q(s)[X+Y] \,, \tag{13}$$

if states $(l,l+1,\dots,\bar{s})$ are divided in $(l,l+1,\dots,m-1)$, where $X+Y \geq T_A$ holds, and in $(m,m+1,\dots,\bar{s})$, where $X+Y < T_A$ holds. The market value of bank B's claim would then be:

$$F_B = T_B \sum_{s=1}^{k-1} q(s) + \sum_{s=k}^{m-1} q(s) \max\{X+Y-T_A-U, 0\} . \tag{14}$$

Adding the market values of (13) und (14) to the market value F_{oo} of the debt, if A is totally secured, one receives:

$$F_{oo} = T \sum_{s=1}^{k-1} q(s) + \sum_{s=k}^{m-1} q(s) \max\{X+Y-U, T_A\} + \sum_{s=m}^{\bar{s}} q(s)[X+Y] . \tag{15}$$

Comparing (15) with the market value F of the debt given in (3), which refers to the unsecured debt, one can see that the market value of the debt is:

$$F_{oo} = F + \sum_{s=k}^{m-1} q(s) \max\{0, T_A + U - (X+Y)\} + U \sum_{s=m}^{\bar{s}} q(s) \geq F_o \geq F , \tag{16}$$

if the claim of bank A is totally secured. Corresponding to this derivation it could be easily confirmed that the market value of the debt could be raised, if bank B's debt would be also secured. The risk transfer to U is obtained independently of the chosen form of collateralization. Whether the securities which serve as collateral are ordered in a ranking (first and second mortgage e.g.) or a securities pool is of no importance.

If no receivables U have to be considered, (16) shows that since $U = 0$ and $X \geq T_A$ holds for $s = k,k+1,\dots,l-1$, resp. $X+Y \geq T_A$ holds for $s = l,l+1,\dots,m-1$, the market value of the debt, if debt A is totally secured, equals the value of the debt without collateralization. Thus, if the chosen collateral is only the liquidation proceeds X, as described in section 2.2, a market value rise can neither be achieved, since if $U = 0$ in (11), one gets:

$$\max\{X+Y, T_A\} = (X+Y) \quad \text{in} \quad s = k,\dots,l-1 \quad \text{and}$$
$$\max\{X+Y, X\} = (X+Y) \quad \text{in} \quad s = l,\dots,\bar{s}$$

and thus

$$F_o = T \sum_{s=1}^{k-1} q(s) + \sum_{s=k}^{\bar{s}} q(s)(X+Y) , \tag{17}$$

and therefore

$$F_0 = F . \tag{18}$$

With F from (3') and $U = 0$ one gets the result that although the collateral causes a creditor's risk transfer from bank A to bank B, the debt policy is irrelevant for the amount of the market value of the total debt and therefore also irrelevant for the market value of the firm, if all claims on the firm are valued on the market.

References

Adams, M. (1980): Ökonomische Analyse der Sicherungsrechte, Königstein

Baltensperger, E. (1976): The Borrower-Lender Relationship, Competitive Equilibrium and the Theory of Hedonic Prices, American Economic Review 66, 401-405

Barro, R.J. (1976): The Loan Market, Collateral and Rates of Interest, Journal of Money, Credit and Banking 8, 439-456

Benjamin, D.K. (1978): The Use of Collateral to Inforce Debt Contract, Economic Inquiry 16, 333-359

Drobnig, U. (1980): Sicherungsrechte im Deutschen Konkursverfahren, in: Rabels Zeitschrift für ausländisches und internationales Privatrecht, Bd. 44, 784-807

Drukarczyk, J. (1983): Kreditverträge, Mobiliarsicherheiten und Vorschläge zu ihrer Reform im Insolvenzrecht, in: Zeitschrift für Betriebswirtschaft, vol. 53, 328-349

Drukarczyk, J. (1984): Credit Contracts, Collateral-Based Security Agreements, and Bankruptcy, in: G. Bamberg, K. Spremann (ed.), Risk and Capital, Berlin, 139-159

Gerth, A. (1980): Atypische Kreditsicherheiten, 2nd.ed., Frankfurt

Hirshleifer, J.; Riley, J.G. (1979): The Analytics of Uncertainty and Information, in: Journal of Economic Literature, vol. 17, 1375-1421

Jaffee, D.M.; Russell, Th. (1976): Imperfect Information, Uncertainty and Credit Rationing, in: Quarterly Journal of Economics, vol. 90, 651-666

Kalay, A. (1982): Stockholder-Bondholder Conflict and Dividend Contraints, in: Journal of Financial Economics, vol. 10, 211 ff.

Meckling, W.H. (1977): Financial Markets, Default and Bankruptcy: The Role of the State, in: Law and Contemporary Problems, vol. 41, 13-38

Milde, H. (1980): Kreditrationierung, Zinsdispersion und Segmentialsuche, in: Zeitschrift für die Gesamte Staatswissenschaft, vol. 136, 266-285

Milde, H. (1981): Adverse Selektion und Kreditsicherheiten, in: H. Göppl; R. Henn (ed.), Geld, Banken und Versicherungen II, 1089 ff.

Modigliani, F.; Miller, M.H. (1958): The Cost of Capital,Corporation Finance, and the Theory of Investment, in: American Economic Review, vol. 48, 261-297

Myers, St.C. (1977): Determinants of Corporate Borrowing, in: Journal of Financial Economics, vol. 4, 147-175

Plaut, J.E. (1985): The Theory of Collateral, Journal of Banking and Finance 9, 401-419

Rudolph, B. (1974): Die Kreditvergabeentscheidung der Banken, Opladen

Rudolph, B. (1982): Können die Banken ihre Kreditsicherheiten "vergessen", in: Kredit und Kapital, vol. 15, 317 ff.

Rudolph, B. (1984): Kreditsicherheiten als Instrumente zur Umverteilung und Begrenzung von Kreditrisiken, in: Zeitschrift für betriebswirtschaftliche Forschung, vol. 36, 16-43

Schildbach, Th. (1983): Sicherheiten versus par conditio creditorum, in: Betriebs-Berater 34, 2129-2136

Schmidt, R.H. (1981): Ein neo-institutionalistischer Ansatz der Finanzierungstheorie, in: E. Rühli, J.-P. Thommen (ed.), Unternehmensführung aus finanz- und bankwirtschaftlicher Sicht, 135-154

Scott, J. (1977): Bankruptcy, Secured Debt, and Optimal Capital Structure, in: Journal of Finance, vol. 32, 1-19

Smith, C.W. (1980): On the Theory of Financial Contracting - The Personal Loan Market, Journal of Monetary Economics, vol. 6, 333 ff.

Smith, C.W.; Warner, J.B. (1979a): Bankruptcy, Secured Debt, and Optimal Structure: Comment, in: Journal of Finance, vol. 34, 247 ff.

Smith, C.W.; Warner, J.B. (1979b): On Financial Contracting - An Analysis of Bond Covenants, in: Journal of Financial Economics, vol. 7, 118 ff.

Stahlschmidt, D. (1982): Schutzbestimmungen in Kreditverträgen, Wiesbaden

Stiglitz, J.E.; Weiss, A. (1981): Credit Rationing in Markets with Imperfect Information, in: American Economic Review, vol. 71, 402 ff.

Swoboda, P. (1975): Betriebswirtschaftliche Kapitaltheorie, in: Handwörterbuch der Betriebswirtschaft, 4th.ed., Stuttgart, 2129 ff.

Swoboda, P. (1982): The Relevance of Securing Debts, manuscript Graz.

Asset Pricing in a Small Economy: A Test of the Omitted Assets Model*

Eduardo S. Schwartz and Michael J. Brennan

Summary: In this paper we are concerned with testing the asset pricing model in a small economy where the issue of integration or segmentation of different national markets cannot be decided a priori. Because of the limited power of tests based on portfolio data, we are unable to reject the null hypothesis that a value weighted Canadian market portfolio is the tangency portfolio for the efficient set formed from Canadian stocks alone; that is, that the Sharpe-Lintner version of the asset pricing model holds for Canada during the sample period. Turning next to issues of international asset pricing, we are also unable to reject the efficiency of the Canadian market index against the alternative hypothesis that the efficient portfolio is a linear combination of Canadian and U.S. stocks (Canadian bonds). On the other hand, we are able to reject the hypothesis that the Canadian and U.S. markets are integrated and satisfy a global asset pricing model. Thus from a Canadian perspective the hypothesis of a national asset pricing model seems to be preferred to that of a North American asset pricing model.

Table of Contents:

* Research support from the Corporate Finance Division of the Department of Finance, Ottawa, and the Centre of International Business Studies, University of British Columbia, are gratefully acknowledged. This paper has benefitted from stimulating discussions with Richard Roll, Richard Stehle and our colleagues at the University of B.C., though we do not with to implicate them in the views expressed here.

Capital Market Equilibria. Ed. by G. Bamberg and K. Spremann

1. Introduction

As Roll (1977) has pointed out in a classic and widely cited paper, a test of the generalized or Zero Beta[1] asset pricing model is equivalent to a test of the mean-variance efficiency of some particular portfolio with respect to a given set of risky assets, while if the Sharpe-Lintner version of the model is tested the sets of assets with respect to which efficiency is assessed also includes the riskless asset.

In the absence of a riskless asset there are an infinite number of efficient portfolios, while if a riskless asset is included the number of efficient portfolios of risky assets shrinks to one. Thus the first problem that must be addressed in formulating an empirical version of the asset pricing model is the choice of a portfolio to be assessed for efficiency. Since the asset pricing theory states that it is the market portfolio of all assets which is efficient, and since the theoretical market portfolio is inherently unobservable, the adequacy of the asset pricing paradigm can only be assessed in terms of the efficiency of some portfolio which can be regarded as a reasonable empirical counterpart of the market portfolio of the theory. There are many portfolios which may be chosen to correspond to the market portfolio and some may be efficient and others not, so that, as Roll has emphasized, we can never hope to determine whether the asset pricing model holds in some absolute sense: we can only hope to determine whether it offers an adequate description of security returns for some particular operational definition of the market portfolio.

It is of course highly unlikely that any particular portfolio chosen *a priori* would turn out to be exactly mean-variance efficient with respect to a given set of assets. It is therefore useful to be able to test more general hypotheses derived from the asset pricing model which assert, not that a particular portfolio is efficient, but that there exists a member of a specified class of portfolios which is efficient with respect to the given set of assets. We shall test such a hypothesis in this paper, the class of portfolios consisting of all convex combinations of a basic set of 'index' portfolios. For the sake of example, suppose that an investigator has available to

---

1) See Black (1972)

him returns on all New York Stock Exchange (NYSE) stocks, the NYSE index, an index of bond returns and an index of real estate returns. He may wish to test the hypothesis that a 'market' portfolio consisting of investments in the NYSE index, in bonds, and in real estate is mean-variance efficient with respect to a broader set of assets including the set of NYSE stocks under consideration:[1] beyond hypothesizing that the weights in the efficient portfolio are all non-negative he may not be able to impose further prior restrictions on the composition of the portfolio, either because he lacks data on the market values of individual asset classes or because he suspects for example, that legal restrictions partially segment the market, so that only a fraction of the outstanding bonds are available for inclusion in the portfolio of investors who also hold stocks. The procedure described in this paper allows the investigator to test the hypothesis that some combination of the three indices is efficient with respect to a set of assets including NYSE stocks, and that the NYSE index omits some specific class of assets (bonds, real estate) which is included in the mean-variance efficient portfolio. For this reason we refer to the hypothesis as the omitted assets version of the asset pricing model, or, more simply, as the omitted assets model.[2]

The specific context in which we employ the omitted assets model is an examination of pricing in the Canadian equity market. It has been conventional to test asset pricing model hypotheses in terms of the efficiency of some national market index with respect to the common stocks of that national market. However, there are grounds for questioning the plausiblility of such hypotheses since they neglect entirely the possibility of international portfolio diversification. Simple international asset pricing theories[3] suggest that investors

---

1) Although in this paper we consider combinations of only two index portfolios, extension to a larger number is straightforward in principle.

2) The terminology is that of Mayers (1972) who first examined the consequences of employing a market proxy which omits a class of assets which belongs in the efficient portfolio. More recently Kandel (1984) has reached mainly negative conclusions about the possibility of testing for mean-variance efficiency of a portfolio, some of whose assets are omitted. The main difference between his analysis and ours is that he assumes that the covariances between included assets and omitted assets are unknown, whereas we assume that they are known, or at least can be estimated.

3) Solnik (1974); Stulz (1981a).

will tend to invest proportionately in each national equities market, and more elaborate theories allowing for taxes on foreign investment and other frictions[1] suggest that investors will still invest abroad, but less than is predicted by the simpler models.

In Canada individual residents are free to invest in U.S. equities as well as in Candian equities. However, investment in Candian equities receives preferential tax treatment, and for institutions as well as for individual retirement accounts there are restrictions on the permissible amount of foreign investment. For these and perhaps for other reasons most Canadian portfolios consists largely of Canadian stocks: this would suggest that a purely Canadian market portfolio should be efficient relative to the universe of Canadian stocks. On the other hand, to the extent that the aforementioned taxes and institutional restrictions can be avoided, the asset pricing theory would suggest the value weighted combination of Canadian and U.S. market indices as a candidate for efficiency. We shall therefore test the hypothesis that the Canadian market index is efficient against the alternative hypothesis that it omits U.S. stocks which belong in the mean-variance efficient portfolio.

The only other study relating to the integration of U.S. and Canadian equity markets is by Berges (1982). His specific hypothesis is derived from the Arbitrage Pricing Theory[2] and the assumption that the markets are integrated, and asserts that the risk premium associated with a given factor or source of risk should be the same for Canadian and U.S. stocks. His findings are mixed. Risk factors associated primarily with U.S. securities appear not to earn the same risk premium for Canadian securities, which suggests that the markets are segmented rather than integrated. On the other hand, risk factors associated primarily with Canadian stocks do appear to be priced the same in both countries.

An earlier study which has tested for the integration of international capital markets is that by Stehle (1977). His analysis is similar to ours in spirit but examined whether NYSE stocks were priced in a segmented national market or an integrated world market.

---

1) Black (1974); Stulz (1981b)

2) see Ross (1976).

His findings were not statistically significant although they were mildly supportive of the hypothesis of an integrated world market. However he did not explicitly test for the efficiency of his national or world market portfolio proxies.

Even given a portfolio candidate for efficiency, there remain formidable econometric problems in conducting a test. These arise primarily from the impossibility of estimating a variance-covariance matrix for a large set of asset returns given only a limited time series. There appear to be two possible approaches to resolving this problem. First, the variance-covariance matrix could be estimated if sufficient prior restrictions were imposed on it, for example, by assuming a particular factor structure for returns.[1] The simpler and more common approach, and the one we shall adopt is to form the assets into portfolios and to test the efficiency of the candidate portfolio relative to a restricted set of assets - namely the portfolios. As discussed in the following section, this is a much weaker test of efficiency than a test employing the full set of asset returns would be.

The remainder of the paper is organized as follows. In Sections 2 and 3 we discuss the limitations of portfolio based tests of efficiency and present a more detailed analysis of the omitted assets model in the Canadian setting. The data are described in Section 4. Section 5 presents some standard tests of the asset pricing model in Canada, and Section 6 is concerned with the omitted assets version of the model and the issue of integration or segmentation of North American capital markets.

2. Portfolio Based Tests of Efficiency

Since the tests of portfolio efficiency we employ in the paper, like the earlier tests of Gibbons (1980) and Stambaugh (1982),[2] use data on a limited number of portfolios rather than on individual securities, it is important to understand the limitations of these tests.[3] In figure 1 AA is the efficient set constructed from the

---

1) This is the approach followed by Litzenberger and Ramaswamy (1979) who assumed a single factor model in estimating the parameters of a tax augmented asset pricing model. A single factor model would appear too restrictive an assumption for testing for efficiency.

2) As Roll (1977) has pointed out, the earlier asset pricing studies of Black, Jensen and Scholes (1974) and Fama and MacBeth (1973) so not attempt to test for the efficiency of their market portfolio proxies.

3) For a more formal discussion see Roll (1977).

set of assets under consideration ; BB is the efficient set constructed from a set of portfolios formed from the original assets. BB can be thought of as a constrained efficient set of the original assets, where the constraints are derived from the portfolio construction rules, and this implies that BB lies within (but possible touches) AA .

It follows from the mathematics of the efficient set that a candidate portfolio which is a linear combination of the original portfolios will be found to be efficient as assessed by the linearity of the relation between expected return and beta for the portfolios if the candidate portfolio lies on either AA or BB . In other words, the generalized asset pricing model will be accepted by the test if the market portfolio proxy lies either on the unconstrained efficient set AA or on the constrained efficient set BB , while of course the model will actually hold for that portfolio only if the portfolio lies on AA . If the candidate portfolio lies at any other point in the space the generalized asset pricing model will be rejected. It is the possibility that the candidate portfolio lies on BB and not on AA which greatly reduces the power of portfolio based tests of the generalized asset pricing model.

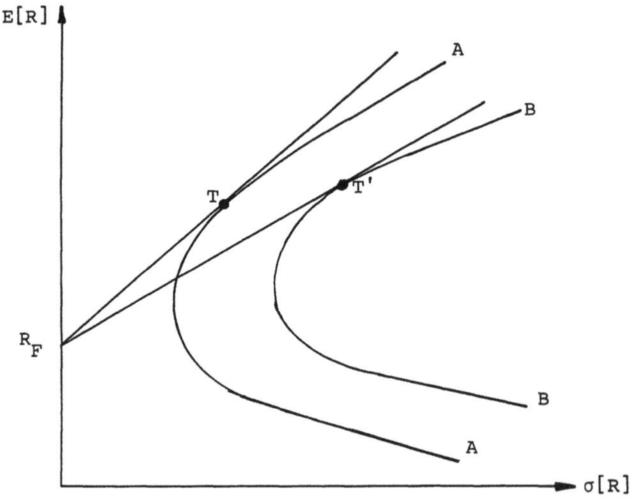

Asset Pricing Inferences with Portfolio Data

Figure 1

Considering next the Sharpe-Lintner version of the asset pricing model, this states that the market portfolio lies at the point of tangency between the efficient set and a ray drawn through the riskless rate, R_F , so that the market portfolio is the only portfolio of risky assets which is efficient in the presence of a riskless security. With a riskless security a candidate portfolio will be found to be efficient using portfolio data only if the portfolio risk premia are proportional to their betas computed with respect to the candidate portfolio. It follows again from the mathematics of the efficient set that this will be the case only if the candidate portfolio is either the true tangency portfolio T or the tangency portfolio of the constrained efficient set T' . That the candidate market portfolio should be chosen as the exact linear combination of the portfolios corresponding to T' will occur on a set of measure zero, so that if the candidate market portfolio is found to be efficient with respect to the risky asset portfolios and the riskless security, then we may be reasonably assured that it is because the portfolio is at the point T and the Sharpe-Lintner version of the model holds.[1)]

Thus, while the use of portfolio rather than individual security returns significantly weakens the power of tests of the asset pricing model, the effect is much less for the Sharpe-Lintner model than for the generalized asset pricing model.

3. Omitted Assets

3.1 The Model

Let R_E be the return on a market index E which is hypothesized to be efficient with respect to a set of assets. Then the fundamental result of asset pricing theory is that the risk premium on those assets is a linear function of their covariances with R_E :

$$E[R_j] - R_F = a + k\ \mathrm{cov}(R_j, R_E)\ ,\ k > 0 \tag{1}$$

where R_j is the return on security j and R_F is the riskless return.

---

1) Only reasonably assured because of course our statistical tests will reject the model only if the candidate portfolio is not close to the tangency portfolio.

Let R_I be the return on the value weighted portfolio of a subset of the assets, the included assets, and let R_O be the return on the value weighted portfolio of the assets omitted from the subset under consideration. Then

$$R_E = x R_I + (1 - x) R_O \quad , \quad 0 \leq x \leq 1 \tag{2}$$

where x is the (possibly unknown) fraction of the efficient portfolio accounted for by the included assets. Using (2) and the properties of the covariance operator, (1) may be written as

$$E[R_j] - R_F = a + kx \; \text{cov}(R_j, R_I) + k(1 - x)\,\text{cov}(R_j, R_O) \; . \tag{3}$$

Then, noting that β_j^I and β_j^O , the betas of security j with respect to R_I and R_O , are given by

$$\beta_j^I = \frac{\text{cov}(R_j, R_I)}{\sigma^2(R_I)} \quad , \quad \beta_j^O = \frac{\text{cov}(R_j, R_O)}{\sigma^2(R_O)}$$

equation (3) may be written as

$$E[R_j] - R_F = a + b\;\beta_j^I + c\;\beta_j^O \tag{4}$$

where $b = kx\;\sigma^2(R_I)$, $c = k(1 - x)\sigma^2(R_O)$.

Alternatively, define v as the residual from the regression of the return on the omitted assets on the return on the included assets:

$$R_O = f + g\;R_I + v \; . \tag{5}$$

Then using (3) and the fact that v is orthogonal to R_I we have

$$E[R_j] - R_F = a + k[x + g(1-x)]\text{cov}(R_j, R_I) + k(1-x)\text{cov}(R_j, v) \; . \tag{6}$$

Equation (6) may also be written as

$$E[R_j] - R_F = \gamma_0 + \gamma_1\;\beta_j^I + \gamma_2\;\beta_j^V \tag{7}$$

where β_j^V is the beta of security j with respect to v , the orthogonal component of the return on the omitted assets.

Under the Sharpe-Lintner model $a = 0$ in equation (4) and $\gamma_0 = 0$ in equation (7), so that the Sharpe-Lintner hypothesis will be rejected for the index R_E if $a \neq 0$. If $x = 1$ so that the efficient index does not include any of the omitted assets then $c = 0$ in equation (4) and $\gamma_2 = 0$ in equation (7); using this result it is possible to test whether the efficient index includes any of the omitted assets. Finally, following Gibbons (1980) we shall be able to test the efficiency of the candidate portfolio R_E by examining how well equations (4) and (7) describe returns on the subset of assets under consideration - the included assets.

3.2 Integrated and Segmented Capital Markets

In our context R_I will be return on a value weighted index of Canadian stocks and R_O will be the return on a portfolio of U.S. stocks or of Canadian Bonds. Figure 2 illustrates the omitted assets model in the context of integration and segmentation of U.S. and Canadian equity markets. In this figure CC is the efficient frontier of Canadian stocks alone; UU is the efficient frontier constructed from U.S. stocks alone, and GG is the global efficient frontier which is attainable by combining U.S. and Canadian stocks. M_c is the Canadian market portfolio, M_u is the U.S. market portfolio and M_G is the global market portfolio consisting of a weighted combination of the two national market portfolios.

Figure 2a represents a situation in which the Sharpe-Lintner model holds for the integrated capital market: neither the U.S. nor Canadian market portfolios are efficient with respect to their national equity markets, but a weighted combination of them is efficient with respect to all stocks. Recalling that x is the fraction of the efficient portfolio accounted for by Canadian stocks, this corresponds to the case in which $x > 0$ and E is efficient. Equations (4) or (7) will then describe the pricing of Canadian stocks (and U.S. stocks) with $a = \gamma_0 = 0$ and $c, \gamma_2 > 0$. If the generalized asset pricing model holds but not the Sharpe-Lintner version then $a \neq 0$ $(\gamma_0 \neq 0)$.

Figure 2b represents the case of complete market segmentation in which the Sharpe-Lintner model holds on a national basis but not on a global basis. Under these circumstances equations (4) and (7) describe the pricing of Canadian stocks with $a = \gamma_0 = 0$, $c, \gamma_2 > 0$. If only the generalized asset pricing model holds on a national basis then $a \neq 0$ $(\gamma_0 \neq 0)$.

Figure 2c corresponds to the case in which the asset pricing model does not hold at all. In this case equations (4) and (7) will not describe the pricing of Canadian stocks for any values of the model parameters.

Finally, it is possible, though unlikely, that the Canadian market portfolio is efficient with respect to Canadian stocks, and the global portfolio M_G is also globally efficient. In this case x in equations (4) and (7) is indeterminate since the coefficient vectors consisting of $\beta_j^O(\beta_j^V)$ and β_j^I are linearly dependent.

Figure 2(a)(b)(c): Integrated and Segmented Capital Market

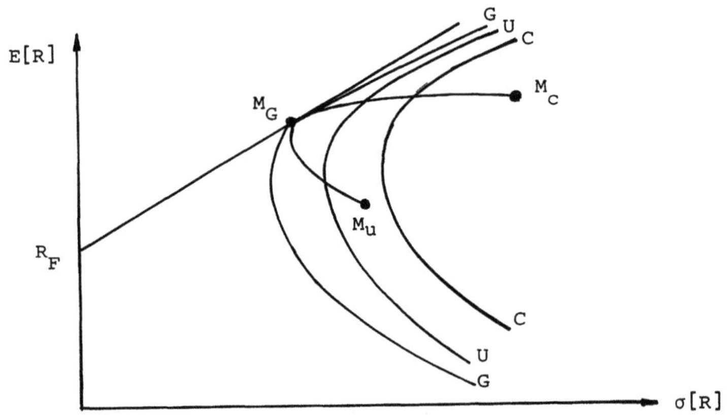

(a) Integrated

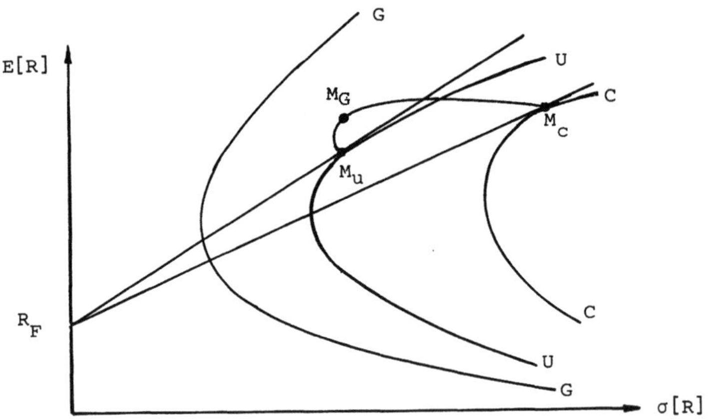

(b) Segmented

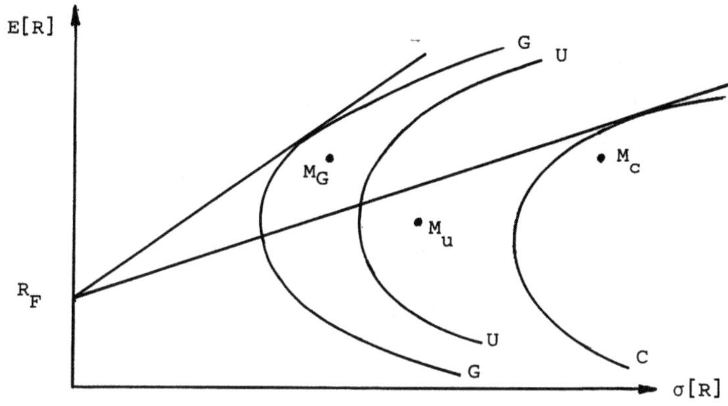

(c) No Asset Pricing Relation

4. The Data

The primary data for the tests reported below are monthly rates of return on Canadian securities calculated from the Laval Securities Tape[1] for the period January 1963 to December 1980. The Laval tape contains virtually all firms listed on the Toronto Stock Exchange during this period, a total of 982 securities, all of which are common stocks. Since security betas were estimated using 60 months of data, all securities with less than 60 consecutive months of data were eliminated, reducing the sample size to 731. The monthly return on the Canadian market index, R_{ct} was calculated as the value weighted average of the returns on all outstanding securities meeting the above listing requirements.[2]

The risk free rate R_{Ft} was calculated from yields on 90-day Government of Canada bills taken from the Bank of Canada Review. An index of Canadian bond returns R_{Bt} was constructed from the index of yields on Government of Canada Bonds with maturities in excess of 10 years reported in the Bank of Canada Review. The calculation treated these yields as consol yields. The U.S. market index was taken as the return on the CRSP value weighted index adjusted for changes in the exchange rate as reported on the CRSP tape.

---

1) For a detailed description see Morgan and Turgeon (1978).

2) The Laval tape reports the number of shares outstanding only on a calendar year basis. We assumed that the number of shares outstanding adjusted for split etc. remained constant throughout the year.

5. Efficiency of the Canadian Market Index

In this section we report the results of tests of the asset pricing model on Canadian equity returns, using procedures similar to those employed by Fama and MacBeth (1973) and by Gibbons (1980). Both of these procedures require that securities be assigned to portfolios and that the tests be conducted on these portfolio returns.[1] 20 portfolios were formed initially in the following manner.

For each January from 1968 to 1980 a beta was estimated for each qualifying security using the prior 60 months of returns. A security qualified for inclusion in a given year if it had been listed continuously for the previous 60 months. The number of securities qualifying for inclusion ranged from 251 in 1968 to 426 in 1978.

5.1 Beta Estimation under Thin Trading

To take account of the sporadic nature of trading in many Canadian securities,[2] the Dimson (1979) aggregated coefficients estimator[3] with two lead and two lag terms was employed by estimating the regression

$$R_{jt} - R_{Ft} = a_j + \sum_{i=-2}^{2} b_j^i (R_{c,t+i} - R_{F,t+i}) + e_{jt} \; . \qquad (8)$$

The Dimson beta estimate is given by the sum of the b_j^i $(i = -2,\ldots,2)$.

In each year the securities were assigned to one of 20 portfolio according to the estimated value of beta, the first portfolio consisting of the securities with the lowest beta, and so on. These (equally weighted) portfolios are the basic data on which the tests to be described below were carried out.

---

1) The Fama-MacBeth procedure requires portfolio assignments to mitigate problems caused by errors in the estimated betas; the Gibbons approach requires that the data set be reduced from the full security sample to avoid singularity of the estimated variance-covariance matrix.

2) Fowler, Rorke and Jog (1980) report that of 1800 securities which were listed on the Toronto Stock Exchange for at least 12 months during the period January 1970 to December 1979, only 78 traded on the last day of each month they were listed, 679 traded in every month, and for the remaining 1043 there was at least one month in which no trade was recorded.

3) Fowler and Rorke (1983) have pointed out that Dimson's estimator is inconsistent if the return on the market portfolio is serially correlated, and have proposed a correction. This seems to make a negligible difference in the current context.

First, betas where estimated for each of the 20 portfolios using all the available returns. Four different techniques were employed: a simple regression of the portfolio excess return on the market excess return; the Dimson procedure represented by equation (8) above; the Scholes-Williams procedure,[1] and the Scholes-Williams extended procedure.[2] The simple regression estimator is known to suffer from bias when trading is sporadic; the remaining three estimators are intended to correct this bias. The Scholes-Williams estimator presupposes that securities trade each month but not necessarily at the month's end. The Dimson estimator allows for months in which no trades occur and the Scholes-Williams extended estimator corrects the bias in the Dimson estimator when the market return is serially correlated. The resulting estimates are shown in Table 1. The differences between the simple regression estimates and any of the other three are substantial, confirming that thin trading must be taken into account when estimating betas with Canadian data, even when the returns are measured over a period as long as one month - for portfolio 1 the Dimson estimate exceeds the simple regression estimate by 40 %. The three remaining estimates which correct for the thin trading bias are quite similar, and the Scholes-Williams extended estimator is very close to the Dimson estimator. In what follows we shall rely mainly on the Dimson estimator since it lends itself to a simple adaption of the Gibbons' maximum likelihood procedure.

5.2 Preliminary Estimates

Following Fama and MacBeth, portfolio excess returns are regressed on the beta estimates each month:[3]

$$R_{jt} - R_{Ft} = a_t + b_t \hat{\beta}_j + e_{jt} \ . \qquad (9)$$

The Sharpe-Lintner model predicts that $b = E[b_t] = E[R_{ct}] - R_{Ft}$, $a = E[a_t] = 0$, while the generalized or Zero Beta asset pricing model simply predicts $E[b_t] = b > 0$. Table 2 reports the estimates of a and b obtained by averaging the monthly estimates, and the standard errors as computed from the time series of these estimates. For comparison, the results are reported for the three beta estimators

1) Scholes and Williams (1977).

2) See Fowler and Rorke (1983).

3) Unlike Fama and MacBeth we assume that the beta for each portfolio is an intertemporal constant.

Portfolio	Portfolio Beta Estimates			
	Dimson	Simple Regression	Scholes-Williams	Scholes-Williams Extended
1	1.42 (0.20)	1.05 (0.09)	1.49	1.49
2	1.30 (0.15)	1.02 (0.07)	1.39	1.37
3	1.16 (0.15)	1.04 (0.07)	1.34	1.18
4	1.14 (0.15)	1.03 (0.07)	1.29	1.16
5	1.07 (0.14)	0.96 (0.06)	1.21	1.09
6	1.20 (0.12)	0.93 (0.06)	1.26	1.26
7	1.20 (0.12)	0.95 (0.05)	1.27	1.25
8	1.06 (0.13)	0.89 (0.06)	1.13	1.09
9	0.95 (0.12)	0.83 (0.06)	1.06	0.98
10	0.98 (0.12)	0.87 (0.05)	1.04	1.00
11	1.03 (0.12)	0.80 (0.05)	1.06	1.07
12	0.72 (0.11)	0.66 (0.05)	0.83	0.74
13	0.90 (0.11)	0.76 (0.05)	1.03	0.93
14	1.08 (0.11)	0.85 (0.05)	1.06	1.11
15	0.85 (0.10)	0.70 (0.04)	0.87	0.88
16	0.78 (0.11)	0.68 (0.05)	0.90	0.80
17	0.82 (0.11)	0.68 (0.05)	0.81	0.84
18	0.76 (0.12)	0.75 (0.05)	0.94	0.77
19	0.77 (0.11)	0.68 (0.05)	0.87	0.80
20	1.14 (0.16)	0.69 (0.07)	1.14	1.22

(Standard Errors in Parentheses)

TABLE 1

which account for thin trading. For both the Dimson and Scholes-Williams extended estimator of beta the point estimates of the parameters conform remarkably well to the predictions of the Sharpe-Lintner version of the asset pricing model, both the intercept from and the slope coefficient differing from their theoretical values by only about one tenth of 1 % per month, this difference not being statistically significant; furthermore, we can reject the null hypothesis that the slope coefficient is non-positive at the 5 % level under conventional assumptions. With the Scholes-Williams estimator of beta the results are only slightly less favourable to the Sharpe-Lintner model and still do not allow us to reject the model.

As Gibbons has pointed out however, tests of the foregoing type lack power relative to a restricted non-linear regression model in which the betas and the parameters a and b are estimated simultaneously, and the restrictions imposed by the asset pricing model are tested using the likelihood ratio.

Asset Pricing Model Estimates: January 1968 - December 1980

$$R_{jt} - R_{Ft} = a_t + b_t \hat{\beta}_j$$

Beta Estimator		$\bar{a}_t$	$\bar{b}_t$	$\overline{R_{ct} - R_{Ft}}$
(i)	Dimson	0.0011 (0.0033)	0.0077 (0.0045)	0.0066
(ii)	Scholes-Williams	-0.0016 (0.0036)	0.0095 (0.0047)	
(iii)	Scholes-Williams Extended	0.0017 (0.0036)	0.0068 (0.0041)	

(Standard errors in parentheses)

TABLE 2

5.3 Maximum Likelihood Estimation

To develop the Gibbons test note that the generalized asset pricing model (1) may be written as

$$E[R_{jt}] = a_t + \beta_j \{E[R_{ct}] - a_t\} \qquad (10)$$

where a_t is the expected return on a portfolio with a zero beta. Assuming that intertemporal variation in the interest rate is mirrored in the zero beta return, $a_t = R_{Ft} + \gamma$ where γ is an intertemporal constant. Then (5) may be written as

$$E[R_{jt}] - R_{Ft} = \gamma + \beta_j \{E[R_{ct}] - R_{Ft} - \gamma\} \ . \qquad (11)$$

If $\gamma = 0$ then (11) is the Sharpe-Lintner model.

Assuming stationarity of the joint distribution of rates of return in excess of the riskless interest rate, realized returns also satisfy

$$R_{jt} - R_{Ft} = a_j + \beta_j (R_{ct} - R_{Ft}) + e_{jt} \ . \qquad (12)$$

Comparing (11) and (12) it follows that $a_j = \gamma(1 - \beta_j)$. Then substituting for a_j in (12) and solving for e_{jt} we have:

$$e_{jt} = R_{jt} - R_{Ft} - \gamma - \beta_j (R_{ct} - R_{Ft} - \gamma) \ . \qquad (13)$$

If V , the variance-covariance matrix of e_{jt} , defined in (13) is known, then the maximum likelihood estimator of γ and β_j is obtained from:

$$\min_{\{\hat\beta_j\}, \hat\gamma} L = \min \hat e' V^{-1} \hat e = \min \sum_{t=1}^{156} \hat e_t' \Omega^{-1} \hat e_t \qquad (14)$$

e_t is the vector of errors for period t and we have assumed that e_t is multivariate normally distributed. $E[e_t e_t'] = \Omega$, $E[e_t e_s'] = 0$ for $s \neq t$. Then $\hat e_t$ is the vector of estimated errors whose typical element is

$$\hat e_{jt} = R_{jt} - R_{Ft} - \hat\gamma - \hat\beta_j (R_{ct} - R_{Ft} - \hat\gamma) \ . \qquad (15)$$

Moreover, it can be shown that under the null hypothesis that the generalized asset pricing model restriction is valid, the statistic

$$-2 \ln \lambda = 156 \{ \ln |\hat e' \hat e| - \ln |\hat e_u' \hat e_u| \} \qquad (16)$$

asymptotically follows a χ^2 distribution with degrees of freedom one less than the number of portfolios. In (16), $\hat e_u$ is the vector of errors from the unrestricted regressions (12).

In the present application the variance-covariance matrix Ω is not known and therefore the estimation was carried out using an asymptotic maximum likelihood procedure suggested by Malinvaud (1966), which is described in the Appendix. The estimated value of γ was -0.0052 with a standard error of 0.0033, and the maximum likelihood estimates of the portfolio betas were only marginally changed from the corresponding simple regression estimates. However, the value of the log likelihood ratio statistic (16) was $\chi^2 = 37.37$ with 19 d.f. which is highly significant, pointing to the rejection of the generalized asset pricing model with the candidate market portfolio.[1]

A major limitation of the Gibbons test in this context is that, unlike the Fama-MacBeth type of tests described above, it takes no account of the effects of thin trading on the beta estimates and we have already observed that these are substantial. Therefore the procedure was modified as follows. Equation (12) was replaced by the Dimson regression model:

$$R_{jt} - R_{Ft} = a_j + \sum_{i=-2}^{2} b_j^i (R_{c,t+i} - R_{F,t+i}) + e_{jt} \quad (12')$$

Recalling that $\beta_j = \sum_{i=-2}^{2} b_j^i$, this implies the asset pricing model restriction $a_j = \gamma(1 - \sum_{i=-2}^{2} b_j^i)$, so that (13) becomes

$$e_{jt} = R_{jt} - R_{Ft} - \gamma - \sum_{i=-2}^{2} b_j^i (R_{c,t+i} - R_{F,t+i} - \gamma) \quad (13')$$

The maximum likelihood estimation was then repeated with errors calculated from (13'), and for the unrestricted regressions from (12'). Since for this estimator it was necessary to estimate 5 individual coefficients for each portfolio, it was computationally infeasible to carry out the maximum likelihood procedure for all 20 portfolios. The estimation was therefore carried out using returns on 10 portfolios which were obtained by averaging the returns on adjacent pairs of the original 20 portfolios.

---

1) Stambaugh (1982) suggests that the likelihood ratio test is biased towards rejection of the null hypothesis when the number of portfolio is large relative to the number of time series observations. This is unlikely to be the problem here when we have 20 portfolios and 156 time series observations.

The result of this estimation, which combines the Dimson approach to estimating beta with the Gibbons maximum likelihood approach to estimation of the asset pricing model parameters, are reported in the first two columns of Table 3. The first column presents the unconstrained Dimson beta estimates from regressions of the type (12'); the corresponding maximum likelihood estimates are shown in the second column. While the estimate of γ is little changed from the value obtained for the simple beta model, it is striking that the χ^2 statistic which formerly pointed to rejection of the model is no longer significant at conventional levels. Thus, after allowing for the biases due to thin trading by using the Dimson beta estimation technique, it is no longer possible to reject the hypothesis that returns are described by the zero beta version of the asset pricing model.

The Dimson-Maximum-Likelihood estimation was then repeated, imposing the prior restriction that $\gamma = 0$, which corresponds to the Sharpe-Lintner model. The resulting beta estimates are shown in the third column of Table 3. The χ^2 statistic at the foot of the column is from a test of the restriction that $\gamma = 0$ against the alternative of no restriction on the values of a_j . Again we cannot reject the null hypothesis that returns are described by the Sharpe-Lintner model.

We have found in this section that we could not reject either the generalized asset pricing model or the Sharpe-Lintner model against an unspecified alternative hypothesis. In the following section we also test the null hypothesis of efficiency of our Canadian market index but now against the alternative that this market index omits a specified class of assets which belong in the efficient portfolio.

Maximum Likelihood Estimation of the Asset Pricing Model with Dimson Betas

Portfolio Betas

Unconstrained Regression	Maximum Likelihood Estimates Zero Beta Model	Maximum Likelihood Estimates Sharpe-Lintner Model
1.40	1.37	1.41
(0.15)	(0.14)	(0.14)
1.16	1.22	1.21
(0.13)	(0.11)	(0.12)
1.15	1.22	1.20
(0.12)	(0.10)	(0.11)
1.14	1.17	1.17
(0.11)	(0.10)	(0.10)
0.97	1.00	0.99
(0.11)	(0.10)	(0.10)
0.88	0.93	0.91
(0.10)	(0.09)	(0.10)
0.99	1.06	1.03
(0.10)	(0.08)	(0.09)
0.82	0.86	0.83
(0.09)	(0.08)	(0.08)
0.79	0.83	0.80
(0.10)	(0.08	(0.09)
0.95	0.95	0.95
(0.12)	(0.10)	(0.11)
	$\hat{\gamma} = -0.0049$	$\gamma = 0$
	(0.0036)	
	$\chi^2_9 = 7.28$	$\chi^2_{10} = 9.10$

(Standard errors in parentheses)

TABLE 3

6. Tests of the Omitted Assets Hypothesis

As a first step in determining whether the Candian market index whose efficiency we have been unable to reject omits assets which belong in the portfolio which is efficient relative to a broader set of assets including Canadian stocks, we estimate equation (4). The indices of omitted assets are first the U.S. market index with returns R_{ut}, and secondly the Canadian government bond index with returns R_{Bt}. The equations to be estimated are then:

$$R_{jt} - R_{Ft} = a + b\ \beta_j^{CAN} + c\ \beta_j^{US} + u_{jt} \tag{17}$$

$$R_{jt} - R_{Ft} = a + b\ \beta_j^{CAN} + c\ \beta_j^{BON} + u_{jt}\ . \tag{18}$$

u_{jt} is the unanticipated return on security j; β_j^{CAN} is the beta, already described, with respect to the Canadian market index; β_j^{US} and β_j^{BON} are the betas calculated with respect to the U.S. market index and the Canadian bond index respectively.

It will be recalled that under the null hypothesis that the Canadian market index is efficient $c = 0$ in equation (17) and (18). In addition to interpreting c in (18) in the context of the omitted assets model it is possible to interpret it also in the context of Merton's (1973) intertemporal capital asset pricing model: in this model the expected return on an asset may depend on its covariance with unanticipated changes in the investment opportunity set. One possible index of the investment opportunity set is the interest rate series, so that β_j^{BON} may proxy for the covariance of asset's return with shifts in the opportunity set. A non-zero value of c would thus be consistent with Merton's model.

The tests, whose results are reported below, were carried out on four sets of nine portfolios sorted according to bond and U.S. betas, as well as the Canadian betas. Two sorting procedures were employed leading to two sets of A portfolios and two sets of B portfolios. The procedure for constructing the A portfolios was as follows. Each January from 1968 to 1980 the qualifying securities were divided into three portfolios according to their (Dimson) Canadian beta estimates derived from the prior 60 months of returns. Each of these three portfolios was further subdivided into three portfolios based on the Dimson estimate of the U.S. (bond) beta also estimated over the previous 60 months. For each of the two sets of 9 portfolios the Canadian betas and U.S. (bond) betas were then estimated using the whole time series of returns on the portfolios. These A portfolios are constructed to maximize the spread of Canadian betas and hence will not provide an efficient estimator of the effects of the U.S. (bond) betas. Therefore two sets of nine B portfolios were constructed by sorting first on the U.S. (bond) betas and then on the Canadian betas.

The portfolio excess returns were regressed on the Canadian and U.S. betas each month and the resulting coefficients averaged to yield the results reported in the top half of Table 4. For the A portfolios the coefficient of β_j^{CAN} is of the same order of magnitude as reported in Table 2 but it is not longer statistically significant. The coefficient of β_j^{US} is small and negative but also statistically insignificant. For the B portfolios neither coefficient is significant. Thus we can reject neither the hypothesis that the Canadian market portfolio is efficient $(x = 1)$ nor the hypothesis that the U.S. portfolio is efficient relative to Canadian stocks.

Omitted Assets Model: U.S. Market Index

$$R_{jt} - R_{Ft} = a_t + b_t\, \hat{\beta}_j^{CAN} + c_t\, \hat{\beta}_j^{US}$$

	$\bar{a}$	$\bar{b}$	$\bar{c}$
A Portfolios	.0021	.0098	-.0034
	(.0041)	(.0092)	(.0104)
B Portfolios	.0025	.0011	.0064
	(.0042)	(.0129)	(.0155)

Omitted Assets Model: Canadian Bond Index

$$R_{jt} - R_{Ft} = a_t + b_t\, \hat{\beta}_j^{CAN} + c_t\, \hat{\beta}_j^{BON}$$

	$\bar{a}$	$\bar{b}$	$\bar{c}$
A Portfolios	-.0005	.0096	.0013
	(.0039)	(.0053)	(.0049)
B Portfolios	-.0014	.0105	.0011
	(.0035)	(.0050)	(.0042)

(Standard errors in parentheses)

TABLE 4: Averaged estimated coefficients

The lower part of Table 4 reports the results of similar tests where the omitted assets portfolio is a proxy for a portfolio of Canadian government bonds. Again, the results for both A and B portfolios are inconclusive. We turn therefore to the more powerful maximum likelihood tests of the omitted assets model.

Since the index of included assets is the return on the Canadian market portfolio the omitted assets model (7) implies

$$E[R_{jt}] - R_{Ft} = \gamma_0 \quad \gamma_1\, \beta_j^{CAN} + \gamma_2\, \beta_j^{v} \tag{19}$$

where β_j^v is the beta with respect to v, the orthogonal component of the omitted assets index. Assuming stationarity of the distribution of the excess return on the Canadian market index, define the unexpected return on this index by

$$r_t^c = R_{ct} - R_{Ft} - \{E[R_{ct}] - R_{Ft}\} . \tag{20}$$

Then

$$R_{jt} - E[R_{jt}] = \beta_j^{CAN}\, r_j^c + \beta_j^v\, v_t + e_{jt} . \tag{21}$$

Combining (19) and (21) and solving for e_{jt}, we have

$$e_{jt} = R_{jt} - R_{Ft} - \gamma_0 - \beta_j^{CAN}(r_t^c + \gamma_1) - \beta_j^v(v_t + \gamma_2) . \tag{22}$$

Under the null hypothesis that the markets are segmented and that the Canadian market index is efficient, $\gamma_2 = 0$. If, in addition, the Sharpe-Lintner version of the asset pricing model holds, $\gamma_0 = 0$.

The parameters of (22) were estimated in the following manner when the candidate index of omitted assets was the U.S. market index. r_t^c was computed as the deviation of the excess return on the Canadian market index about its sample mean. v_t is the residual from the regression of the U.S. market index on the Canadian market index. Finally, to take account of thin trading (22) was modified to[1]

$$e_{jt} = R_{jt} - R_{Ft} - \gamma_0 - \sum_{i=-1}^{1} b_{ij}^{CAN} (r_{t+i}^{c} + \gamma_1) - \sum_{i=-1}^{1} b_{ij}^{v} (v_{t+i} + \gamma_2) \qquad (22')$$

The parameters $\gamma_0, \gamma_1, \gamma_2, b_{ij}^{CAN}$ and b_{ij}^{v} were estimated by a maximum likelihood procedure similar to that described in the previous section, employing the returns on the A and B sets of nine portfolios. The results are summarized in the first panel of Table 5. We find first that for neither the A portfolios nor the B portfolios does the beta with respect to the U.S. market index residual play a significant role in pricing; secondly γ_1, the reward for Canadian market risk, is significantly different from zero; thirdly, the intercept γ_0 is insignificantly different from zero. Finally, the likelihood ratio statistic testing the asset pricing restrictions is well within the acceptance region. Thus we are not able to reject the null hypothesis that the Canadian market index is efficient against the alternative that the efficient portfolio is a linear combination of the U.S. and Canadian market indices.

The lower panel of Tabel 5 summarizes the analogous results when the index of omitted assets is the return on a Canadian bond index. Again we cannot reject the null hypothesis that the efficient portfolio contains no bonds, while the estimate of γ_1, the reward for Canadian market risk, is significantly different from zero.

---

1) Computational consideration forced us to restrict the Dimson estimator to one lead and one lag term.

Maximum Likelihood Estimates of Omitted Assets Model				
1. U.S. Market Index				
	γ_0	γ_1	γ_2	χ^2_6
A Portfolios	.0002 (.0040)	.0110 (.0038)	-.0072 (.0070)	7.51
B Portfolios	-.0012 (.0042)	.0113 (.0040)	-.0050 (.0087)	8.33
2. Canadian Market Index				
A Portfolios	-.0040 (.0036	.0078 (.0035)	.0001 (.0041)	5.78
B Portfolios	.0011 (.0030)	.0069 (.0033)	.0007 (.0037)	5.69

TABLE 5

Our results thus far indicate that we cannot reject the null hypothesis that the U.S. and Canadian market are completely segmented and that the Sharpe-Lintner version of the asset pricing model holds for the Canadian market. These results will be of only limited interest, however, if we are also unable to reject the null hypothesis that the U.S. and Canadian markets are integrated.[1] Therefore to test the hypothesis of integration we formed a 'global' market portfolio whose returns are a weighted average of the returns on the Canadian and U.S. market indices.[2] The model was then re-estimated with the global index taking the place of the Canadian market index and v_t defined as the residual from the regression of the Canadian index on the global index. As before, nine A portfolios were formed by sorting first on Canadian betas and then on global betas, and B portfolios were formed by sorting in the reverse order. γ_1 is now the reward for global market risk and γ_2 is the reward for Canadian market risk. If the markets are integrated and the asset pricing model holds we expect $\gamma_2 = 0$. The results shown in Table 6 do permit us to reject the null hypothesis of market integration since for the A portfolios the estimate of γ_2 is significantly different from zero. On the other hand the estimate of γ_1 is never significant. Thus, while we were not able to reject the

---

1) We are grateful to R. Stehle for pointing this out.

2) Annual market values for Canadian and U.S. equities were obtained from Ibbotson, Carr and Robinson (1982). The monthly market values required to compute the weights were then approximated by taking the values at the beginning of each year and adding the monthly returns.

hypothesis that the U.S. and Canadian markets are segmented we are able to reject the alternative hypothesis that they are integrated, though this finding should be tempered by recognizing the imperfections of our global market index.

A Test of Market Integration

$$E[R_{jt}] - R_{Ft} = \gamma_0 + \gamma_1 \beta_j^G + \gamma_2 \beta_j^V$$

	$\hat{\gamma}_0$	$\hat{\gamma}_1$	$\hat{\gamma}_2$	χ^2_6
A Portfolios	-.0004 (.0039)	-.0001 (.0059)	.0117 (.0053)	6.59
B Portfolios	-.0022 (.0039)	.0038 (.0020)	.0087 (.0068)	7.76

β_j^G - beta with respect to global portfolio

β_j^V - beta with respect to orthogonal component of Canadian market index

(Standard errors in parentheses)

TABLE 6

Appendix: Iterative Maximum Likelihood Procedure

Let $\hat{e}_{jt}(\lambda)$ represent the error in the prediction of the excess return on portfolio j in period t as a function of the model parameters to be estimated given by the vector λ.[1]

Consider an estimator of $\lambda, \lambda(S)$, which minimizes

$$L(\lambda,S) = \Sigma_t \hat{e}_t(\lambda)' S \hat{e}_t(\lambda) \tag{A-1}$$

where S is a positive definite matrix and $\hat{e}_t$ is a vector.

Then $\lambda(S)$ satisfies the necessary condition for a minimum:

$$H(S,\lambda) = \Sigma_t Q_t(\lambda)' S \hat{e}_t(\lambda) = 0 \tag{A-2}$$

where

$$Q_t(\lambda) = \left[-\frac{\partial \hat{e}_t(\lambda)}{\partial \lambda}\right]$$

is a matrix.

Starting from a particular value of $\lambda, \lambda^0, H(S,\lambda)$ can be approximated by:

$$H(S,\lambda) = H(S,\lambda^0) + \frac{\partial H(S,\lambda^0)}{\partial \lambda} (\lambda - \lambda^0) \tag{A-3}$$

1) For example, taking account of the thin trading problem as in equation (13'), λ consists of the 5×10 portfolio regression coefficients required for the Dimson beta estimates and γ, the CAPM parameter.

and setting (A-3) equal to zero yields $\lambda(S)$.

The estimator $\lambda(S)$ will be the maximum likelihood estimator if the errors e_{jt} are $N(0,\Omega)$ and $S=\Omega^{-1}$. Since Ω is unknown, an asymptotically MLE is obtained by the following iterative procedure described by Malinvaud (1966):

i) Calculate $\lambda^* = \lambda(I)$ by the above procedure: this is the (non-linear) OLS estimator

ii) Calculate the residuals $\hat{e}_{jt}(\lambda^*)$, and their covariance matrix Ω^*

iii) Calculate the estimator $\lambda^{**} = \lambda(\Omega^{*-1})$.

This estimator is asymptotically normal with variance - covariance matrix

$$\left\{\sum_t \left[\frac{\partial e_t(\lambda^{**})}{\partial \lambda}\right]' \Omega^{*-1} \left[\frac{\partial e_t(\lambda^{**})}{\partial \lambda}\right]\right\}^{-1} .$$

References

Bergés, A. (1982): Some Tests of the Arbitrage Pricing Theory and Integration in the U.S. - Canadian Stock Market, unpublished paper

Black, F. (1972): Capital Market Equilibrium with Restricted Borrowing, Journal of Business, 45, 444-455

Black, F.; M.C. Jensen; M. Scholes (1972): The Capital Asset Pricing Model: Some Empirical Tests, in: M.C. Jensen (Ed.) Studies in the Theory of Capital Markets, Praeger, New York

Black, F. (1974): International Capital Market Equilibrium with Investment Barriers, Journal of Financial Economics, 1, 377-352

Dimson, E. (1979): Risk Measurement when Shares are Subject to Infrequent Trading, Journal of Financial Economics, 7, 197-226

Fama, E.F.; J.D. MacBeth (1973): Risk, Return and Equilibrium: Empirical Tests, Journal of Political Economy, 81, 607-636

Fowler, D.J.; H. Rorke; V. Jog (1980): Thin Trading and Beta Estimation Problems on the Toronto Stock Exchange, Journal of Business Administration, 12, 77-90

Fowler, D.J; H. Rorke (1983): Risk Measurement when Shares are Subject to Infrequent Trading, Journal of Financial Economics, 11, 279-284

Gibbons, M. (1980): Multivariate Tests of Financial Models: A New Approach, Journal of Financial Economics, 10, 3-28

Ibbotson, R; R. Carr; A. Robinson (1982): International Equity and Bond Returns, Financial Analysts Journal, 38, Nr. 4 (July-August), 61-83

Kandel, S. (1984): On the Exclusion of Assets from Tests of the Mean-Variance Efficiency of the Market Portfolio, Journal of Finance, 39, 63-75

Litzenberger, R.; K. Ramaswamy (1979): The Effect of Personal Taxes and Dividends on Capital Asset Prices: Theory and Empirical Evidence, Journal of Financial Economics, 7, 163-196

Malinvaud, E. (1966): Statistical Methods of Econometrics, North-Holland

Mayers, D. (1972): Non-Marketable Assets and Capital Market Equilibrium under Uncertainty (M.C. Jensen, Ed.), Studies in the Theory of Capital Markets, Praeger, New York

Merton, R. (1973): An Intertemporal Capital Asset Pricing Model, Econometrica, 41, 867-887

Morgan, I; G. Turgeon (1978): Development of a File of Canadian Stock Market Monthly Returns, ASAC Conference, University of Western Ontario

Roll, R. (1977): A Critique of the Asset Pricing Theory Tests, Journal of Financial Economics, 4, 129-176

Ross, S.A. (1976): The Arbitrage Theory of Capital Asset Pricing, Journal of Economic Theory, 38, 343-362

Scholes, M.; J. Williams (1977): Estimating Betas from Non-synchronous Data, Journal of Financial Economics, 5, 309-328

Solnik, B. (1974): An Equilibrium Model of the International Capital Market, Journal of Economic Theory, 36, 500-524

Stambaugh, R. (1982): On the Exclusion of Assets from Tests of the Two Parameter Model, Journal of Financial Economics, 10, 237-268

Stehle, R. (1977): An Empirical Test of the Alternative Hypothesis of National and International Pricing of Risky Assets, Journal of Finance, 32, 493-502

Stulz, R. (1981a): On the Effects of Barriers to International Investment, Journal of Finance, 36, 923-934

Stulz, R. (1981b) : A Model of International Asset Pricing, Journal of Financial Economics, 9, 383-406.

The Simple Analytics of Arbitrage

Klaus Spremann

Summary: Arbitrage theory becomes particularly transparent if a finite discrete framework is taken as basis. The simple structure and mathematical background are shown and connections to other topics such as production theory are pointed out. Arbitrage techniques are applied to construct free lunches, to determine issue prices, and to derive the classical one-period call-price formula.

Table of Contents:

1. General Equilibrium, Modern Finance, and Arbitrage Theory

1.1 General Equilibrium

Many economists assert there is a striking concept that is basic to their science: the concept of general equilibrium. It is the idea of attaining an efficient allocation of resources through a competitive market mechanism, where all individuals behave upon own interests, where decision making occurs in a decentralized way, and where prices provide sufficient information in order to coordinate the many single acts of economic cooperation. Adam Smith (1723 - 1790) and his epigones made this concept of general equilibrium an issue of political ethics and established the laissez-faire principle as the indispensable basis of welfare policy.

Capital Market Equilibria. Ed. by G. Bamberg and K. Spremann

Other economists realized the mathematical problems involved in the analysis of the competitive market process. Leon Walras (1834 - 1910), Vilfredo Pareto (1848 - 1923), Abraham Wald (1902 - 1950) contributed to the mathematical foundation of general equilibrium theory. However, the most comprehensive presentation of economic equilibrium theory as a mathematical structure in linear spaces, goes back to 1960 and is mainly due to Kenneth Arrow and Gerard Debreu: In their description, the number of commodities determines the dimension of the underlying linear space, and production processes and trading possibilities between individuals define convex sets. Then, under certain assumptions, the separation theorems of functional analysis assert the equivalence between the notion of equilibrium and the existence of a price vector which establishes a property of optimality: if and only if a market is in equilibrium, each individual finds the allocation of commodities best with respect to the initial endowment and the price system.

The analysis presented by Arrow and Debreu with its deep connection between economics and mathematics is elegant and well-rounded. As a consequence, most of the papers published subsequently, are sometimes classified as sophisticated but not suited to enlarge our economic understanding of the concept of equilibrium.

1.2 Modern Finance

It was apparently time to proceed to another field of research or paradigm, as Thomas Kuhn described "The Structure of Scientific Revolutions" (1962). While the mathematical requisites of equilibrium theory became more and more sophisticated, a new paradigm emerged: finance, the theory of pricing risky assets and futures contracts.

This new field of research in mathematical economics has two independent origins. The first origin of modern finance is the analysis of the investor's problem of portfolio selection and goes back to Harry Markowitz. The second origin of modern finance, due to Franco Modigliani and Merton H. Miller, is the analysis of the problem of capital structure or the question of an "optimal" debt-equity ratio of a firm. Modigliani and Miller demonstrated in their seminal 1958 paper the irrelevance of corporate financial policy. Their idea is strikingly simple in a world of perfect markets, where there are neither transaction costs nor time delays in the tâtonnement process. Financial policies of the corporation, such as leverage and payment of dividends, are irrelevant to the shareholders, if the shareholders have access to the same means as the firm.

Let us turn to the first origin of modern finance. In 1952, Harry Markowitz suggested describing the random return of risky assets by two parameters only, the expected value and the variance of return. Markowitz displayed the rich field of research left open by the restriction to the mean-variance world. A portfolio is composed of several types of risky assets in certain quantities. These quantities and the parameters of the joint distribution of the returns of all single assets, in particular the correlation structure, determine the mean and the variance of the return resulting from the whole portfolio. Although the particular portfolio an investor chooses will depend on initial wealth and individual risk aversion, no investor decides for an inefficient portfolio. Thus, independent of individual characteristics, only "efficient" portfolios (those not dominated with respect to mean and variance) are acceptable candidates. Markowitz designed an algorithm to determine all portfolios that are efficient.

Portfolio theory was then improved, enlarged, and completed in several directions. Let me mention two of these lines of research. One group of subsequent papers concerns the consistency between the mean-variance world and decision theory. We know that only a combination of restrictions on tastes - concerning the class of admissible utility functions - and on beliefs - concerning the class of admissible probability distributions - allows for a sound foundation of the mean-variance world in a decision-theoretical framework. Another direction of research within the mean-variance world is the Capital Asset Pricing Model (CAPM). The CAPM aggregates portfolio decisions of many investors, although their beliefs must be homogeneous. Equilibrium prices of shares as well as market values of whole firms can then be derived, within the CAPM, from the aggregate demand for risky assets. Thereby, the prices are expressed in terms of what is called "market portfolio".

These remarks should turn out important aspects: Modern finance deals to a large extent with situations under "risk" rather than "uncertainty". A situation was called "risk" by Frank Knight, if a decision maker is willing and able to base his choices on probabilities. Assumptions and restrictions on beliefs (concerning the distributions of returns) as well as on tastes (concerning the individual's risk aversion) seemed to be an indispensable prerequisite in order to get results in modern finance.

1.3 Arbitrage

The theory of finance is a paradigm which attracts many mathematical economists. Is it in contrast or harmony with equilibrium theory? To give an answer, we look at what today is called the theory of arbitrage.

Arbitrage is a traditional microeconomic tool to derive the conditions that must prevail in equilibrium. Arguments of arbitrage are largely independent of individual characteristics such as endowments and preferences, initial wealth and particular attitudes toward risk. Perhaps the only assumption is that individuals are non-saturated: more of any commodity is better than less. If a commodity is traded at two different prices, and if transaction costs are negligible, an economic agent can make profits: he or she just buys the commodity at the low, and sells at the high price. Thus, prices are unique in equilibrium, an economic law that was originally stated by William S. Jevons (1835-1882).

Arguments of arbitrage become somewhat more difficult, if there are no isolated considerations for single commodities. Remember that buying at the low and selling at the high price refers to an exchange bargain which involves only one commodity and money. Rather, we have to consider processes of exchange that involve several types of commodities simultaneously. Production is one example for these more complicated processes of "exchange", and entrepreneurs are indeed incessantly in quest of profitable arbitrage possibilities through the transformation of inputs into outputs. Another example of such an exchange process that involves several different commodities is a futures contract. Several different points of time and several events determine the circumstances of the exchange process called "futures contract". But, from a methodical point of view, arbitrage in a commodity space of inputs and outputs of production has the same mathematical structure as arbitrage in a contingent space of futures and of risky assets.

Consequently, we might expect that arbitrage theory provides a link between the theories of general equilibrium and of finance. We will see, indeed, that arbitrage theory bridges between both paradigms. Moreover, some of the most important results in finance, which have been demonstrated in the risk framework and under restrictions on tastes and beliefs, could be proved by arbitrage arguments in a fairly general framework. This framework is based on uncertainty rather than on risk, no particular assumptions are made concerning probabilities and preferences.

The use of arbitrage arguments in finance is not an invention of the last ten years. Perhaps the first was John M. Keynes who developed in 1923 his Interest-Rate-Parity Theory of foreign-exchange rates along arbitrage lines. Modigliani and Miller demonstrated their 1958 result on the irrelevance of corporate capital structure through arbitrage. On the other hand we have the Pricing of Options. Option pricing, as an outstanding application of arbitrage theory, was initiated in 1973 by Fischer Black and Myron Scholes, in 1976 by John C. Cox and Stephen A. Ross, in 1979 by Cox and Mark Rubinstein.

This paper is an introduction to the basics of arbitrage theory.

2. An Example, its Generalization, and the Question

2.1 A Portfolio of Savings Bonds and Term Deposits

Let us start with a concrete situation in which an individual is making a portfolio decision.

We assume that the investor can buy several types of assets. To keep notation simple only three points of time are considered for all types of assets considered. Today, t_0, is the moment of making the investment decision and of paying the corresponding prices. The investor will get returns in one year, at t_1, and in two years, at t_2, from now on. We restrict our example to the case of pure certainty: with all types of assets there is no uncertainty about the corresponding pay back at future times t_1 and t_2.

Three financial assets are offered. The first is a two-year termed saving bond of type A ; one \$ today brings a \$ 0.10 interest payment at t_1 and, in addition, \$ 1.10 at t_2. The second financial asset is the same savings bond but type B ; no interest is paid at t_1 such that each \$ today is transformed into \$ 1.21 at t_2. The third asset is a simple one-year term deposit; each Dollar at t_0 can be exchanged with \$ 1.12 at t_1.

SITUATION 1 Payment in \$ at points of time	t_0	t_1	t_2
Savings bond type A	-1	0.10	1.10
Savings bond type B	-1	0	1.21
One-year term deposit	-1	1.12	0

Some remarks on the particular terms of these contracts in situation 1 are apt. Firstly, there is nothing contradictory that a 10% as well as a 12% rate of interest is offered because one rate refers to a one year term deposit whereas the other rate holds for the two-year termed savings bond. Secondly, it is not unusual that an investor can choose between type A and type B of savings bonds with the same rate of interest and the same maturity time.

Accordingly, an investor would not find anything unusual with this offer by a bank. Today, a substantial sum of money is available for investment. Corresponding to individual time preference, the investor knows exactly how much returns she wants to receive at each of the future points of time t_1, t_2. Thus, she decides on a specific investment plan, allocating her money among the three financial assets.

Definition: The result of this investment decision is called "original portfolio".

Both, size and composition of the original portfolio depend, of course, on all individual characteristics such as initial wealth and time preference. However, we are neither interested in knowing the investor's wealth and preferences, nor are we inquiring in the exact size and composition of the original portfolio.

2.2 Is a Free Lunch Possible?

Neither the investors' individual characteristics nor the size and composition of the original portfolio belong to the given data. Nevertheless we are looking for criteria to test whether the investor made a good or a bad portfolio selection. To be more precise: can we judge from the data of situation 1 whether the investor could get an immediate free lunch by reconsidering and eventually revising her original portfolio: Is there any modification which today costs less, but nevertheless guarantees at least the same returns as the original portfolio at times t_1 and t_2, respectively?

Without knowing the investor's individual characteristics such as wealth and preferences and just judging from the data of the situation 1 we can conclude, indeed, that a free lunch is possible. Consequently, the original investment planning was poor.

The only two assumptions we have to make for discovering this are: firstly, all three assets are contained in positive quantities in the original portfolio, and secondly, the investor is non-saturated in the sense that she prefers a free lunch to having nothing.

To see that such a possibility for profitable arbitrage exists, follow this suggestion to revise the original investment planning:

(1) The investor should reduce the amount invested in the savings bond type A by, let us say, \$ 10,000 . The consequence at t_1 is \$ 1,000 less interest payment. In order to maintain the original level of return at t_1 , there is only one way:

(2) She has to increase her term deposit by $\$ 1,000 / 1.12 = 892.86$. The consequence at t_2 is \$ 11,000 less in redemption and interest. In order to maintain the originally desired return at t_2 ,

(3) she has to increase her investment in savings bond type B by $\$ 11,000 / 1.21 = 9,090.91$. Thus, the returns at both points of time t_1 and t_2 in the future keep the originally intended levels.

But what are the consequences of this modification of her original portfolio today, at t_0 ? On the one hand, (1) the investor keeps \$ 10,000 more because of her reduced investment in the savings bond type A and, on the other hand, (2),(3) she must spend additional $\$ 892.86 + 9,090.91 = 9,983.77$ for her increased engagement in the term deposit and savings bond type B .

Summing up, the revised portfolio costs $\$ 10,000.00 - 9,983.77 = 16.23$ less, although both the returns at t_1 and at t_2 keep the same level. The investor gets a free \$ 16.23 lunch today.

2.3 Events and Futures

The demonstration that profitable arbitrage exists in situation 1 is, as already stated, independent of the particular preference of the investor.

Further, it is of no importance that we thought of the event t_1 to denote the point of time in one year from now on and that we thought of t_2 to denote two years ahead. Profitable arbitrage exists also if we give t_1 and t_2 the interpretation of "in 15 months" and "in 28 months", respectively. To pursue this line, the events t_1 and t_2 can likewise denote uncertain states of the nature, such as "the price of gold surmounts the $ 13,000-per-kilogram level". The term "uncertain state of nature" means that each of the assets results in the corresponding returns (shown in the table), if and only if this state of nature occurs. Clearly, we suppose that the relevant states of nature can be observed without error by each of the contracting individuals.

In a similar way, events such as t_1 and t_2 can refer to the transfer of goods rather than the transfer of money. Each event must then specify the type of commodity, the location, the point of time and the condition, under which the transfer will be carried out. Thus, t_i could have the meaning of "barrels of Arabian light in the port of Amsterdam on July 1, this year, if and only if condition x becomes true during the next week". Instead of financial asset we would then better speak of futures contracts. But the structure remains the same.

In the "Theory of Value", Gerard Debreu wrote: "A contract for the transfer of a commodity now specifies, in addition to its physical properties, its location and its date, an event on the occurence of which the transfer is conditional. This new definition of a commodity allows one to obtain a theory of uncertainty free from any probability concept and formally identical with the theory of certainty developed ... A contract for delivery of wheat between two agents takes for example the form: the first agent shall deliver to the second agent, who shall accept delivery, five thousand bushels of wheat of a specified type at location s , at event e . If e does not obtain, no delivery takes place" (1959, 88 - 89).

Consider a set of n events $k = 1,2,\ldots,n$ which unambiguously determine among a group of contracting persons,

- currencies or commodities to be transferred,
- locations, at which transfer is to take place,
- fixed points of time at which the transactions occur,
- the conditions and states of the nature under which the transactions occur and which today are still uncertain.

A financial asset or futures contract j is then completely described by its price a_j (which is denoted as a negative entity because the holder of the portfolio has to pay it) and by the returns b_{jk} under events $k = 1,2,\ldots,n$. The entities $b_{j1}, b_{j2}, \ldots, b_{jn}$

for asset j denote the amounts of money or the quantities of commodities which should be given to the holder of the asset at the locations, times, and under the conditions of the events $k = 1,2,\dots,n$.

Assume that an individual can buy m assets or futures contracts $j = 1,2,\dots,m$. Assume that this agent can buy each of the assets in any nonnegative quantity wanted and that linearity holds in the sense that the total amount to be paid for a portfolio consisting of contract j in quantity q_j is the amount of $q_1a_1 + q_2a_2 + \dots + q_ma_m$. Then a table describes the data for the portfolio problem. The m lines in the table correspond to the contracts, and there are $n+1$ columns to show the current prices a_j as well as the returns b_{jk} at the events $k = 1,2,\dots,n$:

GENERAL SITUATION	current price	events 1	2 ...	k ...	n
contract 1	a_1	b_{11}	b_{12}	b_{1k}	b_{1n}
contract 2	a_2	b_{21}	b_{22}	b_{2k}	b_{2n}
...					
contract j	a_j	b_{j1}	b_{j2}	b_{jk}	b_{jn}
...					
contract m	a_m	b_{m1}	b_{m2}	b_{mk}	b_{mn}

The negative numbers $a_1,a_2,\dots,a_m$ show the present values or buying prices of the contracts $1,2,\dots,m$. Those who wish may visualize all a_j equal to -1 . We form a vector $a = (a_1,a_2,\dots,a_m)'$ of all these buying prices.

The numbers b_{jk} are either positive or equal zero. For a contract j , of course, some of these futures $b_{j1},b_{j2},\dots,b_{jn}$ can equal zero, but not all together. On review, which can only take place at a later stage after all the contracts have been transacted, the case can arise where the holder of the contract j does not receive a return for investment a_j . This is the case when none of the events $k = 1,2,\dots,n$ with positive b_{jk} did occur. This however, is not known in advance at the time when the agent selects his portfolio. Insurance policies are a standard example.

The returns b_{jk} $(j = 1,2,\dots,m$ and $k = 1,2,\dots,n)$ of the m financial assets in the n events are arranged in a matrix B .

Definition: The terms of the m futures contracts $j = 1,2,\dots,m$, (that is both the vector a of buying prices and the matrix B of future returns under events $k = 1,2,\dots,n$) determine the "situation" or the "capital market".

2.4 The Question: Should the Original Portfolio be Revised?

Let us now observe an investor, who as a result of motivated action buys financial assets in positive quantities and incorporates all of them into his portfolio, which we term as the original portfolio. A recomposition of this original portfolio is a vector $x = (x_1, x_2, \dots x_m)'$ with partly positive, and partly negative components. The vector x specifies a revised portfolio where the number of asset j is increased by x_j. Thus, if x_j is positive, additional assets type j are bought for the amount of $x_j a_j$. And all assets type j, where x_j is negative, are sold for the amount of $|x_j a_j|$.

Definition: A recomposition $x = (x_1, x_2, \dots, x_m)'$ is called "arbitrage", if two conditions hold:

Firstly, in each event $k = 1,2,\dots,n$ the revised portfolio should give the investor returns no smaller than the original portfolio, that is,

$$x_1 b_{1k} + x_2 b_{2k} + \dots + x_m b_{mk} = \sum_{j=1}^{m} b_{jk} x_j \geq 0$$

or written in matrix notation,

$$B'x \geq 0 .$$

Secondly, the recomposition x should require less positive payments (for the assets j with positive x_j) than negative payments (for those assets j with negative x_j), that is,

$$a_1 x_1 + a_2 x_2 + \dots + a_m x_m = \sum_{j=1}^{m} a_j x_j = a'x > 0 ,$$

or, in short, a free lunch $a'x > 0$ is possible.

The main question of the arbitrage theory can be stated as: Under which condition is arbitrage possible in a situation created by the vector a of buying values and the matrix B of futures quantities? For an answer we begin in the next chapter with a consideration motivated by economic reasoning, and then we wish to discern the formal mathematical background in a separation theorem of functional analysis.

3. Arbitrage Versus Equilibrium

3.1 Some Borrowing from Production Theory

Let us leave, for a moment, the theory of finance in order to see whether problems of similar structure are already solved in other fields of economics or management science. It turns out that the analysis of arbitrage plays a key role in the microeconomic theory of the firm. And sometimes, each kind of business can be viewed as a form of arbitrage. In particular, think of production. Each production process transforms inputs into certain outputs. The simplest view of the entrepreneurial role is that the firm, endowed with a technology, i.e. a set of feasible production processes, is constantly observing the spot prices of relevant inputs and outputs. Arbitrage is possible, if a production process is feasible for which the input cost is less than the sum of the spot prices multiplied with the resulting output quantities. The entrepreneur will consequently activate this production process and realize it in the highest possible scale.

In the view of an equilibrium theorist, however, the prevailing price system cannot represent a market equilibrium, if there exist production processes with positive profit. In fact, the moment the entrepreneur activates a profitable production process, the prices for the demanded inputs increase, and the prices for the offered outputs decrease. These price movements will continue as long as the entrepreneur activates his production process. And the entrepreneur, in turn, will run his production process as long as the input costs are lower than the output returns. On the other hand, the entrepreneur will reduce the activity of any production process for which the cost at spot cost increase the spot returns.

Result: A price system is a market equilibrium if and only if the value of inputs equals the value of outputs for all activated production processes.

Thus, in a market equilibrium no profitable arbitrage is possible through increasing or decreasing the scales of production processes. In other words: either there are some possibilities of arbitrage or there exists a price system so that for each activated transformation process the value of inputs equals the value of outputs.

3.2 Either Arbitrage is Possible or Equilibrium Prices Exist

The above knowledge acquired from microeconomic production theory can directly be transferred to finance. Here the processes of transformation are futures contracts. The types of outputs are the events $k=1,2,\ldots,n$. The buying price of contract j is denoted by a_j ; and $b_{j1},b_{j2},\ldots,b_{jm}$ are the quantities of the resulting outputs or better futures. The above result states: If a portfolio contains all m futures contracts $j=1,2,\ldots,m$ in positive numbers, then either arbitrage is possible or there exists a system of prices $p_1,p_2,\ldots,p_n$ for the events $k=1,2,\ldots,n$ such that for each contract $j=1,2,\ldots,m$ the buying price equals the value of the futures. That means, either arbitrage is possible or there exist numbers $p_1,p_2,\ldots,p_n$ such that

$$p_1b_{j1}+p_2b_{j2}+\ldots+p_nb_{jn} = -a_j$$

holds for all contracts $j=1,2,\ldots,m$.

The existence of such a price system $p=(p_1,p_2,\ldots,p_n)'$ with this equilibrium property, which can once again be stated in matrix notation,

$$Bp = -a$$

is therefore the desired condition for a situation to be free of arbitrage. If, on the other hand, the linear system $Bp=-a$ has no solution p , arbitrage and a free lunch are still possible.

3.3 The Lemma of MINKOWSKI-FARKAS as Mathematical Background

Not surprisingly, our economic way of reasoning can be formalized and demonstrated to be correct in a rigorous way. Since the linear structure of the transformation processes is best described in linear spaces, the mathematical support of our argument is given by one of the theorems of linear algebra. The formal result belongs to the class of separation theorems and bears the names of Hermann Minkowski (1910) and the Hungarian mathematician J. Farkas (1902).

Lemma: Given is a vector a different from the null vector and a matrix B with m rows and n columns. Then,

(i) either there is a vector $x \in \mathbb{R}^m$ such that both $a'x>0$ and $B'x\geq 0$ hold

(ii) or there is a solution $p\in\mathbb{R}^n$, $p\geq 0$ of the linear system
$$Bp = -a .$$

For a proof of this Lemma see for example Akira Takayama (1974, 42) or Hukukane Nikaido (1968, 38).

The alternative (i) is the possibility of arbitrage with a certain recombination x, whereas (ii) refers to the existence of an equilibrium with a vector $p = (p_1, p_2, \dots, p_n)'$ of prices p_k for the events $k = 1, 2, \dots, n$.

3.4 The Derivation of an Issue Price

Let us present a first application for the equilibrium condition $Bp = -a$ and consider for that purpose our first situation with three investment opportunities: Savings bonds A, savings bonds B, and term deposits. If these three financial assets have the given terms, arbitrage is possible. The recombination of the portfolio saw the need to sell type A savings bonds and to invest not only in more term deposits, but also to acquire additional type B savings bonds. Obviously, the buying price of a type A savings bond was too high in relation to those of both other assets.

In practice it is also a fact that when issuing a new financial asset j, the future returns $b_{j1}, b_{j2}, \dots, b_{jn}$ are exactly predetermined in the preliminary stage of issue, and made publicly known to potential investors. The issue price a_j, on the other hand, is fixed only shortly before the time of issue, taking into consideration the spot terms of other investment opportunities. This way, all possibilities of arbitrage are eliminated and the existing equilibrium on the capital market does not get displaced.

Let us view a similar situation. We should determine beforehand the conditions for the type B savings bonds and the term deposit. A type A savings bond, which yields its purchaser \$ 0.10 payment in one year and \$ 1.10 in two years, is available for the current price a_1. We would like to adjust a_1 in such a way that arbitrage is not possible.

SITUATION 2		a_j	b_{j1}	b_{j2}
Savings bonds A	j=1	a_1	0.10	1.10
Savings bonds B	j=2	-1	0	1.21
Term deposit	j=3	-1	1.12	0

Let us try to fix a_1 in such a way, that the equilibrium condition $Bp = -a$ has a solution $p = (p_1, p_2)'$. The equation system reads

$$\begin{aligned} 0.10 \cdot p_1 + 1.10 \cdot p_2 &= -a_1 \\ 1.21 \cdot p_2 &= 1 \\ 1.12 \cdot p_1 &= 1 \end{aligned}$$

The third equation implies $p_1 = 1/1.12 = 0.893$, and the second equation results in $p_2 = 1/1.21 = 0.826$. These values for p_1, p_2 can only satisfy the first equation if

$$0.10 \cdot 0.893 + 1.10 \cdot 0.826 = -a_1$$

holds, and that is exactly the case when we fix a_1 according to

$$a_1 = -0.998 .$$

Under the condition that the terms for the saving bonds B and the term deposit remain steady, this a_1 is exactly the issue price for the savings bonds A which makes arbitrage impossible.

If a certain situation allows for the calculation of the balanced issue price for a particular financial asset from a system of event prices, the contract is called derivative. In this situation, the savings bonds A is treated as derivative contract, whereas the terms of the contracts $j = 2,3$ were considered to be completely determined.

Which contracts are considered to be given and which one is the derivate asset depends on the point of view. Again, we start with situation 1, which still permits arbitrage. But now, we suppose that the terms for both the savings bonds are given and that these terms are so strong, that all what happens in the market is governed by them. The consequence is a variation in the rate of interest for the term deposit. Which, in this situation 3, is the equilibrium rate of interest for a one-year deposit?

SITUATION 3		a_j	b_{j1}	b_{j2}
Savings bond A	j=1	-1	0.10	1.10
Savings bond B	j=2	-1	0	1.21
Term deposit	j=3	-1	b_{31}	0

Let us try to derive the value of the variable b_{31} for which the equilibrium condition $Bp = -a$ has a solution $p = (p_1, p_2)'$ in the situation 3. The equation system is now

$$1.10 \cdot p_1 + 1.10 \cdot p_2 = 1$$
$$1.21 \cdot p_2 = 1$$
$$b_{31} \cdot p_1 = 1$$

The second equation implies $p_2 = 1 / 1.21 = 0.826$, and with that, the first equation results in $p_1 = 0.909$. This price p_1 can satisfy the third equation if and only if $b_{31} = 1.10$ holds, which means an equilibrium rate of interest for one-year deposits of 10 % .

3.5. Summing up the Results

The theory of arbitrage, insofar, supplies us with a condition of equilibrium $Bp = -a$.

Firstly, this condition can be applied as a proof test in a particular situation, where all the terms, i.e. all the components a_j of the vector a and all the elements of the matrix B are given. One can quickly test whether or not arbitrage is possible. If a solution $p \geq 0$ exists, no free lunch can be gained. If, on the other hand, no nonnegative solution p exists, there is possibility of arbitrage, although the theory gives no advice how to choose an appropriate recombination x of the original portfolio.

Secondly, there is the case where the terms of the futures contracts are not completely determined. If it is nevertheless possible to calculate prices of the events from the available data, these prices can be used to fix or adjust free parameters for derivative contracts such that equilibrium prevails.

Thirdly, consider a situation where $Bp = -a$ has either no nonnegative or no unique solution p , that is, either there is still the possibility of arbitrage or so few terms are already fixed that free parameters cannot be derived in a unique way. Then, arbitrage theory fails to provide us hints on the particular equilibrium that will be reached in such a situation. In fact, the final equilibrium will depend on supply and demand functions, i.e. on aggregates of characteristics of individual agents, which do not enter into the analysis of arbitrage.

4. Derivative Contracts in Complete Capital Markets

4.1 Complete Capital Market

Definition: If a situation or capital market given by vector a and matrix B permits the determination of a unique system of equilibrium prices p with $Bp = -a$, then the capital market is called to be "complete". Given a complete capital market with events $k = 1,2,\ldots,n$ and a futures contract j which refers to these events only. If one of the terms $a_j, b_{j1}, b_{j2}, \ldots, b_{jn}$ is not yet given and can be determined through the equilibrium condition $b_{j1}p_1 + b_{j2}p_2 + \ldots + b_{jn}p_n = -a_j$, then the contract j is called "derivative".

4.2 One-Period Option Pricing

An option is a contract entitling the holder to buy or sell a designated security at or within a certain period of time at a particular price. Edwin J. Elton and Martin J. Gruber indicate that options must be derivative contracts par excellence: "There are a large number of types of option contracts, but they all have one element in common: the value of an option is directly dependent on the value of some underlying security" (1981, 441). Thus we might suspect that arbitrage theory provides the tool to derive buying prices for options.

Perhaps, the most common type of an option is a call. A call gives the holder the right to buy a fixed number of shares of a stock at a fixed price, either before (America) or at (Europe) a fixed expiration date. The exercise price, of course, will in general be different from the spot stock price.

We now determine the buying price of a European call in a simple situation. The situation is simple because we start with one stock only and assume that there are only two possible realisations for the stock price at the expiration date. Thus, there are two events, $k = 1,2$ and the relative rate of returns for the stock are denoted by r_k, where $r_1 < r_2$. Denote by s the current price of a share. In addition to this equity contract, we consider a debt contract which provides the holder with rate of interest i independent of which event will realize.

SITUATION 4		a_j	b_{j1}	b_{j2}
debt	j=1	-1	1+i	1+i
equity	j=2	-s	$s(1+r_1)$	$s(1+r_2)$

This situation is an equilibrium for any set of parameters i, r_1, r_2 as long as $r_1 < i < r_2$ holds. Moreover, the situation is a complete capital market because the prices p_1, p_2 for the events are uniquely determined. Solving the equilibrium condition $Bp = -a$ results in:

$$p_1 = \frac{r_2 - i}{(1+i)(r_2 - r_1)}$$

$$p_2 = \frac{i - r_1}{(1+i)(r_2 - r_1)} \quad .$$

These event prices can be interpreted as product of a discount factor $1/(1+i)$ and a pseudo probability, which amounts to $(r_2 - i)/(r_2 - r_1)$ for the event 1, and which is equal to $(i - r_1)/(r_2 - r_1)$ for the event 2. Both the pseudo probabilities are positive and sum up to 1 .

Now the situation 4 is modified through the introduction of a call. The call entitles the holder to the option of buying one share at the exercise price e at the point of time, when it is known whether event 1 oder event 2 comes true. We can assume

$$s(1 + r_1) < e < s(1 + r_2)$$

because otherwise the option would be trivial. The holder, of course, will exercise the call exactly when the better rate of return r_2 comes true (event $k = 2$), for then he can obtain the amount $s(1 + r_2) - e$. If event $k = 1$ occurs, the holder will not exercise the option since the spot price of the share $s(1 + r_1)$ is then below the exercise price e . Consequently, the returns for a call are given by the third row $(j = 3)$ of the subsequent table. The buying price a_3 for the call is not yet fixed and should be derived such that no arbitrage is possible.

SITUATION 5		a_j	b_{j1}	b_{j2}
debt	j=1	-1	1+i	1+i
equity	j=2	-s	$s(1+r_1)$	$s(1+r_2)$
call	j=3	a_3	0	$s(1+r_2)-e$

The call is introduced as a new contract into the complete capital market of situation 4 and is derivative. Immediately follows $(s(1+r_2)-e)p_2 = -a_3$ and consequently

$$|a_3| = \text{option price} = \frac{(i-r_1)(s(1+r_2)-e)}{(1+i)(r_2-r_1)} \quad .$$

Briefly worded, the buying price for a call is equal to the discounted pseudo expected value of the future returns.

References

Arrow, K.J. (1974): General Economic Equilibrium, Purpose, Analytic Techniques, Collective Choice, American Economic Review 64, 253-272

Arrow, K.J. (1964): The Role of Securities in the Optimal Allocation of Risk-Bearing, Review of Economic Studies, 91-96

Black, F.; Scholes, M. (1973): The Pricing of Options and Corporate Liabilities, Journal of Political Economy, 637-654

Breeden, D.T.; Litzenberger, R.H. (1978): Prices of State-Contingent Claims Implicit in Option Prices, Journal of Business 51,4, 621-651

Brennan, M.J. (1979): The Pricing of Contingent Claims in Discrete Time Models, Journal of Finance 34, 637-659

Brenner, M. (1983) (Ed.): Option Pricing. Theory and Application, Lexington

Cox, J.C.; Ross, S.A. (1976): A Survey of some New Results in Financial Option Pricing Theory, Journal of Finance 31,2, 383-402

Cox, J.C.; Rubinstein, M. (1979): Option Pricing: A Simplified Approach, Journal of Financial Economics 7, 229-263

Debreu, G. (1959): Theory of Value, Wiley, New York

Dreze, J.H. (1970/71): Market Allocation under Uncertainty, European Economic Review, 133-165

Elton, E.J.; Gruber, M.J. (1981): Modern Portfolio Theory and Investment Analysis, 2nd. Ed. Wiley, New York

Geske, R. (1978): The Pricing Of Options with Stochastic Dividend Yield, Journal of Finance 33, 617-625

Harrison, J.M.; Kreps, D.M. (1979): Martingals and Arbitrage in Multiperiod Securities Markets, Journal of Economic Theory 20, 381-408

Hsia, Ch. (1983): On Binomial Option Pricing, Journal of Financial Research 6,1, 41-50

Hubermann, G. (1982): A Simple Approach to Arbitrage Pricing Theory, Journal of Economic Theory 28, 183-191

Knight, F.H. (1921): Risk, Uncertainty and Profit, Houghton Mifflin, New York

Kuhn, T.S. (1970): The Structure of Scientific Revolutions, University of Chicago

Markowitz, H.M. (1952): Portfolio Selection, Journal of Finance, 77-91

Merton, R.C. (1977): On the Pricing of Contingent Claims and the Modigliani-Miller Theorem, Journal of Financial Economics 5, 241-249

Müller, S. (1985): Arbitrage Pricing of Contingent Claims, Berlin-Heidelberg-New York-Tokyo

Nikaido, H. (1968): Convex Structures and Economic Theory, Academic Press, New York

Rendleman, R.J.; Bartter, B.J. (1979): Two-State Option Pricing, Journal of Finance 34,5, 1093-1110

Roll, R.; Ross, S.A. (1980): An Empirical Investigation of the Arbitrage Pricing Theory, Journal of Finance 35,5, 1073-1103

Ross, S.A. (1976): The Arbitrage Theory of Capital Asset Pricing, Journal of Economic Theory 13, 341-360

Ross, S.A. (1978): A Simple Approach to the Valuation of Risky Streams, Journal of Business 51,3, 453-475

Rubinstein, M.E. (1975): Securities Market Efficiency in an Arrow-Debreu Economy, American Economic Review 65,5, 812-824

Rubinstein, M.E. (1976): The Valuation of Uncertain Income Steams and the Pricing of Options, Bell Journal of Economics and Management Science 7, 407-425

Smith, C.W.jr. (1976): Option Pricing -A Review, Journal of Financial Economics 3, 3-51

Spremann, K. (1985): Finanzierung, Oldenbourg-Verlag, München

Takayama, A. (1974): Mathematical Economics, Dryden Press, Hinsdale, Illinois

Wilhelm, J. (1981): Zum Verhältnis von Capital Asset Pricing Model, Arbitrage Pricing Theory und Bedingungen der Arbitragefreiheit von Finanzmärkten, Zeitschrift für betriebswirtschaftliche Forschung 33,10, 891-905.

Wilhelm, J. (1985): Arbitrage Theory, Berlin-Heidelberg-New York-Tokyo.

About Contributors

GÜNTER BAMBERG (* 1940) studied mathematics at the universities of Saarbrücken and Bonn. He got his diploma degree at the University of Saarbrücken in 1966, his doctoral degree at the same university in 1968 (thesis on game theory), and his Habilitation at the Technical University of Karlsruhe in 1970. Since 1970 he is full professor of statistics, University of Augsburg, where he stayed despite calls to Osnabrück and Heidelberg. He is co-editor of the Statistical Papers and Mathematical Systems in Economics. His books and articles deal with statistics, econometrics, Operations Research, and decision theory.

MICHAEL J. BRENNAN (* 1942) holds the Albert E. Hall chair of finance at the University of British Columbia, Vancouver B.C., Canada. He studied in Oxford (B.A. 1964, B. Phil. 1965) and Pittsburgh (M.B.A. 1966). His Ph.D. thesis on "Investor Taxes, Market Equilibrium and Corporate Finance" (M.I.T. 1970) was supervised by Franco Modogliani. His professional activities are widespread. He was editor of the Journal of Finance from 1980 to 1983 and is currently co-editing several professional journals. His papers cover topics such as dividend policy, insurance, regulation, convertibles and option pricing.

VOLKER FIRCHAU (* 1948) is Privatdozent at the department of economics, University of Augsburg. He received the Diplom-Mathematiker degree from the University of Münster (1974), whereas he passed his doctoral promotion (1978) and his Habilitation in Augsburg. His current interest of research include decision theory, problems of insurance, and statistical methods. Two monographies on advanced topics of informational economics were recently published.

ROBERT GESKE (* 1944) is Professor of Finance at the University of California, Los Angeles (UCLA). He serves on the editorial boards of the Journal of Financial and Quantitative Analysis and the Journal of Portfolio Management. He was the recipient of a Hubner Foundation Grant for research on "Mutual Fund Insurance", a Q-Group Grant for "Studies in Biases in Option Models", and a Federal Home Loan Bank Board Grant for "Studies of Hedging Interest Rate Risk." He has authored (and co-authored) many papers on option theory, applications, and empirical tests, and on the interactions between real activity and inflation and their effects on asset prices.

BERND RUDOLPH (* 1944) is professor of finance at the Johann Wolfgang Goethe Universität in Frankfurt. He got three degrees from the University of Bonn: Diplom-Volkswirt 1970, Dr.rer.pol. 1972, Habilitation in business administration 1978. He had offers from the universities of Mannheim and Saarbrücken and was Visiting Professor in Vienna. His publications in professional journals as well as his books deal with various topics of banking, financial intermediation, and investment policy.

EDUARDO S. SCHWARTZ (* 1940) is the W.M. Young Professor of Finance at the Faculty of Commerce and Business Administration, University of British Columbia, Vancouver B.C., Canada, where he graduated (M.Sc. 1973, Ph.D. 1975) and is working since 1976. He was visiting professor at the University of California, Berkeley (1978), and at the London Business School (1982 - 1983). He is Associate Editor of the following three journals: The Journal of Finance, The Journal of Financial and Quantitative Analysis, and Finance (Revue de L'Association Française de Finance). His numerous publications, most of them jointly with Michael J. Brennan, were published in professional journals.

KLAUS SPREMANN (* 1947) studied mathematics at the Technical University of Munich, where he got his Diplom-Mathematiker degree in 1972. His doctoral dissertation 1973 was on dynamic optimization, his Habilitation 1975 (Technical University of Karlsruhe) on economic theory. Since 1978 he is full professor at the University of Ulm. Klaus Spremann was Visiting Professor at the UBC, Vancouver B.C., in 1982 and won two offers from the Universities of Bielefeld and Graz (Austria). He published numerous papers on finance, micoreconomic modelling, intergenerational contracts, aggregation problems, and the theory of the firm.

SIEGFRIED TRAUTMANN (* 1951) is currently Assistant Professor at the Faculty of Economics, University of Karlsruhe, were he also graduated as a Diplom-Wirtschaftsingenieur (1974) and received his doctoral degree (1979). He is teaching in the fields of finance, and accouting, and he conducts computer-aided business games. His current interests of research are finance and the application of Management Science to problems of corporate management.

Author Index

Subject Index

MIX
Papier aus verantwortungsvollen Quellen
Paper from responsible sources
FSC® C105338

If you have any concerns about our products,
you can contact us on
ProductSafety@springernature.com

In case Publisher is established outside the EU,
the EU authorized representative is:
Springer Nature Customer Service Center GmbH
Europaplatz 3, 69115 Heidelberg, Germany

Printed by Libri Plureos GmbH
in Hamburg, Germany